A TEXTBOOK OF TI
STRATEGIES IN
MANAGE

CW00618081

David Guest is Senior Lec
tions at the London School
tutor in charge of the Dipl
agement. Before joining the
Personnel Department at British Rail and on a research secondment with the Manpower and Training Division of the National Ports Council. For
several years he has been one of the IPM's chief
examiners, responsible for Training and Development and he was closely involved with the introduction of the new examination scheme. He is currently undertaking a major research programme on
the nature and effectiveness of the personnel function
and has written extensively on this and many other
topics including, in particular, worker participation
and motivation at work. He is an industrial psychologist by training, and was a recent chairman of the
Occupational Psychology Section of the British
Psychological Society.

Terence Kenny is Personnel Director for several
business groups within the Bowater Corporation.
His career has seen a regular alternation between
academic and industrial jobs. The academic posts,
all in the management education field, were with
Bristol University, the Manchester Business School
and Brighton Polytechnic. Previous industrial jobs
were with Albright & Wilson and the British Printing Corporation. He has been a Vice-President of
the Institute of Personnel Management and Chief
Examiner for the general personnel management
papers in the IPM examination scheme. He has served
on the national negotiating team of the British Printing Industry Federation and currently serves on the
Industrial Relations Advisory Committee of the National Federation of Building Trades Employers. Before this he was a member of the management training committee of the PPITB and served on the
Training Research Advisory Committee of the then
Training Services Agency. He has published many
articles over the years on personnel subjects and is a
long standing member of the editorial advisory committee of *Personnel Management*.

A TEXTBOOK

OF

TECHNIQUES AND STRATEGIES

IN

PERSONNEL MANAGEMENT

Edited by David Guest and Terence Kenny

Institute of Personnel Management

Note: wherever appropriate the convention has been followed whereby *he* and *him* are used to cover *she* and *her*

Printed and bound in Great Britain by
Butler & Tanner Ltd, Frome and London

British Library Cataloguing in Publication Data

Guest, David
  A textbook of techniques and strategies in personnel management.
  Vol. 1
  1. Personnel management
  I. Title   II. Kenny, Terence
  658.3   MF5549

ISBN   0–85292–269–8

Contents

Authors

Christine Holroyd BSc (Soc) FIPM has been a personnel practitioner all her working life. She has worked in the clothing, chemical and pharmaceutical and paper, packaging and printing industries and is currently the personnel director of St. Regis International. She has twice set up personnel departments from scratch.

A past chairman and chief negotiator of the British Fibreboard Packaging Employers Association, she has been a member of the Industrial Tribunal panel for England and Wales since 1973.

Barbara Dyer is currently Personnel Executive at the British Medical Association. She was formerly Personnel Adviser at the Industrial Society where she edited the third edition of their *Personnel Systems and Records*, the standard work in this field. She is a magistrate and serves on industrial tribunals.

Andrew West, an industrial psychologist by training, is personnel operations manager for Europe and the Far East for British American Tobacco before which he was BAT's Recruitment and Selection Adviser. Prior to joining BAT, he was the head of research in the Manpower and Training Section of the National Ports Council.

Clive Fletcher is Senior Lecturer in Psychology at Goldsmith's College, University of London. Before this he worked in the Behavioural Sciences Research Division of the Civil Service where he specialized in selection, appraisal and promotion systems. He is one of the countries leading experts on appraisal systems, advises a number of companies on their procedures and has written many publications on appraisals and related topics.

John Bramham was Manpower Planning Manager at British Gas headquarters before moving to his present post as Assistant Industrial Relations Manager at Northern Gas. His book *Practical Manpower Planning* has long been a best seller for IPM, for which he is now preparing a text on personnel records and information.

Bev Walters has worked in both the industrial and academic fields. He taught at Kingston Polytechnic and more recently was head of the department of management studies at the South Bank Polytechnic. He has been management development adviser to British American Tobacco and is now Management Development manager with Costains.

David Jenkins is a Consultant with the Engineering Industries Training Board (EITB) where he has helped many companies over the past seven years to design training schemes. Before joining the EITB he had wide industrial training experience, principally with the fast growing BTR. He has published a book and many articles on industrial training.

Judith Davies is currently employed by Shell International at their Hague headquarters in Holland where she is particularly concerned with the recruitment field. She has been a lecturer in quantitative methods at Middlesex Polytechnic from which she went to the Research Department at Ashridge Management College where she specialized on questions of training evaluation. She was seconded from there to the Imperial Group.

Duncan Wood is currently the visiting Nancy Seear Personnel Management Fellow in the Department of Industrial Relations at the London School of Economics. After a number of jobs in personnel management with Dunlop, SC Johnson and The Crown Cork Company he spent 15 years as a management consultant with Binder, Hamlyn Fry and Co. During this period he established a reputation as a leading expert on payment systems, a subject on which he has advised many organizations.

Clive Moody is Personnel Director at the Oxford University Press. Originally a consultant in the pensions industry he moved into manufacturing industry as an employee benefits manager with BPC, where he came to be involved in all aspects of personnel work.

Acknowledgements

Several people have made an important contribution to this book. We would like first and foremost to thank the authors who have written the various chapters. We imposed difficult demands upon them, sometimes asked them to do a great deal of extra work and occasionally took considerable liberties with their text. In return, they have for the most part been patient and cooperative. We would also like to thank our secretaries Anne Morris and Pat Rowlands for their forebearance in typing various drafts of the manuscript. Sally Harper and her colleagues at the Institute of Personnel Management have been both patient and supportive in helping to ensure that this book eventually saw the light of day.

Preface

The chapters in this book share a common concern to present and discuss the practical aspects of personnel management work. However despite common guidelines each chapter in certain respects reflects the preferred style of the author. We took an editorial decision to retain this diversity where at all possible. There are therefore quite considerable variations in presentation; some make use of case studies while others find them less helpful; some write in a conventional prose style while others prefer to combine it with a more abbreviated note form for some sections; and some authors make extensive use of references to publications while others omit this almost entirely.

At the end of each chapter, the references are presented in full. Where these are few in number, there is guidance on further reading. In addition to this, of course, anyone seeking to develop a comprehensive knowledge of the field of personnel management should also refer to one of the complementary texts on the subject such as George Thomason's *Textbook of Personnel Management*.

In selecting personnel strategies and techniques as the focus for particular chapters, we have had to make a number of arbitrary choices. We have been guided by two principles. The first is the need to include material on at least some of the necessary but often rather neglected areas of personnel work. The second is to ensure coverage of the mainstream topics which most personnel managers can expect to encounter at some stage in their career. The book is therefore directed at those obtaining professional qualifications and embarking upon a career in personnel management and also at established personnel managers who wish to learn about the appropriate procedures and techniques in a part of personnel management which may be relatively unfamiliar to them.

To provide sufficient space for each topic the book has had to be divided into two volumes. The provisional list of topics for Volume II is as follows:

1 Job analysis and job evaluation
2 Job design
3 Working conditions, working hours and working life
4 Welfare and counselling
5 Organization development
6 Communication and consultation
7 Negotiation and collective bargaining
8 Grievances, disciplinary systems, dismissals and disputes
9 Redundancy
10 Labour turnover and absenteeism
11 Accidents and safety
12 New techniques
13 Finding out for yourself

Section One

This section contains the introductory chapter. It stands on its own in so far as it sets the scene and outlines the thinking behind the book and the approach adopted within it. It also presents a view of the personnel management process by identifying the types of decisions involved. This process is then compared with other types of management and some of the issues and problems specific to personnel management are high-lighted. The chapter, therefore, provides a rationale for what follows and helps to set the context for it.

1

Chapter one

Introduction: personnel management strategies, procedures and techniques

WHY A NEW TEXTBOOK?

The growth of personnel management has been accompanied by a rapid expansion in the number of books written for personnel managers. To add yet another textbook to the list requires some explanation. The typical textbook sets out to delineate, describe and analyse the major areas of personnel management, usually offering a framework for integrating the field. It will therefore contain chapters on central areas of personnel, such as recruitment and selection, manpower planning, training, payment systems and industrial relations. It will probably discuss the legislation that affects personnel management; and it will invariably cover aspects of the social sciences including the historical development of the subject, the influence of social, cultural and organizational factors and individual issues such as leadership and employee motivation. All this is very important; indeed it serves as an essential background for effective personnel management. But, even in the discussion of specific topics such as recruitment or training, the presentation is invariably one step removed from the operational level and is of indirect rather than direct help to the individual concerned with how to 'do' personnel management.

The aim of this textbook is to provide an outline of personnel management at the operational level. It therefore seeks to answer the question 'What do I do?'. It aims to help the personnel manager who, perhaps for the first time, is confronted with the need to recruit for a new and

3

unclearly specified technical post, to extend a job evaluation system, to design an appraisal scheme or to deal with an alcoholic worker.

To meet this aim, it is necessary to start from an analysis of how the more effective personnel managers get things done. Although it may not be recognized by the managers themselves, it is possible to break their actions down into a series of stages or component parts. In doing so, we are attempting to be both descriptive and normative; that is to say we are describing how some personnel managers *do act* but, more important in the present context, we are also outlining how managers *should proceed*[1].

PERSONNEL MANAGEMENT IN PRACTICE

The practice of personnel management, when applied to a specific aspect of the field, can be considered as a series of stages. These can be described as follows:

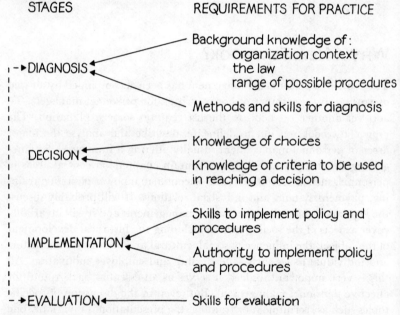

Each of these stages is discussed in this section.

DIAGNOSIS

Personnel managers wishing to conduct a useful diagnosis of problems and take effective action, must possess certain kinds of background knowledge and information, without which their judgement and decision-making may be impaired.

Knowledge of the organizational context

Personnel managers should be familiar with the organization structure, the technology and the products or services provided. They should also be familiar with the key characteristics of the workforce, including the stability, skill mix and orientations of the workers. In addition they should be able to characterize the key features of the local labour market and the community. For example, any proposals to change the hours of work or to introduce a new system of shift-working must take into account factors outside the workplace ranging from transport facilities to community values and school starting and finishing times. In this context, a knowledge of the behavioural sciences is essential to appreciate the significance of certain types of technology, market or worker orientation on structure and action within the organization. Some knowledge of the research concerning the impact of, for example, shift-working on health and home life would also be helpful.

Knowledge of the law

In many areas of their work, personnel managers are now constrained by the law. A knowledge of what the law permits or requires is therefore essential background for many personnel decisions. It is useful, in a number of circumstances, to view the law as an opportunity rather than a constraint. For example, a sufficiently detailed knowledge of the equal opportunities legislation or the Health and Safety at Work etc Act can provide a lever for action. There can be considerable difficulties in keeping up to date, particularly with the Employment Appeals Tribunal decisions, but without this information, personnel managers sometimes run the risk of taking inappropriate action. The subsequent repercussions can be very damaging for both the organization and the personnel function.

Knowledge of procedures

Personnel managers must know what steps to take, once they have chosen a particular path of action. It is not enough, for example, to know what the major forms of job evaluation are and to be able to identify their strengths and weaknesses. Personnel managers must know what steps are involved in actually undertaking job evaluation. The same is true, for example, of cost-benefit analysis in the evaluation of training and for many other aspects of personnel work. It is necessary to know, or to be able to find out quickly, about the procedures associated with action. The danger of not knowing or of taking the view that it is possible to find out about procedures when the time comes, is that decisions about the choice of procedure, taken in the absence of sufficiently detailed knowledge about procedure, may be unrealistic and inappropriate.

Many textbooks on personnel management discuss aspects of the organizational context and the law and these are not covered, except incidentally, in this textbook. They also discuss procedure, but seldom at a sufficiently detailed level to indicate appropriate lines of action. This book will therefore be examining personnel procedures in some detail.

Methods and skills of diagnosis

Knowledge of procedures, techniques and of the criteria which influence choice of approach is part of the picture. In addition, personnel managers must know how to obtain, analyse and assemble relevant information. Over the years, this is an area where the reputation of the personnel function has been poor. Too often the quality of personnel information is less impressive than that of most other management functions and this can reduce the influence of a personnel management perspective on general management decisions.

In part, the poor quality of *some* relevant personnel management information is inevitable. How, for example, is the personnel manager to identify levels of power and influence, organization climate or employee attitudes? The behavioural sciences have developed diagnostic techniques for these types of issue and it is helpful for the personnel manager to be aware of them[2]. In practice it will often prove unfeasible to use many of them and even if they are used, the assistance of an industrial psychologist will often be required. At a more specific level, personnel managers have some control over information on topics such as labour turnover, absenteeism, rates for completion of appraisals, attendance on training courses and the like. To improve diagnosis and decision-making, there should be a sensible personnel information system. To achieve this goal personnel managers must possess the skills to understand, analyse and present this information in the most useful way.

DECISION MAKING

Knowledge of the organizational context, of the law and of personnel procedures is an essential background to action. In practice, however, there is often a choice of procedures available to personnel managers and they have to decide which to use. A series of decisions will often be required each flowing from, and partly determined by, the preceding one. For example, if a vacancy arises, the first decision is whether it

6

should be filled, a second may be whether to recruit internally or externally and successive decisions may concern recruitment method, selection method and the final selection decision. This may be viewed as one procedure (the recruitment and selection procedure) but this hides the fact that at each point there are choices and the actual choice determines the subsequent detailed procedures. For example a company has to decide whether to advertise itself or use selection consultants; whether to use tests or group exercises; whether to use individual or panel interviews.

The implications of this analysis are that personnel managers should possess a knowledge of the choices available, an understanding of the criteria on which to base a choice and the skills to carry out the necessary diagnosis.

Knowledge of choices
This is really an extension of the discussion of procedures. Personnel managers must be aware of the range of, for example, performance appraisal methods and the procedures associated with each before making a decision about which is the most appropriate. Clearly a decision based on limited knowledge of the range may be sub-optimal. This is, in effect, a warning to guard against the view that there is one best way and that others can therefore be ignored. The practical problem is that there is a great variety of personnel techniques and it is almost impossible to possess a comprehensive knowledge across more than a fairly narrow range of personnel activities.

Criteria for choosing a procedure
Given that there is often a range of possible procedures, a key to effective personnel management is obviously to select the most suitable. A straightforward approach might be to select the technically soundest procedure for achieving the particular goal, be it recruiting the most promising applicants, eliminating discrimination in promotion or linking pay and performance. However in practice the procedure which has the greatest technical strengths may have considerable drawbacks; it may be too costly, too time-consuming, too difficult; too unpopular with key managers and too progressive for the organizational climate. Faced with these constraints, the technically superior approach may not get the best results.

The personnel manager must therefore know both about the range of possible procedures and about the criteria which should be taken into account in making a choice. To take a specific illustration, how should the personnel manager in a particular plant respond to the opportunity

7

to send supervisors on an off the job training course? The personnel manager believes that the supervisors need training and development, but also believes that a problem-centred approach, close to the workplace, would be more appropriate. However, knowing that a problem-centred approach would be difficult to get off the ground, the personnel manager may prefer to use the off the job programme as the most feasible path to pursue. It can be used as a basis for subsequent follow-up activity within the plant; indeed the evaluation process after the training may facilitate the setting up of the problem-centred activity.

The range of criteria to take into account in considering the choice of procedure or technique is both complex and varied. The illustration above implies that sometimes the personnel manager will have to adopt a long-term and rather indirect strategy. On other occasions the issue will be much more straightforward. In this context, an understanding of the behavioural sciences and the kind of analysis and insights which they can offer on the nature of organizations and the influences on change in organizations is invaluable[3]. They point to the need to be aware of and consider the following range of issues:

technology, markets and organization structure

existing procedures and the historical context within which action is being considered

the attitudes, expectations and power of the key interest groups

the power and influence of the personnel function

the nature of the workforce; its skill level and motivation

the economic climate within the organization and wider economy

the organizational climate with particular reference to control systems, reward systems, communication systems and levels of trust

the administrative and resource implications of the alternatives under consideration.

The skill lies in the ability to weigh up and balance the various factors. A contingency approach, if it aims to point to the 'one best way' will often be inappropriate because it is unclear how the contingencies, or influences, should be weighted. Therefore a systems approach, which recognizes that there is more than one feasible choice is perhaps a better working model. This would recognize that part of the input into a final decision on choice is individual judgement on, for example, how to interpret aspects of history and culture within the organization. This in turn will be influenced by personal values; here the professional ideology and ethics often associated with a professional body such as the Institute of Personnel Management could be important.

A final point to consider, in what is inevitably a somewhat abstract discussion, is that the choice of action may be influenced by the stability of the goal. Personnel management goals, no less than those in many other aspects of management, are often flexible. For example within the context of collective bargaining, a set of goals concerning labour costs, size of pay award, maintenance of a good image with customers and continuity of production may all vie for priority. In many cases, this means that the effective personnel manager must learn to live with ambiguity and uncertainty. The temptation in such circumstances is often to play safe and stick to well-tried procedures. This may make life easier in the short-term but it may also stifle innovation and change, with harmful consequences in the long-term.

Implementation

Skills to implement policies and procedures

Once an approach or procedure has been agreed, the personnel manager must possess the operational skills to implement it. At the heart of the personnel manager's job lie a range of social skills, such as facilitating discussion, eliciting information, listening, showing sympathy, instructing and persuading[4]. Like all skills, these can be learned although it is all too easy for inappropriate learning to occur. Personnel managers must recognize this and constantly seek ways to improve their performance. In addition to these social skills, a range of analytical skills, including statistical analysis, are also required. Training in a range of skills, such as interviewing, lecturing, negotiation, presentation of tribunal cases and job analysis and evaluation is likely to be helpful. The need for detailed practical training of this kind is recognized and built into the current Institute of Personnel Management examination scheme.

Authority to implement policy and procedures

Without the necessary authority to implement policies and procedures, nothing may happen and much time and effort will have been wasted. Legge's (1978) analysis indicates that in this respect, personnel management is often weak. In seeking to enhance their power and indispensibility, personnel managers have perhaps been too willing to accept numerous tasks cast off by other managers—to act, in Drucker's terms, as a kind of trash can. Engaged in relatively trivial tasks, they are excluded from key policy decisions, yet forced to implement them, even

9

where there are negative personnel repercussions. The failure to demonstrate sufficient commitment to handed-down policies and to implement policy effectively reinforces a view of limited competence and, in the eyes of other managers, justifies the exclusion of personnel managers from key policy decisions. Guest and Horwood (1980) reinforce this view, on the basis of their research which indicates that personnel managers at the operational level are so busy on a wide range of tasks, many of which are short-term, fire-fighting issues, that they seldom have the time to take on a considered view of policy options. Both Legge and Guest and Horwood indicate ways of breaking out of this vicious circle, recognizing the fact that effective personnel management will invariably require increased authority for and competence within the personnel function.

Problems of personnel authority may reside in relations between personnel and line management but may also result from conflicts between levels within the personnel function. Typically, these concern policy guidelines and procedures developed at the centre to which operational personnel managers at local level have low commitment. Brewster and Richbell (1982) have highlighted the distinction between what they term espoused and operational policy, although the analysis can be extended to procedures. Espoused policies are those which are formally agreed; operational policies are those which are carried out in practice. A sizeable gap between the two will usually reflect a problem of authority and in this respect, there is ample evidence that many espoused personnel policies and procedures are not implemented in practice.

This analysis identifies a particular problem for the personnel function, although it is one from which other functions are seldom totally immune. It also highlights the difficulties faced by personnel managers who, working in a service function, invariably require the help or co-operation of other managers to get things done. Inevitably, therefore, the concern for the authority and power of personnel management is a crucial and recurring issue.

Recognizing some of these problems, personnel managers should weigh up their authority and in choosing a particular policy or procedure, consider their ability to implement it. This will involve consideration of the strength of the barriers and of the pressures that can be brought to bear. Inevitably intra-organizational conflicts and politics will play an important part in this process. At the same time, personnel managers should be constantly seeking ways to enhance the authority of their roles and of the function as a whole, since this is a key to effective personnel management. Discussions of power and politics in organizations can sometimes seem somewhat remote to personnel officers in junior positions, but an understanding of their importance is invariably an essential prerequisite to effective personnel practice at all levels.

MONITORING, REVIEW AND EVALUATION

A final stage, which should be built into all policies and procedures is a system for monitoring progress to enable periodical reviews and at some stage a more significant evaluation to take place. This implies the need for personnel information systems. It is important to recognize that evaluation will take place anyway, through a more or less formal process and will be made by those both inside and outside the personnel function. Often it will be difficult to make a clear attribution of success or failure; nevertheless, armed with good quality evaluation data of their own, personnel managers are in a much better position to argue for the positive impact of their work.

Many procedures, which work effectively for a time, have a habit of wasting away. Therefore appraisal schemes, disciplinary procedures, payment systems, training courses and the like all require occasional review and adjustment. In effect, this can become a more or less continuous feedback loop, influencing decisions on whether or not to introduce new or amended policies and procedures.

AUTONOMY AND THE PRACTICE OF PERSONNEL MANAGEMENT

The emphasis on choice and decision-making in personnel work could be taken to imply that our concern is mainly directed towards middle and senior management posts. It is therefore important to recognize that the activities that make up most personnel management jobs involve varying degree of discretion. As part of the LSE research project, Guest and Horwood (1980, p 20) developed an autonomy classification to identify the varying degrees of discretion. This contained the following five levels:

tasks involving overall direction and leadership of the function

tasks involving research into and development of concepts and policy proposals

tasks involving provision of specialist expertise or professional services in support of line management

11

tasks involving implementation of policy within broadly prescribed limits, but with scope and need for creative input and judgement

tasks involving implementation of administrative systems providing little scope for independent judgement.

The research showed that while some personnel managers at corporate level only engaged in tasks at the first two levels, almost none of the junior personnel staff were confined to implementing administrative procedures. Indeed many personnel jobs contain tasks at three or four of these levels. There is, therefore, even in the most junior personnel posts, scope for choice.

PERSONNEL MANAGEMENT IN PERSPECTIVE

It would be wrong to over-emphasize the uniqueness of personnel management work. Indeed Mintzberg (1973) describing the nature of managerial work in general identified six central characteristics. These were:

managers perform a great quantity of work at an unrelenting pace

management work is typically varied, fragmented and brief

managers prefer to deal with current, specific, *ad hoc* issues

managers sit in the middle of a network of contacts

managers prefer verbal media

most managers exert some control over their own activities.

With respect to all these characteristics there are exceptions; with respect to the last point, for example, Mintzberg acknowledges that some managers become puppets responding to crises. More explicitly, he insists that we are unlikely to over-estimate the complexity of managerial work. However in an effort to characterize it, he identifies three central types of behaviour concerned with interpersonal contact, information processing and decision-making.

Stewart (1982) has recently presented a view of managerial work which is similar to the process outlined earlier in the chapter. She distinguishes management work, managers' behaviour and managers' perception. In doing so, she emphasizes that each manager will carry out what may be ostensibly the same job in a rather different way. Any managerial job imposes certain demands, carries certain constraints and offers certain choices, which can be described as choices concerning what to do and how to do it. These choices will be influenced by the personal input and individual characteristics of each manager. Interestingly, her research shows that managers get carried along by the momentum of the job and are not always aware of the choices, even if in practice choices are constantly being made.

Personnel managers are therefore not alone in fire-fighting and rushing from one task to another; indeed both Mintzberg and Stewart suggest that managers in general could profitably spend more time thinking and planning. Nor are personnel managers alone in seeing the hustle, bustle and unpredictability of their work as one of its major attractions. Nevertheless there are a number of features of the personnel manager's role which suggest that the problems of performing effectively in it may be particularly acute.

The first factor is the quantity and diversity of tasks and knowledge associated with the job. Inevitably, this has led to division of the role and specialization within the function. However personnel managers who have responsibility at the unit level, in the factory, office or hospital often have to perform across the full range of personnel tasks and this places considerable demands upon their capacities. The second factor is the role of personnel as a service function which is further compounded by the fact that managers of all types invariably undertake a certain amount of what can be termed personnel activity. This results in constant concern for management of the boundaries of the role and for the establishment of non-substitutable knowledge and skills. In particular there is a dilemma about how much personnel activity to undertake or to press upon line management. The third factor is that personnel managers are concerned with human resources, which are less predictable and invariably more problematic than material resources. Furthermore, as Legge emphasized, because it is less tangible and less direct, it is more difficult to demonstrate successful management of human resources and even more difficult to demonstrate the part played by personnel managers. Finally, the human resource is generally recognized as a key factor in industry, yet personnel managers who are supposed to possess the expertise and skills to deal with it are often unable to exert as much influence as they would like. In other words, other managers claim a stake in the personnel managers' territory and a share of their expertise.

These four factors indicate that there will often be particular kinds of pressure upon personnel managers and that they face various types of dilemma and choice in determining how to pursue their goals. There is, therefore a need to think about these issues, to plan as carefully as possible and to consider alternative paths to effective performance. This requires a greater emphasis upon the proactive development of policies, procedures and competence than has been found in the existing studies of personnel managers. It is in part a question of strategy. Strategic issues are usually considered to exist only at a senior level in organizations, while managers at lower levels deal with tactics. In practice, as we have emphasized, there are invariably choices at all levels within the personnel function. Adjusting the scale a little, personnel strategy can be conceived of in terms of choice of policies and procedures, while tactics concern the process of implementation and the level of techniques. The use of the concept of strategy emphasizes the need to recognize choice and to consider planning ahead. The four factors also reflect the challenge, the attraction and the excitement of personnel management. Part of the satisfaction also comes from a recognition that despite what others may sometimes claim, the personnel manager's job is frequently demanding and difficult.

THE STRUCTURE AND APPROACH OF THE BOOK

The aim of the book is to describe personnel management work at the operational level reflecting the kind of approach outlined earlier in this chapter. This means that it must highlight choices and influences on the choices and also describe specific procedures. Since the book is intended to deal with applied and practical issues, it was decided that the bulk of it should be written by practitioners. Each topic is examined in some detail, but in the space of one chapter no subject can be comprehensively covered. The chapters can therefore be viewed as detailed introductions to the operational level of personnel management and at the end of each one further reading is indicated. In many but by no means all chapters, particular approaches have been illustrated with short case studies.

The authors have assumed little prior expertise or background knowledge of the subject. The book therefore introduces those who have to apply a specific aspect of personnel management for the first time to the relevant applied issues and procedures. It should therefore be of value to two main groups. The first are students studying personnel management; they should regard this book as a complement to, rather than as a substitute for existing texts which focus on a more general level of knowledge and of which the best known is probably Thomason's (1982) *Textbook of Personnel Management*. The second group are practitioners who are required to operate for the first time in an unfamiliar area of personnel management; the trainer who has to get involved in selection; the recruiter required to do some work on payment systems; or the industrial relations expert who is confronted with the need to consider job design. In practice, the student and the fairly junior practitioner will often overlap. For both, this is intended to be a practical source book.

The decision on what topics should be included is inevitably arbitrary. However an attempt has been made to provide a comprehensive coverage of the main applied areas within personnel management. To do this in sufficient detail requires two volumes. This first volume is divided into four main sections and the introduction to each section briefly elaborates upon the choice of topic and the particular approaches adopted by the authors.

REFERENCES

BREWSTER, Chris *and* RICHBELL, Susanne (1982). 'Getting managers to implement personnel policies.' *Personnel Management*. Vol. 14, No. 12, 34–37.

CHILD, John (1977). *Organization*. London, Harper and Row.

COOK JD, HEPWORTH SJ, WALL TD *and* WARR PB (1981). *The Experience of Work*. London, Academic Press.

GUEST, David *and* HORWOOD, Robert (1980). *The Role and Effectiveness of Personnel Managers: A Preliminary Report*. London, London School of Economics.

LEGGE, Karen (1978). *Power, Innovation and Problem-Solving in Personnel Management*. London, McGraw-Hill.

MINTZBERG H (1973). *The Nature of Managerial Work*. New York, Harper and Row.

STEWART R (1982). *Choices for the Manager*. London, McGraw-Hill.

THOMASON, George (1982). *A Textbook of Personnel Management*. Third ed., London, Institute of Personnel Management.

THURLEY, Keith *and* WIRDENIUS, Hans (1973). *Approaches to Supervisory Development*. London, Institute of Personnel Management.

TORRINGTON, Derek (1982). *Face-to-Face in Management*. London, Prentice Hall International.

NOTES

1 One of the major reasons for emphasizing this approach is the experience gained while acting as Chief Examiner for the Institute of Personnel Manage-

ment. It is clear that students are far more comfortable presenting knowledge than using the knowledge to tackle applied problems.

2 An excellent analysis of relevant organizational factors can be found in Child (1977). A more detailed consideration of strategies of change, particularly in relation to training and development is presented in Thurley and Wirdenius (1973).

3 There are a number of books which present, describe and evaluate some of the major types of measure used by industrial psychologists. A good and up-to-date example is the book by Cook *et al* (1981).

4 A discussion of several of the main contexts within which personnel managers have to utilize their social skills can be found in Torrington (1982).

Section Two

This second section contains two chapters concerned with establishing the administrative context of personnel management. The first of these chapters (chapter 2), by Christine Holroyd, deals with the setting up of a personnel department. This is a topic which has been largely ignored by textbooks on personnel management; indeed the existence of a personnel department is generally taken as given. In practice, however, many personnel practitioners, at all levels, can find themselves in a situation where they have to either create a new department or, more modestly, a new role. In both cases, the essential problem is the same, namely how to 'muscle in' on established practice and convince others that you can introduce significant improvements. The chapter identifies a set of stages in this process and outlines the problems, issues and choices for the practitioner at each stage. It does not provide detailed guidance on specific aspects of personnel practice such as training or payment systems. These are covered in the later chapters.

Chapter 3, by Barbara Dyer, examines the process of developing and maintaining personnel records. The importance of good quality personnel records and information as an essential prerequisite for effective personnel management is now generally recognized. The systems for recording personnel information are undergoing rapid development with the availability of a range of flexible computer systems. The chapter examines the choices available in determining what sort of records to keep and how to store them. The bibliography indicates further reading for those interested in examining the more technical aspects of some of the recent systems.

Chapter two

Setting up a personnel department

INTRODUCTION

New organizations and new departments within organizations are being set up every day. Yet surprisingly little advice is available on how to go about setting up a new department including, in this case, a new personnel department. Much energy has been directed towards advice on specific personnel systems, ie employee selection, manpower planning, appraisal, counselling, etc, assuming that a personnel department already exists. Part of the explanation for the lack of guidance available may lie in the difficulty of giving specific advice, since the appropriate action will vary widely depending on the organizational context and the objectives of the exercise. In this, as in so many aspects of personnel management, there is no one best way.

What can be identified, however, is a set of stages which can be used both to describe what often happens in practice and to provide some idea of the issues that ought to be considered in setting up a personnel department. In this chapter, the setting up of a personnel department will therefore be considered in terms of the following stages:

1 identifying and establishing the need
2 determining the role and appointing a person
3 induction
4 getting started
5 becoming established.

IDENTIFYING AND ESTABLISHING THE NEED FOR A PERSONNEL DEPARTMENT

The title of this chapter assumes that the decision to set up a personnel department has already been taken. There are at least six fairly common reasons for the decision to establish a personnel department.

GROWTH IN THE SIZE OF THE ORGANIZATION

As organizations grow in size and the management process becomes more complex, division of labour and the development of specialist activities becomes inevitable. The key dimension of size, as far as the personnel function is concerned, is usually the number of employees. The type of employees, including their skill mix, availability in the labour market and salary or wage levels may also be important. The point at which a specialist personnel department is set up will vary according to the perceived needs of the company and the circumstances in which it is operating, so there are dangers in specifying a particular number.

PROBLEMS ARISING FROM THE MANAGEMENT AND CONTROL OF THE WORKFORCE

Many organizations set up personnel departments to deal with the problems presented to the management by the workforce. A typical example might be an increase in trade union activity which has exposed the lack of adequate personnel policies and practices. Other examples include difficulties in recruitment of specialists, problems of poor pay structures and the proper application of national agreements.

PROBLEMS ARISING FROM THE GROWTH OF KNOWLEDGE AND INFORMATION

As the amount of knowledge required to manage the workforce increases, so too does the risk that organizations will become dated in their practices unless they possess specialists who can keep abreast with new developments. The most obvious area within the personnel field is the need to keep abreast of employment legislation and ensure that it is being noted and correctly applied. A painful experience at the hands of an industrial tribunal may underscore this need.

ANTICIPATED GROWTH IN THE BUSINESS

Wise organizations will plan ahead and any anticipated expansion in the workforce, bringing with it the need for more attention to selecting, training, developing and rewarding employees may point to the need to establish a personnel department.

SETTING UP A NEW SITE

Where a subsidiary of a larger parent body is being set up, an established personnel department can participate from the beginning in the planning of the new organization. Indeed a personnel department may exist on the drawing board and a personnel specialist may be appointed before the operation gets underway. Such a move makes considerable sense when the early critical activity includes recruiting and training a workforce, establishing terms and conditions of employment and allocating roles.

RESPONDING TO FASHION

Some organizations decide to set up a personnel department, in much the same way as they decide to buy a computer or hire economic forecasters, because others are doing so and it seems the fashionable thing to do. In the 1970s there was certainly a sense in which organizational problems were defined in personnel and industrial relations terms and the solution therefore seemed to be to have a personnel department. This was most noticeable in the public sector. Reviews or consultancy reports led to the establishment of a full-scale personnel function in the health service, in local government and in the central civil service to replace the old 'staff', 'establishment' or 'administration' sections. The problem with this approach, as we have seen recently in the context of the Civil Service, is that fashions can change and the need for a personnel department can in its turn be questioned.

Each of the above reasons for setting up a personnel department may, in their own context, be valid. They do, however, illustrate the variety of reasons for the decision and emphasize the need for careful diagnosis and analysis of the thinking behind the decision prior to the establishment of plans and priorities for the department.

One further issue needs to be considered in analysing the decision stage. It concerns the question of who took the decision. There are three possible options:

1 the existing management team
2 outside consultants
3 the headquarters personnel function staff decide to set up a personnel
   department in a subsidiary.

The answer is important because it could have a bearing upon the
priorities for the new department, on its power base and on its chances of
making an effective contribution. In particular, it is likely that the
existing management team, unless they have sought outside advice, may
be in a poor position to understand either the potential or the appropriate
structure for a new personnel department. Equally, as the health service
and civil service illustrate, a decision by outside consultants, imposed
from the top of the organization, may encounter opposition from established employees who feel that their position is threatened.

For all these reasons anyone appointed to a newly established personnel department must examine closely the influences behind the decision
to set up the department and be sensitive to the disturbance that the
department causes to established systems and power bases. Equally, those
influencing and involved in the decision, perhaps from a headquarters
base, must look closely at these factors and give appropriate support if
they are to ensure that the move will be a success.

DETERMINING THE ROLE AND APPOINTING A PERSON

These two issues must be looked at from two sides, first from the point of
view of the organization making the appointment and secondly from the
perspective of the individual who may be given the job of setting up the
new department.

The key decisions for the management, concern the type of personnel
department they envisage and therefore the type of person they wish to
appoint to manage it. Prior to recruitment of a personnel manager,
preliminary decisions will have to be made about the duties and responsibilities, the reporting relationships, the resources for the department
and about terms and conditions for the employment of the manager. At
the same time it is necessary to consider how much flexibility should be
built into the role and the terms and conditions to accommodate the
skills and experience of the most attractive candidate. The type of role
will depend upon two features of the organizational context. First, in
subsections of public sector or large private sector organizations, the

pattern established at other locations may be used by headquarters staff to shape the role. Second, in organizations which are expanding and have no obvious 'model' of a personnel role to follow, there will be a temptation to combine roles. Some of the more popular combinations include Personnel and Administration, Personnel and Accountancy and Management Services and Personnel. The danger with this approach is that it may deter personnel professionals who will be unhappy at the prospect of stepping outside their main areas of expertise.

The major choices in selecting the new personnel manager are whether to choose someone from inside or outside the existing organization and/or someone who is already experienced in personnel management. When a personnel department is about to be established (perhaps as a result of rapid growth) there is an overwhelming case for appointing an experienced outsider. Indeed the lack of internal expertise is likely to justify the use of selection consultants to assist in the appointment. Where the personnel department is going to be set up at a new site or expanding site and the appointment is likely to be controlled by the personnel department of the parent organization, there are more options. It may, for example, make sense to appoint someone from within the existing personnel function, either at headquarters or at another location.

In considering whom to appoint, two further points are worth bearing in mind. First, there is a case for appointing someone who has worked in at least two personnel departments, and thus knows that there is more than one right way of doing things. Secondly, it is important to remember that to make a success of the job requires energy, determination and patience. It should therefore not be someone who is too inexperienced and impatient, nor too old and lacking in energy.

Turning now to the perspective of the person about to be appointed as the new personnel manager, it is understandable and tempting, particularly when unemployment among personnel managers is high and the alternative may well be the dole queue, to accept any job offer gratefully and not to ask any difficult questions until the contract of employment has been signed. On the other hand, if a success is to be made of the job, it is very important to clarify a number of key issues.

It is essential that detailed discussions take place before the appointment is finalized and that the exchange of information is thorough and frank. Once it is clear to the candidate that he (or she) is likely to be offered the post, he must take the initiative to discuss the way in which the function might operate, the way in which it would relate to other functions, the sort of objectives that it would be expected to achieve and so on. It is at this stage that a candidate should establish the reporting relationship, the extent of coverage of the function (in case, for example, there are any residual notions that the department will deal with shop-floor employees only) and the limits on finance and support staff which are envisaged. Finally his or her own terms and conditions of employment must be drawn up. This is particularly important when the person charged with making the appointment may have only the slimmest idea of what personnel management is all about and what its scope and contribution can be. It is also desirable to meet as many members of the senior management team as is practicable in order to allay doubts on both sides.

At this stage it is important for the new incumbent to probe the reason for the establishment of a personnel department as listed earlier. Not only does it give vital background knowledge but will provide the newly-appointed personnel manager with some valuable time to plan the early approaches before starting the job. Another matter worth raising (with delicacy) is the question of the announcement that may or may not precede the personnel manager's arrival. A badly-worded or erroneous statement written by someone else may take years to live down, therefore, the prudent personnel manager will seek to draft his own.

A further point which should be discussed at the pre-appointment stage is the question of the personnel manager's own induction. It is worth aiming at having an agreed minimum period (three months would be ideal) before taking up any specific duties. For this halcyon period the new person may ask any questions he likes, may forget and have to be reminded of names, may use layman's words rather than industry jargon and may be forgiven for not knowing by heart every phrase of the union agreements; thereafter, total knowledge will be expected.

So, the period of detailed interviews and exploratory discussions is over and our new personnel manager knows a great deal about the organization, the industry in which it operates, the reasons for the decision to set up a personnel department, the nature and scope of its activities and where the early priorities will lie. He would also be well advised to make enquiries outside the organization to learn what is available about its local and industry reputation as an employer, about its financial standing and past business performance (if it is a commercial or industrial concern) and what the long-term trends are likely to be.

INDUCTION OF THE PERSONNEL MANAGER

After the introductions and tour of the organization, the personnel manager must begin the induction programme. The process will vary according to the context and in particular according to whether he is entering an established organization or a new site. The rules of common sense apply but, in meeting and talking to new colleagues, the personnel manager should request facts and figures and then seek to categorize the information. The following guidelines apply to most situations:

'INDUSTRY' INFORMATION

The term 'industry' is meant to cover the type of organization whether it be retail distribution, hospital service, banking and insurance, local government, university education or manufacturing industry. What constitutes the 'competition'; how do terms and conditions compare; is there a common body such as an employers' association; are there industry agreements with the trade unions? In due course the personnel manager will be required to know almost as much about the competition as about his or her own organization, so careful study and documentation is desirable. A number of exchange visits with counterparts might be planned at the later stages of the induction.

'LOCAL' INFORMATION

As well as wishing to become known at the local offices of the Departments of Employment and Health and Social Security and the main schools and colleges in the area, the personnel manager should try to make contacts with other local personnel people. 'Cold calling' may be a little difficult so early participation in the activities of the nearest IPM group may yield considerably better results. Study of the local press is also useful to assess its potential for recruitment advertising.

TRADE UNION INFORMATION

Careful study of all existing agreements is, of course, essential. So too is discussion with managers who have operated the agreements to establish where deviations have crept in: even in organizations which claim to follow their agreements very closely, it is unusual to find total compliance with the written word. Early discussions with shop stewards, branch and area officials is necessary and in due course courtesy visits to national officers should be arranged.

'Technical' information

However non-technical the personnel manager may feel himself to be, serious efforts should be made to get to grips with the technology and jargon of the enterprise: ignorance in this area will be exposed in due course and reduce the standing of the personnel manager: on the other hand, detailed knowledge (or at least intelligent understanding) will prove an asset. The acquisition of this information comes from discussions with technical colleagues, (who, generally, are delighted to explain their particular speciality to anyone who will listen) line managers, supervisors, maintenance engineers, sales and production staff. During the induction programme time should be made for a period on the shop floor either for close observation or, if practicable, for personal participation. In the course of this period, someone should be asked to list the common jargon of the business and provide definitions: this glossary can be used later in the induction programme for other new employees.

'Source' information

The personnel manager starting a department will discover that his basic data has to be gathered from many sources. These may include the company secretary, the payroll office, the chief executive, the chief accountant, the work study department, the pension scheme secretary, the production or senior line manager, the industrial nurse or chief first-aider, to name but a few. Total co-operation in providing this data is not to be expected: all the human relations skills possessed by the personnel manager will have to be brought to bear in obtaining this information freely and voluntarily. Other source material will be obtained from publications such as the organization's annual report, monthly accounts, sales or promotional literature, and, if they exist, safety and training policies.

'Systems' information

It will be useful at the induction stage for the new personnel manager to learn about the operation of various systems in his new organization: for example, how and when budgets are compiled, how monthly accounts are prepared, how and when expense accounts have to be submitted.

It may be that the personnel department is being established within a unit of a larger organization where a personnel function already exists. If this is the case, clearly a third dimension is introduced and close regard will have to be paid to 'group' policies, procedures and priorities.

During the induction period, the new personnel manager should anticipate possible problems. First, he or she should be prepared at all times for popular misconceptions about this new department: in the view of some people, the prime function will be sick visiting, for others it will be hiring and firing, for others, taking a grip on the canteen and sports and social club. Secondly, the personnel manager should have his senses alert to the sound of grinding axes and the sight of chip-laden shoulders: in the nature of things, all organizations have their share of people who feel badly done by and the advent of a personnel manager is seen by many as the opportunity to have their wrongs righted and it is essential for the personnel manager to recognize when he is being lobbied and to be carefully non-committal unless it is something that he can solve. Thirdly, the personnel manager must anticipate opposition from colleagues who feel threatened by his presence, either because he will be taking over certain responsibilities which others do not want to release or because he might discover errors and inadequacies in current practices. Here, again, considerable sensitivity and the exercise of social skills will be required. Fourthly, despite the best intentions regarding the induction period, there is a chance that it will be disregarded by colleagues who will begin to expect answers and results fairly swiftly (there are problems in recruiting a new systems analyst; a training course is required; the safety policy manual needs to be modified; bonus system problems are threatening to produce industrial action in the goods inward department, etc, etc) and the new personnel manager will be unusual if his or her desire to display professional competence and to influence important decisions does not come to the fore. All the more reason, therefore, to use the induction period wisely and intensively.

GETTING STARTED

THE ANALYSIS OF THE SITUATION

Having armed himself with a fair amount of background information, the new personnel manager must undertake a careful review of the current situation in the organization under the various headings into which the personnel function divides itself. In a situation where the function is being set up in an established organization, the new personnel manager must expect to find wide variations in personnel practice; after all, as Munro Fraser (1971) says 'every manager is a personnel manager no matter what his job may be ...' and where no-one has been charged with the task of ensuring consistency and common practice, managers will have arrived at their own solutions and made their own decisions. 'Decisions regarding employees' states Dale Beach 'are commonly made under the pressure of the situation without regard for the long-run consequences' (Beach, 1975, p 77).

The review of the various areas of personnel activity is likely to highlight a range of problems and inappropriate practices, some of which can prove disconcerting for the personnel manager whose previous experience has been in organizations with well-established personnel departments. It is, of course, equally disconcerting for anyone who has recently completed professional personnel management training, with its emphasis on how the personnel function ought to work rather than on the actual practice in contexts where it is undeveloped.

There is a large number of areas of personnel activity which will have to be considered at some time. However, it is unlikely that an organization without a personnel function will have an established system of, for example, manpower planning or appraisal. But there will be identifiable practices in areas such as recruitment and selection, payment, records and industrial relations, These will often be priority areas for action and this section concentrates on them, identifying the difficulties that can be presented by the existing practices of non-personnel people and the types of situation with which the new personnel practitioner might be confronted.

Recruitment and selection

Departmental managers will probably have carried out this activity themselves; sometimes there is some rough form of 'grouping', ie the Chief Accountant recruits all 'office' jobs, the Production Manager all manual jobs, the Managing Director all senior executive jobs. It is uncommon to find any interchange of candidates and quite usual to see a number of the company's recruitment advertisements in the same edition of the local press in different formats with replies to be addressed to a number of different people.

Confusion can arise too at the local office of the Department of Employment Jobcentre where the officer submitting applicants may not appreciate the necessity of sending a candidate to see a named individual. The candidate may spend an uncomfortable hour being told by the receptionist that various managers have no vacancies whilst the one he has really been sent to see is off the premises attending to a customer query. Similar lack of uniformity will apply to the methods of selection—

anything from the most cursory one-to-one interviews to a full-scale board of directors grilling. Practice with regard to references and sight of confirmatory documents will be equally variable as will the treatment of rejected candidates. Some managers will meet expenses, others not; some managers will allow 20 minutes per interview, others half a day. Needless to say the records of the interview will range from nothing to three pages of highly detailed information. Performance tests may be used for shorthand typists and aptitude tests for craft apprentices but otherwise probably nothing.

Terms and conditions of employment

The picture here may not be too bleak: with luck, the Contracts of Employment Act will have been observed and the main anomalies removed. If the workforce is unionized, union agreements should have ensured standard terms and conditions for union members. Conditions of service for other employees may have been the subject of written instructions from the Chief Executive, but there may be very large anomalies in the area of non-negotiated wages and salaries, exacerbated by the lack of a formal system of job evaluation and performance rating.

Particular study will have to be made of pension provisions: schemes have a tendency to look alike in their broad outline—for example: based on sixtieths, final salary, five per cent contribution, cash disregard for the State scheme—but vary in detail—for example: provision for dependants, rules for early retirement, commutation clauses, make-up of Trustees. All the particular features of the Company's scheme should be mastered. The extent of pension provision must also be fully understood lest in error the scheme is offered to a new recruit who is ineligible.

Having indicated that negotiated terms and conditions are likely to be reasonably uniform, one subject that may require close attention is that of any production bonus or productivity scheme that is in operation. It is an area fraught with problems and frequently the subject of disputes, accordingly the personnel manager must quickly come to grips with its basis, its method of calculation, its yield when compared with basic pay, how it is updated when production changes occur and so on. Failure to master this topic will expose the personnel manager to both union and management colleagues as someone who has not done his or her homework in an area which is of considerable importance.

Training and development

Unless one executive has been charged with the task of overseeing training and development there is a likelihood of wide variations in practice between departments or functions. Some will have found it relatively easy to recruit suitably qualified people from 'outside' and will have done little or nothing by way of training; others, where there has been a specialist requirement, will have undertaken some sort of training. An enthusiastic and far-sighted management may have recognized training and development as a key function and have achieved very good results: more usually, the position which is inherited will be a function of the need which has been felt to train for business or professional reasons. It is unlikely that training and development will have been linked to any kind of overall manpower or succession planning because, unless the Chief Executive has a personal interest in such matters, there is no-one to cross departmental or functional boundaries.

Industrial relations

The experienced personnel manager should have gained a good 'feel' of industrial relations in the organization during the induction period. Knowing that industrial relations will be a principal interest of the new manager, many colleagues and shop stewards will be keen to give their views on the situation. It is most important to take these opinions into account but it is equally important to carry out a number of independent checks.

The number of trade unions and their relative strength within their 'catchment areas' must be ascertained; the extent of activity based upon the frequency of, and attendance at, meetings should be assessed; the skill with which recent local agreements have been drawn up should be judged and, finally, the extent to which there has been any sort of hostile industrial action should be noted. Clearly, these features must be examined in context—certain industries and certain unions are much more prone to industrial action than others.

Very considerable care must be taken over the industrial relations analysis; the prudent personnel manager will not reach hasty conclusions. Many things can influence, for good or ill, the industrial relations climate of an organization; for example, certain key personalities, local customs, the state of company communications, the relative standing of the terms and conditions, the prosperity of the business during recent times and so on. The natural desire of the personnel professional to make premature changes to what he or she finds should be resisted and any proposed moves should be most carefully considered and discussed with the appropriate line managers.

Communications

This is an interesting area of study for the new personnel manager and a vital one. All sources of communication should be taken into account and given due weighting—formal verbal (the manager or supervisor), informal verbal (the grapevine), the delegate system (employee/management joint council), the written word (notice boards/newspapers/annual reports), and audio visual presentations (closed circuit television), briefing meetings etc. Apart from the obvious need within an organization to have effective communications for an enormous number of purposes, the new personnel manager will have a special and particular need—he or she has the difficult task of conveying to the members of the organization what the role, function, purpose and objectives of the new department are to be, what its systems and methods will be and how it will relate to established institutions within the organization. The personnel function is one that touches the lives of everyone working in the enterprise and doubts, fears and misunderstandings should, as far as humanly possible, be allayed.

Records

The new personnel manager will find that his raw data is spread fairly widely and may be incomplete in a number of respects. The payroll office and the pensions office (or the insurance company) will carry details of dates of birth and service as well as rates of pay; initial recruitment data will probably still be with the manager who did the recruiting while the current manager probably has the training records. In some organizations the position may be easier than this and careful analysis may reveal ways in which small changes may yield all the initial data which is required. It will be sensible at this stage to establish what data processing facilities exist in the organization and to what extent basic personnel files can be set up, with, of course, suitable controls on access and confidentiality. A personnel department which is being newly-established is likely to be short-staffed, and the new personnel manager must, therefore, look for speedy, efficient and labour saving methods of producing his personnel reports and returns.

THE STRATEGY FOR ACTION

The new personnel manager has now gathered together a considerable amount of data and the first drawer of the filing cabinet is well on the way to being filled. Where to start the action? A difficult problem to which there is no absolute or single solution; to a very large extent the sequence of events must be determined by practical considerations and in all probability, despite the desirability of an induction period, the personnel manager will have started to make an initial contribution on a piecemeal basis. However it is essential that at some point towards the end of the initial induction period the personnel manager gives careful thought to his priorities and devises a strategy which will ensure the successful establishment of the personnel department. In doing this a number of general points should be borne in mind:

The key organizational problems and priorities

The personnel manager must not lose sight of the reasons why he was appointed and must take steps to identify and analyse key problems and priorities and, in collaboration with other managers, set initial objectives. When the personnel manager is working in a new unit, the priority may be recruitment, selection and training. In established organizations it may be to develop industrial relations procedures, to meet legal requirements or sort out pay anomalies. In practice there may well be not one but several urgent issues that need tackling and some order of priority must be established. For this to be successful it is clear that the initial period of induction and fact finding is crucial.

Organizational constraints

The size, shape and structure of the organization as well as the nature and success of the business will have an impact upon the new personnel manager's strategy. It may well be that his new organization consists of a number of fairly small units dispersed over a wide area but making the same or similar products; the dispersal may be the same in another case but the product range very diverse; yet again the newly-established department may be in a largish subsidiary of a group which has no central personnel department but has some common personnel policies, the pension scheme for example. Another range of variants arises as a result of overseas ownership of the business: some foreign parents take a close interest in the personnel policies of their overseas subsidiaries others take little or none.

Clearly, the structure of the business will have a profound effect upon the sort of personnel department which can be set up. It is more than likely that the new personnel manager will have to arrive at a number of compromises which will not necessarily be of his or her choice but will be dictated by the circumstances of the operation. Considerable skill and patience is required in weaving together what have hitherto been very disparate personnel policies and practices in units with different histories

32

and management styles. Any early attempts at enforcement will almost certainly be doomed as will a lofty 'professional personnel' approach. It must be realized that the senior people in each unit usually have considerable pride in their operation and have developed systems and methods which work in practice and these will not lightly be surrendered unless the alternative is manifestly better. In consequence, the personnel manager may have to accept a variety of relatively unsatisfactory personnel practices within the organization for a considerable time; early acceptance of such a situation will minimize prolonged and acute frustration!

Staffing and other resources

It is an axiom that the personnel department can only cover those activities for which it has adequate resources. However, the point needs to be underscored because the enthusiastic founder of the function will be sorely tempted to tackle all the activities traditionally encompassed by established departments; the desire to set up an appraisal system based upon the latest theories will run parallel to the wish to sort out the canteen price structure; the urge to breathe participative life into the moribund works committee will compete for time with the desire to see common practices with regard to the provision of protective clothing; the need to study proposed changes to the pension scheme will be at odds with the urgent requirement to produce a written training policy. The new personnel manager must exert considerable self-control in the use of time.

It is possible that the new manager may inherit a member of staff, ie someone who has been performing some personnel duties either full-time or part-time alongside some other activity. The task then will be to assess the extent and quality of this person's contribution to see how it might be harnessed in the future. Reactions to the advent of a new manager may vary from relief to resentment and must be handled accordingly. No matter how unpromising the first impressions, every opportunity, including training, must be given and every sympathy extended to someone whose working life may be substantially disrupted. Apart from the moral considerations, there are the practical considerations. On the positive side, the individual in question is likely to be the keeper of much valuable information and have considerable useful experience to bring to bear; on the negative side, casual or callous treatment will be given wide publicity and will do nothing to enhance the reputation of the new personnel department at a time when all eyes will be upon it.

If there is no such legacy, the new personnel manager will probably

33

wish to recruit a secretary-cum-personnel assistant. For this appointment the natural tendency will be to try to recruit from outside but if the new incumbent believes in internal opportunity first, this is the right moment to display this belief. He may be surprised by the number of capable and knowledgeable secretaries who are longing to 'work with people' as a welcome change from the buying department, the Chief Accountant's office, the production planning section or whatever.

Once the priorities, objectives and scope of the activity of the personnel department has been agreed, it may be possible to demonstrate the need for further staff. However it may well be that other managers need convincing of the value of the personnel department's contribution through action rather than argument before acquiescing in its expansion.

Two other types of resource need to be dealt with at an early stage. The first is money. A provisional budget may have been agreed when the decision to establish a department was taken. Once initial priorities and plans have been agreed this may need to be reviewed. At the same time there may be some flexibility about the allocation of expenses to various departmental budgets. The costs of training, for example, may traditionally have fallen upon the production department and it may continue to carry this cost. How far the personnel manager will wish to renegotiate the budget will depend upon his judgement of the organization climate and the degree of flexibility which exists. He must be careful not to cause a negative impression by trying to enlarge his budget before he has made a contribution. On the other hand, there is a question of how much can be done without adequate resources. In this respect it will help if other senior managers have taken some part in the planning of personnel priorities and therefore can understand and identify with what is being sought.

With regard to physical resources, ie space and equipment, in a rapidly expanding organization there may be pressure on space and many newly appointed managers have found themselves sharing an office or a desk. The nature of personnel work and an adequate filing system means that a good case can usually be made for office space. According to the priorities, the personnel manager may also have to obtain or perhaps re-equip training facilities.

Initial action
Implicit in the discussion of the initial strategy is the need for planning. It is desirable to draw up and obtain senior management agreement for an initial plan of action. This should set out the priorities and goals for the first year and should be arrived at after the analysis of the organiza-

tional context and after discussion and consultation with a wide range of people but with senior management in particular. Care must be taken to ensure that the plan is realistic. An over-ambitious plan might look impressive at the outset but will create false expectations and lead to negative repercussions in the long-term.

From the start it is essential to avoid simplistic or over-optimistic assumptions about what can be achieved or about the knowledge, skills and likely reactions of others. For example it must not be assumed that what has worked elsewhere in the past will readily transplant to the new organization, nor that the new appointment of a personnel manager will be greeted with universal popular acclaim; it must not be assumed that line managers and other functional specialists lack knowledge about the principles and practice of personnel management (the theories of behavioural scientists are now as much a part of the syllabuses of general management courses as of personnel management programmes). Instead of such assumptions, all proposed courses of action should be thought through very carefully: the reason for the action should be clear, all possible obstacles should be anticipated and all possible side-effects taken into account. Inevitably at the 'start-up' of a personnel department there is a great deal to be done, resources are very limited and the temptation to cut corners is great but should be resisted.

A pragmatic view suggests that nothing succeeds like success. In establishing the credibility of the personnel department it is important to be seen to achieve early success in tackling some of the key problems of the company, in particular by helping managers to solve their perceived problems. It is also sensible to be seen as a helpful and available resource. Time-consuming and worrying tasks like recruitment and selection can (with some assistance) swiftly be taken over by the personnel manager. A certain helplessness in the face of an obviously imbalanced salary structure is another area where the new personnel manager may find that his efforts are quickly appreciated (not least by the Chief Executive!). High turnover amongst new recruits may be stemmed by the rapid introduction of a well-balanced induction programme.

It is tempting and in some circumstances probably essential to get the personnel department swiftly established as a useful, credible and seemingly indispensable part of the organization. At the same time it is important to bear in mind the long-term contribution that the department might make. In this respect it is necessary to guard against being overwhelmed by trivia or by becoming what Drucker (1961) termed the 'trash can' of the organization, receiving all the bits of work that no one else wants to deal with. A failure to ensure that other managers face up

35

to their responsibilities for the management of human resources is one of the risks if the personnel department seems all too ready and willing to take them over. Such a course of action may store up future problems for the personnel department and for the organization as a whole.

The first year will be exciting and chaotic; but at some point, perhaps after a year, it is essential to stop and take stock. A good technique is to write the first annual report of the personnel department which reviews the year past but also looks ahead. This is the time to consider longer term issues more carefully. The personnel department has been set up; now it is time to become established.

BECOMING ESTABLISHED

After about a year, a manager of a new personnel department will have developed a 'feel' for the organization, made judgements about his colleagues and evaluated the ease with which it is possible to get things done. He must now try to decide the nature of the longer term personnel contribution. Occasionally this may be rooted, at least partly in a social or business philosophy. One view of personnel management in this context is presented by Maurice Cuming (1968). Replying to the question 'What peculiar contribution does (the personnel manager) make to the efficiency of the organization?' Cuming says:

> The primary justification, as with any other appointment, must be in terms of business efficiency. ... This cannot be done without regard to fundamental concepts of human relations. Clearly no organization can operate efficiently unless its staff are content with what is offered them as human beings by way of job satisfaction, prospects and working conditions. The personnel specialist's task is to identify the needs of employees in these areas, recognize what it is about his organization that fulfils these needs or frustrates them and be able to advise departmental managers on actions that will promote this fulfilment or remove the frustrations. Heads of departments basically have technical responsibilities; the personnel specialist's job is to explain to them reasons for social behaviour which may not be obvious. ... Offering advice to clarify such situations is a task that demands an expert who has been trained to perceive the ways in which individuals and groups interact within an organization, and who can convey his understanding in practical terms to departmental heads who are too preoccupied with their technical activities to have time to consider the social system of the work place as a whole. ... (Cuming, 1968, p 10)

Most organizations do not have an explicit philosophy which has a direct bearing upon the contribution of the personnel function—unless we accept general statements about profits and efficiency. However a philosophy is often embedded in various features of company policy and practice and it is this philosophy which helps to give some employers a good or bad reputation within the labour market. The personnel manager, who may well have undergone professional training, is likely to have views of his own and will wish to help to shape the organization's values and the way it treats its workforce, thus helping to create an organizational style for the management of human resources.

A second, but related long-term issue in establishing personnel management as a central part of the organization is the nature and scope of personnel work. Karen Legge (1978) has documented the failure of personnel managers to participate fully in management planning and policy development. Often this is a consequence of being too fully engaged in day to day issues. Involvement of this sort provides a sense of power through apparent indispensability. At the same time it can be a recipe for ineffectiveness.

Personnel managers have some choice over the way in which a new personnel department develops. Careful thought must be given to means of striking a balance between long-term and short-term issues; between reactive fire-fighting and proactive innovation. One aid in this respect is learning to say 'no' when line managers try to impose more work on the personnel department. This is a step towards creating a clear demarcation between issues for personnel and for other departments. A second possibility, particularly when the personnel department is expanding, is to consider carefully the allocation of the roles within the department, to ensure that sufficient development and planning work takes place. A third approach is to be far more flexible about departmental boundaries. Team working may involve members of other departments in personnel work; at the same time personnel staff could become more involved in production planning and technical design in the hope of forestalling later problems. It becomes progressively more difficult to break out of an established mould so it is all the more important to start considering these issues, which are central to the long-term contribution of the personnel department, at the earliest possible moment.

CONCLUSION

Much has been said in this chapter about timing and the enthusiastic personnel professional is well advised not to expect too much too quickly. This is tedious advice when so much has to be done but in this instance speed is *not* the essence of the contract. It is a good discipline to keep a diary of major discoveries and developments and as time goes by it will really demonstrate that progress has been made and objectives achieved.

Lest the reader disbelieves the time-scale problem, as long ago as 1959 Colonel Urwick, in an IPM Occasional Paper, said:

> There are two centuries of experience of laissez-faire individualistic economics behind the thinking of the workers and of most employers and managers. Their effects cannot be dissipated and a real concern for morale inculcated in any substantial undertaking by a burst of passing interest. My own estimate is that it takes ten to fifteen years of patient, persistent, prudent effort to get any worthwhile results which are really reflected in the attitude of the rank and file.

More than 20 years later one might substitute more current phraseology but nevertheless the point is well made.

And finally, the good news. After all the hard work, the disappointments and delays, the results do begin to show and an enormously high degree of job satisfaction is achieved when the day comes which brings the realization that the personnel department is truly an integral part of the organization and that no major decisions are taken without consideration of their personnel implications.

APPENDIX: CASE STUDY

The Company, part of a larger group, at a time of reasonable economic growth had four locations and a fifth due to open later in the year. There were approximately a thousand employees and no personnel department.

Recognizing that it had moved from being a small to a medium-sized operation the Company had enlisted management consultants to examine its organization and recommend improvements in the management structure where necessary.

The broad approach taken by the consultants was that a divisional framework should be established to provide common management for the small number of operating companies and that a divisional personnel manager should be included amongst the list of new appointments.

The report was accepted by the Company and the consultants were given the task of recruiting the new posts. The need had therefore been identified by external agents and was not generated by management.

The candidate eventually appointed found a curious situation: an embryonic divisional structure, new corporate activities and five new or nearly-new plant managers. The self-induction programme was critical: partly to become familiar with the product, the market and the technology and partly to learn the history of the individual plants, the culture of the Company and to meet key individuals. Data collection in this period became important and copies of contracts of employment, any current union agreements, bonus scheme information, national agreements—in or out of date—were all eagerly swept up for further study and future reference.

Common threads began to emerge gradually. Although there were variants, the plants were all concerned with a similar product range, all were within the compass of one national agreement and one general trade union had the majority membership in four of the five units. This information prompted a round of calls to the employers association and to both national and area union officials. The Company's reputation appeared to stand high and some relief was expressed that there would now be a single point of contact with the Company.

The next requirement was to gather information about Company employees. Personal data was singularly lacking, although the pensions and payroll offices were able to provide a limited amount of basic information. To fill the gap a personal questionnaire was sent to all employees requesting the sort of information contained on a typical job application form. This method had been used in a previous 'green field' situation, had worked well and was now being copied. The result however was markedly different: the whole exercise was greeted with suspicion and hostility, probably because not enough trouble was taken about introducing the document and explaining its purpose. Belated attempts to protest the innocence of the request were largely ignored, blank proforma were consigned to the waste chutes and personal approaches through supervision were frequently met with outright refusals. Thus, the short cut proved to be the long route and much time was subsequently wasted trying to fill gaps.

Soon after the existence of a 'personnel department' (of one person) became a reality rather than a rumour, the work began to arrive although not in the sequence that might have seemed most logical. Initially, because the Company had just experienced rapid growth and because the Training Board had been making its presence felt, the requirement was to provide training of all types for all categories of staff at once. This necessitated a request to the Company for the first additional member of staff, a training manager.

A budget was presented and the reasons for the appointment were stated. Approval was forthcoming and the candidate was appointed. This, for the moment at least, eased the pressure on this front. The departmental managers were given help in preparing their performance appraisals and from these the training needs were developed. The list, as can be imagined, was frighteningly long. The Company, like Topsy, had 'just grown', promotion had largely been vertical and based on service as much as performance. Such a pattern, by no means untypical, based largely upon expediency produced yawning gaps in the basic knowledge of managers and supervisors outside their own immediate spheres. In an attempt to deal with as many demands as possible, no doubt mistakes were made but nevertheless a logical approach was sought.

Supervisors who had displayed some aptitude for training were selected for each unit and given training in the elements of instruction. They then were given the task of carrying out basic job instruction. Next, a crash programme of supervisory training was introduced, action centred leadership widely employed and NEBSS courses started up in collaboration with neighbouring colleges.

The salesmen too had high priority: greater product knowledge was required for the junior men, a better perception of modern sales and marketing techniques for the older. Consultants were employed to assist in the latter programme and the Company's own specialists harnessed to assist with the product knowledge programme.

With the help of a student project team, an attitude survey was carried out into employee communications. The outcome was the establishment of a Company newspaper which in addition to conveying information proved valuable in establishing a corporate identity and in linking the five dispersed locations. The establishment of consultative committees was, sadly, only partially successful: trade union hostility to a body not formally linked to the trade union movement, together with considerable management inertia did not create the right environment for these particular ventures.

With regard to the trade union situation as a whole there was, initially, a certain amount of trying and testing until those concerned had got the measure of each other. In general however, the trade union representatives and committees were helpful and the early task of introducing or rewriting and updating the various agreements proved to be mutually useful. In some units, procedural agreements gave union representatives a greater certainty about their position than they had had and, together with better provision of facilities, brought about a more orderly conduct of union affairs.

Other projects in the initial period included a wholesale redesign of personnel pro-forma, an onslaught on induction programmes to counter very high turnover and a detailed study of the salary structure with a medium-term plan to smooth out the anomalies.

FOOTNOTE

Since those early days, many events have taken place in the Company and trade cycles have caused changes in both personnel policy and practice. Line and general managers are more broadly based and much more skilful in handling their personnel and industrial relations affairs. There is a much greater perception amongst everyone who works in the organization about their inter-dependence and the necessity of treating the customer as pre-eminent. The flow of labour legislation has kept everyone on a high-learning curve, but in general has provided a sensible regulatory framework.

As to that early 'personnel department' it has not been without its vicissitudes, but it remains an integral part of the Company seeking always to ensure that the human side of the enterprise is never overlooked.

REFERENCES

BEACH, Dale S (1975). *Personnel, The Management of People at Work*. London, MacMillan.

CUMING MW (1968). *The Theory and Practice of Personnel Management*. London, Heinemann.

LEGGE, Karen (1978). *Power, Innovation and Problem-Solving in Personnel Management*. London, McGraw-Hill.

MUNRO, Fraser J (1971). *Introduction to Personnel Management*. London, Nelson.

URWICK Lt. Col. LF (1959). *Personnel Management in Perspective*. London, IPM Occasional Paper.

Chapter three

Developing and maintaining personnel records

INTRODUCTION

The growth of personnel management is inescapably linked with the growth of modern 'bureaucratic' management, with its need for systematic recording and use of information. The need to keep personnel records was for many years regarded as a mundane and often time-consuming aspect of personnel work which could also become complex and troublesome as organizations grew in size or changed in character. Very little was written specifically on the subject of personnel records.

Over the past decade the picture has changed. There has been a great deal of new employment legislation which has necessitated more careful collection, recording and presentation of personnel information. Coupled with the increasing need for the personnel function to justify itself in quantitative terms, this has meant that the availability and quality of personnel information has become more central to effective personnel management. Secondly, the advent of computerized personnel information systems has created opportunities for much more sophisticated information storage, analysis and retrieval. These new requirements and opportunities have meant that the subject of personnel records has begun to attract considerable attention.

Nevertheless, record keeping is clearly not the primary function of the personnel department which is concerned now with the total effectiveness of the work force in achieving the objectives of the creation of wealth or the provision of services. However, in order to fulfil this wider role, the personnel department needs to be able to provide information about the

43

employees and to provide it in such a way that it will aid decision making on vital aspects of the business.

Granted the enormous variety of organizations there can be no standard set of personnel records: each company has to develop a personnel information system to meet its own requirements. It is, therefore, necessary to:

define the general aims of a personnel record system

set the objectives for the particular system for the organization in question

specify the records, paperwork and procedures which will be necessary to achieve those objectives.

Before developing our discussion under these three headings it is necessary to be clear on the scope and limitation of the material here presented. The term 'personnel records' is used to include all records and forms used by the personnel department, including statistical as well as individual records, and including forms geared very closely to some immediate action. The discussion is confined largely to setting up and maintaining a system, rather than to the details of its operation. The discussion has a practical aim and is related to real problems for the personnel manager. It is not a disquisition on management information systems generally, of which the personnel system might be seen as a subdivision. Nor is it a plea for an enhanced role for management science and computers in extending the boundaries and the possibilities of information systems, though the chapter ends with some consideration of this. The provision of a sound, even if simple, record system is absolutely basic to personnel management as the following discussion should make clear.

THE GENERAL AIMS OF A PERSONNEL RECORD SYSTEM

The capacity of the human brain to store, retrieve and interpret large quantities of information is all too clearly limited, so that the need to replace the unstructured collection of facts and opinions in managers' minds by formal and structured personnel information systems soon becomes self-evident in a growing organization. One way of doing this could be by classifying the types of information required in a temporal sequence, from recruitment through to final exit from the company.

This could be a helpful way of classifying the range of information required, particularly if one is trying to conceptualize and gain a rough and ready understanding of the whole system. It is not so helpful, however, if one is endeavouring to change and get the most out of systems, where a different analysis can be employed in which the purpose of personnel records is seen as providing:

1 Information about the employee as an individual, often referred to as 'item' information. In the main this will be basic information about the employee and will usually be obtained from his application form.
2 Statistical information which may be used to support decision making in connection with issues such as recruitment, redundancy and management development, or generally in the collection of information about, for example, age distribution. This is often called 'feature' information and provides a 'profile' of the organization. This type of information can be obtained in numerous ways, some of which may be influenced by factors partly outside the personnel manager's control, such as constraints of finance, time and storage space.
3 Essential information to meet the requirements of legislation. The Department of Employment requires a considerable amount of information from most companies over the course of a year (*see* appendix II, p 63) and the legislation covering aspects of employment, recruitment, discrimination, health and safety (all coming on to the statute book since 1971) has had a marked effect on the need for accurate records. In addition, organizations which are members of an employers' association or federation will also require information of this sort to use in connection with national representation to government and unions or for use in central wage bargaining.
4 Indications of general trends such as labour turnover, salary levels and progressions, sickness and absenteeism. These indicators, when analysed, will help the personnel department to recognize problem areas which may be damaging to the company's long-term objectives and, therefore, show a need for control procedures.

SETTING THE OBJECTIVES FOR PERSONNEL RECORDS SYSTEMS

In practice the objectives of any existing system will rarely have been consciously spelled out by any one person or group but will usually have emerged over a period as a result of individual perceptions of gaps or shortcomings in the system. In seeking to tease out the range of implicit objectives and to establish objectives of his own, the personnel manager will find it helpful to distinguish between formal process objectives and substantive objectives. The former are concerned with the operation of a system, the latter with the information that the system should store and reproduce.

SETTING PROCESS OBJECTIVES

The process objectives might include accuracy, speed, cost-effectiveness, confidentiality, flexibility and minimum bureaucracy. Some, like confidentiality, may be regarded as essential, irrespective of the particular organization. Some, like the minimization of bureaucracy, will be chosen because of the individual culture of a firm at a particular time. Thus in a company which is no longer small but retains a very strong paternalistic and traditional culture, it may be quite counter-productive to institute certain rather elaborate management succession development forms and procedures however apparently well suited to the objective needs of the company. Sometimes there will be inconsistencies and even contradictions between objectives.

In many cases contradictions may only point to the need for trade offs between them as, for example, between speed and accuracy. Ideally we will expect to obtain figures of, say, salesmen's achievement of targets and bonus earnings with both speed and accuracy. However, the more speedily we obtain the figures, the less accurate they may be. In such circumstances we would not usually wish to trade off much accuracy for speed, but if the situation were one, for example, where direct selling to the public of encyclopaedias, double glazed windows or the like is concerned, where the principal determinants of profit concern the control and retention of salesmen, it can be much more important to have speed than accuracy. It may be objected that both the objectives of speed and accuracy may be met if enough resources are devoted to improving and maintaining the necessary system, but this merely brings us to the need for a further trade off between the cost of providing the information and the effectiveness of its provision. A principal objective of the system might be the highest degree of simplicity possible and the barest minimum of forms and paperwork. Marks and Spencer are often seen as prime exponents of this approach. However, it is not possible for any large organization simply to follow this line since the organization and management philosophy of Marks and Spencer is distinctive, and is such that their approach can be fruitful. Again, it might be reasonable in some cases that there should be an objective to have a very complex and sophisticated system, giving an enormous amount of useful personnel information.

Here one might consider the case of IBM in the UK. They have a highly sophisticated and remarkably effective personnel information system, yet given the area of their own expertise, the nature of their workforce and the possibility of using the system as a sales aid, then their investment of resources in it seems entirely rational and appropriate. All these illustrations serve to demonstrate that the objectives will vary considerably according to the type of organization, including its size, structure, technology and markets.

THE SUBSTANTIVE OBJECTIVES

Similar considerations apply in what can be called substantive objectives, such, for example as helping to improve the accident prevention record or monitoring industrial relations. The selection of and priority given to these objectives will very much depend on company objectives and for the personnel manager might therefore seem to be largely given, granted that he is properly involved in establishing company objectives. If a multi-location company never moves employees between companies this impacts on one possible objective, and if it has a high accident and injury rate it impinges on another. However this still leaves the personnel manager a large area of choice. He may be aware, for example, that though the number of injuries has been low the rate of hazardous incidents, which have given rise to neither accident nor injury, is high and the potential for serious injury is great. In such circumstances the degree of priority which he gives to this area may be greater than many of his colleagues might find justified given the situation. However all the records and procedures of the personnel manager are vitiated unless the information going in to them is sound, so he has to win the acceptance of a large number of people that the information he seeks is reasonably sought and therefore worth providing.

It must be a prime objective of any system that it provides the information which it is legally required to keep. Even here, however, companies will differ in the extent to which they go beyond the legal requirements. Governments tend to demand from industry no more than well established and reasonably progressive firms are already doing for themselves. Normally we might expect to see broad objectives for a personnel information system as follows:

to support wage and salary administration

to facilitate recruitment and selection

to identify employees of high potential

to determine in-company promotion

to aid management development and training programmes

to monitor industrial relations

to improve health, safety and accident prevention

to provide backup material, when required for judicial purposes, eg
tribunal cases.

These objectives can be refined further by operating managers at different
levels.

When to set objectives

It might seem that the proposal to computerize a system would give an
opportunity to re-think the objectives and to start from scratch, but even
here there is not full freedom of choice because the limitations of the
equipment (hardware) or the associated programs (software) may introduce new constraints. Again, being taken over by a new company may
give an opportunity for a re-think, but here one will encounter the same
problem that a subsidiary company in a conglomerate already faces, that
is, it may as a matter of group policy be required to keep its records in a
uniform group style which would not be necessary or appropriate if it
were independent.

The personnel manager is most likely to bring clear thinking to the
consistency, adequacy or relevance of records when he first takes over an
existing information system. A degree of habituation to a system can soon
set in and more glamorous and exciting tasks than reviewing objectives,
let alone reviewing the operation of the whole system, will soon have
presented themselves. Clearly the size problem is crucial. If the company
is small it will probably already have a rudimentary system and the
updating and retrieval of information from records even in manuscript
form need present no real problems. Even in large companies the cry is
often heard that comprehensive information on, for example, staff appraisal and management development is unnecessary, and it may seem
even more so in the small company. However, whatever the company
size, the personnal manager will need to think through the objectives and
their appropriateness. He must also keep these objectives under review
from time to time, more particularly in this field where rapid developments in computer technology are opening up new opportunities all the
time.

48

SETTING UP THE SYSTEM

There are two obvious but basic questions to be answered. What information is required and how can it be most effectively provided? Having answered them the process of setting up a system can begin. There are however a number of additional questions that have to be asked. For example, how often will the information be used? How often will it need to be updated? How easily can it be updated? Is retrieval easy? Can the information be stored in such a way that it can readily be collated? However the nature of the information required must be assessed first.

First information which employers are required by law to keep is precisely known. The older preoccupation with safety and welfare, particularly of women and young persons, has left its mark on the statute book. For example, 'where young persons are employed in any industrial undertaking, a register of the young persons so employed, and of the dates of their birth, and of the dates on which they enter and leave the service of their employer, shall be kept and shall at all times be open to inspection' (The Employment of Women, Young Persons, and Children Act, 1920). To this older type of legislation a vast new body of industrial legislation, largely concerned with individual rights in employment, was passed in the 1960s and 1970s. Thus, besides welfare and safety, the State had intervened in such important areas as training, race, sex discrimination, redundancy and employment protection. The precise demands of all this legislation provide the minimum information which any system must be designed to handle. In addition companies will require detailed information to meet the kind of objectives already discussed. Some information is sought by almost all companies, eg details of sickness, absence, holidays and education and training courses being taken by employees. Since it seems that every manager has his own needs for particular information, it is easy to fall into the trap of collecting information with no clear idea of its future use. Thus personnel managers find too much of their resources involved in the collation of information which may rarely if ever be used. It is a perceived truth in personnel management that 'if you are not going to use it, don't collect it'. It is, however, a sound practice to have a system capable of development, thus avoiding the necessity to revise the system every time a need for some new, or different, information arises, as it inevitably will. It is also necessary to review the system from time to time in order to ensure that effort is not wasted collecting information which may indeed have been genuinely required at one time but which is now no longer necessary. For anyone setting up a system, or even reviewing an existing one, probably the best place to start is to draw up a flow chart of the recruitment procedure (*see* appendix I on page 62).

This is the clearest way of showing how one procedure affects another, the interaction of various forms, what type of information is duplicated or transferred from one form to another and what use is made of various copies. It shows the need for requisition forms, standard letters, personnel records cards, etc, and at this stage, as it becomes obvious that there must be a limit to the extent of records and forms, some control must be exercised over the paper and the amount of work involved.

There is a strong relationship between payroll, training, personnel and pension records and in smaller firms it is possible to maintain a single data base. At first sight it may seem logical to want all information on employees in one place. In practice, however, this usually becomes too complex and impractical for a number of reasons. Different kinds of information are applicable to different tasks and serve different purposes. The purpose of a wages (payroll) file, for example, is for pay purposes only and much of the data required for payroll purposes (eg taxation details) is of no direct relevance to the personnel records. This does not mean that forms cannot be designed to serve several functions. Also it is important to try to ensure that if there are separate computer-based systems for different aspects of personnel work, they are, where possible, compatible.

For those in a position to review an existing system probably the best way to establish control of the paper is by listing every form in use and its primary objective, the specific information it is intended to provide, or what action it is intended to facilitate and its potential function. It may be useful to arrange all the data elements in a matrix to see the pattern of information gathered and disseminated. Then the following questions need to be asked:

What is the function or purpose of this form?

Why is it necessary?

Is it worth what it costs to produce?

What could be the worst thing that would happen if it were eliminated?

Is there possibly a better way of providing this information or precipitating this action?

Can it easily be kept up to date?

etc . . .

It may well be found that whole files of records are being retained because of one piece of information which could be included in some other record.

At this stage it may be necessary to ask whether it would be possible or cost effective to put the system on a computer. This question is left for separate discussion at the end of this chapter.

COLLECTING THE INFORMATION

DESIGN OF FORMS

Most personnel information, even when it is eventually stored in the most sophisticated of computer systems, is initially collected on some sort of form. It is therefore essential to ensure that forms are well designed. There are many commercial firms who supply forms 'off the shelf' and some who will design the forms and system for the computer. Some of these firms are experienced in the field and can provide good workable systems. Personnel managers need to ensure that if they are buying a ready made system it really meets all of their requirements, otherwise it would be advisable to design a system from scratch. The layout and design of personnel forms will depend very much on the procedures followed and the objectives of the information system. It is helpful if new forms are designed and old ones modified at the same time, particularly if certain forms are used in conjunction with others or if data are recorded from one to another, as in the case of application forms and personal history cards. In this case, relevant information should be in the same sequence and in similar locations on both documents, if possible. The inclusion of every line, every entry, should be made to justify itself, although care must be taken not to exclude features which help to prevent constant queries.

The layout of the form should be clear, uncluttered, logical, easy to complete and easy to read (for illustrations, see Dyer, 1979). Ideally a form should be completed in natural sequence—from left to right and from top to bottom. Items which are always filled in are best located at the left of the form, items which are often completed go in the middle and items which are seldom filled in at the right. This saves time when completing the form.

The main item of identification (the employee's name, for instance) should be wherever it can be most easily seen without drawing the entire form from the file. Filing margins where needed, pre-punched holes, a light rule to show where a form should be folded can all help in the disposition of forms. Where possible forms should be self-explanatory, especially those which are completed by people who are not employees—applicants and referees, for example. Specimen copies of each form should be kept in a special file, with details of how it is used, the supplier, the quantity ordered last with date, price and other relevant information. Notes of problems and ideas for improvement should be inserted as they come up so that they may be considered the next time the form is ordered. To facilitate re-ordering of forms, it is helpful to indicate on the foot of the last page of the form, in the smallest available type, the date, quantity and printer, together with the reference number of the document.

RECRUITMENT

It is not possible to look at all areas of personnel management here but recruitment activity is so important to most that some focus on it is necessary. In smaller firms it is often the practice to replace automatically any employee who leaves and there is no formal procedure for authorizing recruitment. In larger companies a much closer control is exercised and usually no new employee (either new or replacement) may be engaged without authorization by the appropriate line manager. In firms where the importance of manpower planning has been recognized a positive personnel establishment will be agreed for each department and recruitment is handled in accordance with a manpower plan. As an example, where studies have shown that there is an imbalance in the age, sex or racial structure in a department, it may be necessary deliberately to recruit a person against a specification designed to correct the imbalance. A typical employee requisition form may cover any or all of the following items;

Job title

Rate of pay

Urgency of need

Additional or replacement

Hours worked:—part-time, day or shift work, etc

Temporary or permanent

Sex (if genuine occupational qualification)

Special qualifications

Skill or experience

Education requirements.

The form should also indicate the department requiring the staff and be signed by the authorizing manager.

RECRUITMENT INEVITABLY ENTAILS THE USE OF APPLICATION FORMS

These are not only important in the recruitment interview but will provide the basic information for the employee's file. It is also important to remember that the application form has a strong public relations value and the design of the form should reflect the corporate image which the company wishes to display. Essentially, the form should provide information needed for an employer to assess the applicant's eligibility to fill a vacancy and therefore should be designed to do this, bearing in mind the wide range of jobs that it will cover (*see* chapter 4 for fuller discussion of the use of the application form in selection).

The format should be structured so that the information required by each department (personnel, salaries, line, etc) is together. It may even be practicable to include on the application form whole sections that would otherwise have to be maintained separately. If the application form is designed to complement the employee's personal records, the transfer of information from one to the other is made easier and the chance of error minimized. Application forms are not the only type of form used at interview and companies will often supplement these with interview checklists, tests, and finally, with requests for references. Once references are received they should not of course be filed with other personnel records but locked away with other confidential documents.

STORING THE INFORMATION

THE BASIC PERSONNEL RECORD

It is essential for an employer to have a current record of the entire workforce. He must know, for example, the number and type of people in his employment in order to calculate his payments for National Insurance Contributions and his contribution to the Redundancy and Maternity Funds, and to provide information where still relevant to an Industrial Training Board. In addition the employer needs certain basic information about each employee.

This is a task which requires systematic listing of employees. It is advisable to identify records or to keep a separate list of all employees under the age of 18 as their employment is regulated by law. In addition to each employee's name, an employer should record his address, his position in the company, his date of birth and his National Insurance number. It is also a good idea to record the sex of the employee, not least because maternity and retirement benefits for women differ from those for men.

It is also necessary to know the date of engagement, as an employee's years of service may be a factor in calculating his wages or compensation under the Redundancy Payments Act 1965. It is also desirable to include information relating to disciplinary action. Records of formal warnings and other action taken is essential in the event of becoming involved in an industrial tribunal.

The simplest and cheapest filing system available is the ordinary card index box which can be kept on a desk top or in a desk drawer. The cards themselves are stiff enough to withstand frequent handling but flexible enough to be inserted in a typewriter. They are available in different colours to identify the various categories of employees. Rotary wheels are useful where there is a large number of index cards which are referred to frequently. The cards are secure and do not fall out when the wheel is revolved, although they can be easily removed and replaced.

Pre-printed card strips, designed for personnel offices are available for inserting in binders. These card strips are available in various colours and sizes and are thin enough to be inserted in a typewriter for recording personal details.

Larger personnel cards for recording a greater amount of detail are also available and can be filed so that they overlap, showing only the bottom edge containing the most significant information. Many of these traditional methods of storing information are now being superseded by the use of computers. Nevertheless in many contexts, these established methods still have an important role to play.

As the range and complexity of information increases, it can become necessary to establish separate systems. Therefore in certain personnel departments, whether computerized or not, it is possible, in addition to the personal record for each individual to find separate storage systems for information on health and safety, training and development, performance appraisal, pay and pensions.

ANALYSING THE INFORMATION

Periodic and systematic analyses of the personnel records can be used for a number of purposes. First they provide data essential to manpower planning. The analysis may show, for example, shortages of skilled manpower in some areas and surpluses in others. This could indicate a need to recruit specific categories of labour even though the labour requirements of the company as a whole may be decreasing. There may also be a possibility of balancing labour requirements within the company by transfer between departments, or other companies, of surplus labour in certain categories or trades (for the type of information most likely to be required, *see* chapter 6).

Secondly, the analysis can also be used to aid the evaluation of current personnel policies and practices. These may cover a range of topics including attempts to reduce levels of absenteeism, increase the range of the ratings used in the annual appraisal and increase the proportion of women in managerial positions.

Thirdly, an inventory of labour also provides the information needed to complete returns for the Department of Employment, employers' federations and trade associations, and any reports should be presented in such a way that they facilitate the preparation of these returns.

The process of analysing information from traditional personnel records on manual systems will usually be time-consuming and laborious. As a result both the quantity and quality of information will suffer. It is in this context that the advantages of a computer-based system become most apparent.

COMPUTERIZATION

Such is the rapid progress in the whole area of electronic information processing that it is inevitable that many will ask why more personnel managers do not choose to computerize personnel information in order to escape the real problems and restrictions of a manual system. And there are indeed some real problems. The work load involved in maintaining a speedy and accurate system is usually badly underestimated by those not close to it, and peak demands during a big recruitment campaign or at the annual salary review can put great stress on it. Any reasonable speed in retrieval of information is bought at the cost of duplication of records, which apart from its costliness in time and space can give more opportunity for that other inevitable feature of the manual system to come into play, its vulnerability to human error. While there is thus an inbuilt bias against collecting useless information, there is also a deterrent against collecting useful but difficult to process information. Further, the manual system will frequently result in action of some sort for which memos, letters and reports may be necessary but which the system cannot itself produce.

Of course, some of the above difficulties have been ameliorated in many companies by a partial computerization, usually involving payroll and pensions. Much clerical labour has therefore been saved and some analyses useful to the personnel manager have been forthcoming. There remains the problem that usually these sub-systems have been designed with insufficient attention to their relationship with one another or to the personnel information system generally, which retains therefore much of the disadvantages to which reference has already been made. Nor has the advent of the word processor made as great an impact on personnel work as many had expected. A long and complex service contract going through a series of drafts gives ideal work for such a machine, but there is not a great deal of such work in most firms. The word processor may seem to come into its own with its production of largely standardized but apparently personalized letters, but many personnel departments have found the gain questionable. If the printer is good enough, the letter from such a source may make a better impression on the recipient than a standard, pre-prepared personnel department letter, but the standard letter will be cheaper and quicker. Finally, the word processor makes no significant contribution to the production of the reports and analyses which occupy much personnel department time. Therefore a fully computerized personnel information system (CPIS) is often the answer. It has to be said that many personnel managers, frequently coming from a not very highly quantitative background, have been somewhat sceptical about the value of computers in personnel. Some might attribute part of the comparative slowness of growth in computerized personnel as against other commercial and production systems to such a scepticism, as well as to a possible perception of the superior importance of these other fields. However this may be, it is clear that personnel work is particularly difficult to computerize. Computer projects usually cost more and take longer than forecast and personnel computer projects even more so. A healthy scepticism becomes part of the necessary armour of the personnel manager. Yet there have been developments which very much affect the potentialities of the computer for the personnel manager, not least the development of true data-based management systems. The enormous processing and calculative power of the computer will always be valuable for scientific purposes but clearly the personnel manager is more interested in a system where the base of data stored in the computer is structured from the outset for rapid manipulation and retrieval. Instead of data being stored in files with a special application program necessary to link together the information from these files, the information can be more readily retrieved from the indexes which are a feature of the system, while the further flexibility which personnel work requires is helped by the provision of dictionary facilities, whereby the personnel clerk can assess and update through a VDU, without involving an application program, data which changes regularly or frequently.

The cost of computerization is declining as the technology improves. For a current figure of under £12,000, perhaps within the personnel department's own budget limits, a micro-computer system can be installed.

When the personnel manager asks whether it is possible and cost effective to computerize he needs to ask 'What do I need?' rather than 'What can the computer do for me?'. This is not to say, of course, that the personnel manager should be looking simply to put his present system 'on to the computer'. After all, the present system will inevitably have been the result of a compromise of some sort on what information needs it is necessary to supply. For example, a detailed analysis of the changing levels of total earnings between different groups of employees, (often a source of industrial relations problems), could be extremely valuable to many personnel managers but they seldom have this in their present system because of the cost and time needed to achieve it. Conversely, a computerized system could result in less rather than more production of figures, since it may become possible to produce only those figures actually required without dragging in many others. Some reports might be less frequent in a new system rather than more so, since they could be tied more closely to need and less to the mechanics of information gathering.

The precise needs of the personnel manager must be met by the system but he cannot assume that these will be readily understood by data processing (DP) staff. The importance of good communications in both directions cannot be over-emphasized. To which DP specialists should he turn? In a large concern he will need to turn to the internal DP staff. At one time the intrinsic problems about computerizing personnel work meant that such work was not very exciting to them and the personnel manager might have had to turn to a bureau or manufacturer. However, the developments in computing have also affected the positions of DP staff in organizations and tended to reduce the size and power of central

57

computer departments. They look much more therefore to consultancy and co-ordinating roles and are likely to take a renewed interest in personnel work. Insofar as they restrict themselves to this role and do not actively help develop the system, nor help run it in, the personnel manager faces the problem of deciding the type of assistance he needs.

The big decision concerns the question of whether to buy an existing software 'package', or to develop a 'tailor made' system. Only recently have packages reached the degree of sophistication and flexibility which make them a genuine choice for a personnel manager, but problems persist. By definition the package does not fit the necessary tasks exactly. It is a matter of judgement as to how acceptably close it comes to what the salesmen saw as a near perfect identity, and as to what cost may be necessary for any subsequent necessary modification. Yet the choice of a tailor made system is bold. Certainly recent improvements have meant that the massive efforts to think of everything which a system might need (and which helped to ensure some systems took years to develop) are not now so necessary and one can build more easily over time. Even so the amount of development work will be altogether inhibiting for many companies, faced with inevitable uncertainties about the ultimate cost of the development and the time needed to accomplish it. Some organizations, however, like British Rail with their computer-based manpower information system MANIS, have apparently successfully braved and overcome the obstacles.

Whether internal DP staff, an external bureau or supplier helps develop the system will depend on company policy and the personnel manager's judgement on who at the time and over the relevant period can help him most. Whoever is to help him, the nature of the questions to which the personnel manager will require satisfactory answers remains unchanged. He will want to know what hardware is to be used and to be assured of the use of it when his own schedules require it (ie waiting for a batch of work to be processed on the company main frame computer can be as inconvenient as waiting for time in a bureau's computer). Again, some type of information is more securely processed with the personnel manager on hand, rather than churned out at dead of night with only DP staff in attendance. There will be questions about prevention of unauthorized access. Assurances are also needed on the dangers to the system of loss or corruption. How compatible is the existing system with that proposed? If it is proposed to set up and develop the system in a bureau, can it easily be moved to an in-house computer when it is running well? Is it a real time data-based management system, with a high level language? Can personnel staff easily be trained to input and interrogate the system?

How far is it capable of giving the personnel department considerable assistance with reports and action letters and memos? Is it a distributed system which can link up interactively personnel departments at different locations?

But why, in the end, will a personnel manager choose to install a computer-based information system? The ability of the system to help him today is clear, the costs of such a system are lower in real terms, and there are many people able and willing to help him develop a system. Does it help him enough to make the real costs in time and money worthwhile? The answer to this can scarcely be a general one and has to be considered case by case. Sometimes the case may be marginal if the system is seen as only doing better and quicker and probably at a further level of analysis what the present system already does, while the case may become conclusive with new demands on the system, some now clearly, others as yet only indistinctly seen. Thus as far as the present system goes, while the efficiency of record keeping in respect of individuals may not improve much, the preparation of documents for the annual salary review which have to be done somehow, by somebody, can be much assisted. A cost saving of personnel time can be easily calculated in cases like this. Clearly all work involving selective listing (eg how many engineers have we who speak French) is much assisted, but the need for such selective listings may not be so common in reality as in the pages of computer prose. Statistical analysis, of accident rates for example, is clearly assisted, and here once again it is a question for the individual case as to how much help is really needed and what cost saving there may be. It may be that the removal of human error from apparently relatively mundane but nevertheless very important tasks is needed, as for example where those working with materials potentially hazardous in the long run to health may need careful monitoring to see that the right medical examinations are held at the right time. Where the CPIS does much more than the old system, in terms of report generation or in terms, for example, of modelling, the personnel manager will have a clearer case for electing for a new system, even though there will be problems in the quantification of these new modelling benefits. A model which enables the company to predict the implications for the total wage bill of each one per cent rise offered by the employers in a national wage bargain with the unions may be of assistance to their representative on the national negotiating team, but quantifying the benefit of this assistance is clearly difficult. Where sheer size or an immediate obvious and pressing need have not made a CPIS virtually inevitable, a decision to install such a system will largely be influenced by the firm's view of its own future in its own environment. The more it sees the need for early intelligence about changes in this environment and for prompt organizational response to these, the more it will be attracted to a flexible, adaptive personnel system. The more it uses modelling techniques in other business areas, the more it will seek to use modelling facilities within a CPIS. But the personnel manager will still need to think through carefully whether indeed the moment for a CPIS has arrived, to plan it meticulously if it has, and to prepare a well documented case for a bigger capital expenditure than he has probably ever made before, despite the comparative cheapness of modern computing.

MAINTAINING THE SYSTEM AND RETAINING RECORDS

Any system of personnel records must be understood and accepted, not only by the people who are responsible for its successful day to day operation, but by those others whose activities require the use of personnel records and statistics. Procedure manuals should be made available which explain how the records are grouped, what systems are used, where they are located, and the full use that may be made of the information stored within the system. It is also important to identify who should have access to the information. Personnel records must be confidential and need to be treated as such by the personnel department staff.

Just how long personnel records should be retained is a moot point. One needs to consider such factors as space, frequency with which the records are referred to, legal obligations, the particular circumstances of the company, the nature of the work and the firm's own restrictions on former employees; on working for competitors, for example.

Records of names of employees and dates of engagement should be kept permanently as should records of accidents and illnesses contracted as a direct result of working. Application forms of unsuccessful candidates (together with the reason for refusal) may be kept for a short time both to be useful should a similar vacancy arise and to serve as back up material should the company face a claim for discrimination. Certain records concerning wages, working time and holidays should be kept for a period of at least three years.

The Limitation Acts of 1939 and 1954 state that action cannot be brought if six years have elapsed since the date of the occurrence and The Employment Protection (Consolidation) Act 1982 provides certain restrictions on claims made to industrial tribunals. Both of these pieces of legislation must be considered when establishing a retention schedule for the records.

It is useful to establish a retention schedule for each record and to indicate where they are stored. The date for destroying each form or computer tape can be recorded on the form or tape itself.

The feasibility of microfilming certain forms and documents for the purpose of storage should be considered. By reducing the size of documents by photography a company can save on storage space and considerable time can be saved if frequent reference is made to the material. On the other hand, it is difficult with microfilm to identify different coloured cards and impossible to add documents in their normal filing sequence after filming. Microfilming is expensive, but so is storage space, therefore, a careful cost analysis should be undertaken. In this as in other aspects of personnel records, there are many choices available to the personnel manager. In a rapidly advancing field, it is important to keep abreast of new developments and to ignore the traditional unglamorous image of this aspect of personnel work .

REFERENCES

BRITISH INSTITUTE OF MANAGEMENT (1967). *Records Retention*. London, BIM.

CANNON, James (1979). *Cost Effective Personnel Decisions*. London, Institute of Personnel Management.

DYER, Barbara (1979). *Personnel Systems & Records*, 3rd ed. London, Gower Press.

HEALTH AND SAFETY EXECUTIVE *Catalogue* (of forms and publications relating to Factories Acts etc).

HOLMAN, Leonard J (1970). *Basic Statistics for Personnel Managers*. London, Institute of Personnel Management.

IVE, Tony (1982). *Personnel Computer Systems*. London, McGraw Hill.

WILLE, Edgar *and* HAMMOND, Valerie (1981). *The Computer in Personnel Work*. London, Institute of Personnel Management.

APPENDIX I—FLOWCHART OF EMPLOYMENT PROCEDURE

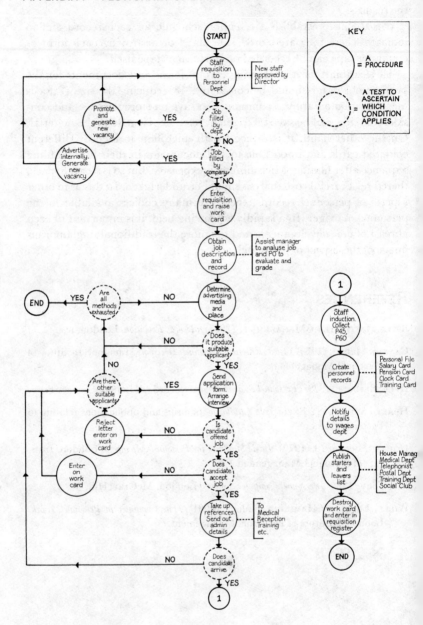

KEY

◯ = A PROCEDURE

◌ = A TEST TO ASCERTAIN WHICH CONDITION APPLIES

START

Staff requisition to Personnel Dept — New staff approved by Director

Job filled by dept — YES → Promote and generate new vacancy

NO

Job filled by company — YES → Advertise internally. Generate new vacancy

NO

Enter requisition and raise work card

Obtain job description and record ····· Assist manager to analyse job and PO to evaluate and grade

Determine advertising media and place

Does it produce suitable applicant — NO → Are all methods exhausted — YES → END

YES

Send application form. Arrange interview — YES → Are there other suitable applicants

NO

Is candidate offered job — NO → Reject letter enter on work card

YES

Does candidate accept job — NO → Enter on work card

YES

Take up references. Send out admin details ····· To Medical Reception Training etc.

Does candidate arrive — NO

YES

1

1

Staff induction. Collect P45, P60

Create personnel records ····· Personal File Salary Card Pension Card Clock Card Training Card

Notify details to wages dept

Publish starters and leavers list ····· House Manag Medical Dept Telephonist Postal Dept Training Dept Social Club

Destroy work card and enter in requisition register

END

62

EMPLOYMENT LEGISLATION — REQUIRING USE OF OFFICIAL FORMS

1 Truck Acts 1831 to 1940
2 Wages Council Act 1945
3 Employment of Women, Young Persons and Children Act 1920
4 Young Persons Employment Act 1938
5 Disabled Persons (Employment) Acts 1944 and 1958
6 Terms and Conditions of Employment Act 1939
7 Payment of Wages Act 1960
8 Factories Act 1961
9 Offices, Shops and Railway Premises Act 1963
10 Industrial Training Act 1964
11 Redundancy Payments Act 1965 and 1969
12 Transport Act 1968
13 Immigrant Acts 1968 and 1971
14 Employers' Liability (Compulsory Insurance) Act 1969
15 Equal Pay Act 1970
16 Contracts of Employment Act 1972
17 Employment Medical Advisory Service Act 1972
18 European Communities Act 1972
19 Employment of Children Act 1973
20 Social Security Act 1973
21 Employment and Training Act 1973
22 Health and Safety at Work etc Act 1974
23 Trade Union and Labour Relations Act 1974 and 1976
24 Rehabilitation of Offenders Act 1974
25 Social Security Pension Act 1975
26 Industry Act 1975
27 Employment Protection Act 1975
28 Sex Discrimination Act 1975
29 Race Relations Act 1976
30 Trade Union and Labour Relations Amendment Act 1977
31 Employment Protection (Variation of Limits) Order 1977
32 Employment Protection (Consolidation) Act 1978
33 Social Security and Housing Benefits Act 1982

Section Three

This section deals with some of the essential aspects of the management of manpower within the organization. Chapter 4 is concerned with the recruitment and selection of people into the organization. Chapter 5 covers the subject of appraisal, which helps to determine the suitability of employees for vertical or lateral movement or further training and development. Chapter 6 examines manpower planning, which is concerned with the whole question of manpower control and anticipation of the demand for and supply of manpower. Each chapter is presented in a rather different way.

The chapter on recruitment and selection is the longest in the book. This is because studies of personnel roles reveal that this is the most commonly undertaken type of personnel work. Many and probably a majority of those in their first or second personnel jobs can expect to be involved in recruitment and selection, even in recessionary times. Andrew West describes the stages in the recruitment and selection process and the key choices and decisions at each stage. He also offers detailed guidance and advice both on how to operate within an existing scheme and on how to improve it by, for example, devising a new application form.

The chapter by Clive Fletcher on appraisals examines the case for appraisals and the steps involved in setting up, operating and maintaining an appraisal scheme. In doing so, he uses a somewhat different approach to that of most of the other contributors by starting from what the research evidence tells us about good practice and using this as a basis for a recommended approach. In a sense, it is, therefore, a more conventional academic perspective while at the same time offering detailed practical guidelines.

The third chapter in this section is by John Bramham who, like Clive Fletcher in relation to appraisals, has already written extensively on the subject of manpower planning. The chapter describes what is involved in setting up and operating a manpower system, concentrating in particular, through a series of illustrations, on the types of information which can usefully be provided. He also poses questions which help the reader to consider the desirability of operating a more or less sophisticated scheme of manpower planning and manpower policy.

Chapter four

Recruitment and selection

INTRODUCTION

Organizations succeed largely through the efforts of the individuals working within them. It follows that selection, whether from outside the organization or within, is of fundamental importance and a cornerstone of good management.

Whilst the benefits of good selection may be clear, the consequences of poor selection are often severe but not always obvious. The cost of advertising, the management time involved in selection and training and the expense of dismissal are relatively easy to calculate; possibly more serious are the debilitating longer term effects such as lowering of morale, reduced quality of product or service and lost business opportunities.

In practice, the selection process consists of a series of decisions of varying complexity. The quality of these decisions depends upon the quality of the information available and upon who is taking the decisions. In many cases selection is often shrouded in mystery; managers frequently talk of having a 'feel' for selecting the right person when in reality they resort to judgements based on quaint and inaccurate criteria.

One sales manager in the office equipment business, believed in keeping his potential salesmen waiting at least two hours before their interview! This he believed, tested their perseverance (an undeniably important attribute) but he failed to realize that candidates with initiative, soon left to seek employment with a more courteous competitor! Good selection is, above all, a methodical approach to the problem of finding the best matched person for the job. A practical framework can be built around the following three questions:

WHAT AM I LOOKING FOR?
analyse the job and formulate the person specification

67

Figure 1
The 'Filters' in the selection process

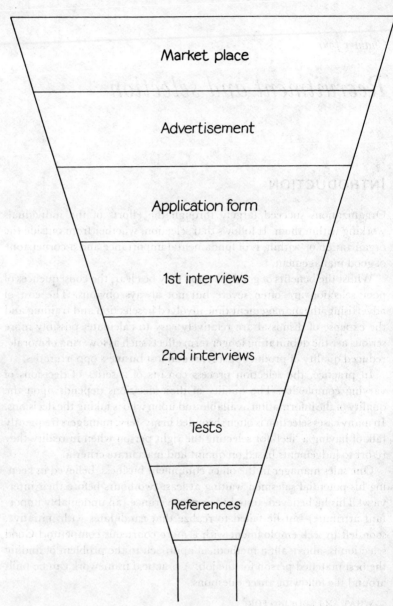

Market place

Advertisement

Application form

1st interviews

2nd interviews

Tests

References

recruit through advertising, agencies, or consultants

screen and select through application forms, interviews, tests and references.

Figure 2
Common methods of recruitment and selection by type of job

Job Types	Methods of recruitment	Methods of selection
Shopfloor	Department of Employment, local advertising, notice boards, friends' introductions	Short interview; simple tests of basic skills and abilities; test for physical requirements eg colour blindness
Mechanics/ Technicians	Regional or local advertising; direct entry from college	Interviews with technical staff; 'trade' tests of knowledge and skill
Sales	National or local advertising; agencies or consultants	Interview; occasionally tests of ability and personality
Office Staff	Direct entry from school/ college; employment agencies	Interviews; simple tests of skill and clerical aptitude
Professional Staff	National advertising	'Technical' interviews; qualifications often regarded as sufficient assessment
Graduates	Almost exclusively through University Careers Centres with supplementary advertising in University papers, careers publications and national press.	Elaborate and difficult: 'milk round' interviews, group selection methods and extensive use of psychometric tests
Managers	National or regional advertising; selection consultants and, at senior levels, executive search consultants. Internal promotion is common	Impossible to generalize; can range from superficial interviews to three-day 'assessment centres'

Selection is like a chain which is only as strong as its weakest link. The links in this case begin with the person specification, move through the recruitment stages and finish with interviews, tests and references. No matter how skilled a manager may be at interviewing, his or her efforts will be in vain if, for example, the person specification was incorrect in the first place.

There are two principles implicit in the selection process. The first is to find candidates with the best match of ability and personality to the requirements of the job. The second is to conduct this matching process by using the various processes of recruitment and selection as a series of 'filters' brought into play one after the other as illustrated in figure 1 on page 68.

The number of filters used in selection and indeed the complexity of the whole process will vary according to a number of factors. These will include the resources available for selection and the nature of the labour market. Some idea of the range of jobs, and selection methods, is provided in figure 2 on page 69.

The central theme in this introductory section is that selection involves a series of complex decisions concerning choice of person, choice of methods to use and choice of information on which to base a final decision. The core of this chapter examines each of the three main stages in the process, namely job analysis and person specification, recruitment and finally, selection. A final section discusses a number of more general issues concerning selection.

STAGE 1 — JOB ANALYSIS AND PERSON SPECIFICATION

ANALYSING THE JOB

A first step in successful selection is an accurate analysis of the job. In many cases no job specification will exist and where one is available, it may be out of date or written for purposes other than selection. It may therefore need updating or completely rewriting. The accuracy of the person specification and of all the subsequent stages in selection will depend on the quality of the job analysis, so it is important to get it right. For shopfloor and sales jobs, observation may help to identify some key skills and provide a flavour of working conditions and atmosphere. However, it is time-consuming and inappropriate for many jobs. In practice, the interview will be used more frequently and the following might be considered as useful interviewees:

the Manager or Head of Department

the present job holder (if available)

other people in similar jobs.

In addition to the interview, useful information may be gleaned from performance records, appraisals and exit interviews.

An initial interview between the person responsible for selection and the head of the relevant department should meet the following main objectives.

decide whether or not to alter the nature of the job

decide whether or not to fill the vacancy

decide on the key characteristics (a) of the job (b) of the person to fill it

decide a time schedule for selection, based on the urgency with which the vacancy has to be filled

decide how the exercise is to be handled: internal/external

decide details of the terms and conditions on which the job will be filled.

For routine vacancies, many of these issues will not arise, but it is therefore important to be able to identify the circumstances in which a more detailed analysis is required. The following criteria might be useful.

a senior vacancy

a newly created job

a 'problem' job, subject to high labour turnover or poor performance

a job where the present job holder has undertaken the job for many years.

In these cases a full job analysis is required using some form of checklist based on the following questions:

The circumstances surrounding the job

How is the department/organization structured?

Where will the newcomer fit in?

What will be his/her major responsibilities?

What are the key qualities and skills required to fulfil these responsibilities?

What remuneration and other benefits are available?

Ways in which good and poor performers differ from each other

Do good performers exhibit certain skills lacking in poor performers?

Is there a difference in qualifications or experience?

71

Is there a difference in circumstances eg do successful job holders live closer to work, are they younger/older?

Difficult aspects of the work
Where are the mistakes made?—therefore, what skills are required?

What previous work experience will minimize the risks of poor performance?

Major sources of satisfaction and dissatisfaction in the job
Can attractive features be useful in 'selling' the job?

What insight do these provide into the personality and motivation required for successful performance?

By a series of questions such as these you will be in a better position to determine what a manager *really* wants. If you are a personnel professional you will be blamed should you fail to find the 'right' candidate even if you acted in good faith by basing your selection decision on some previously agreed but possibly out of date person specification.

Having interviewed the manager and if possible past or present job holders, sufficient information should be available from which to draw inferences as to the skills and personal qualities required of a successful job holder.

THE PERSON SPECIFICATION

In collecting information about the job, much will also have been learnt about the type of person required to fill it. This information must now be turned into a person specification.

The personal characteristics specified should be:

Relevant—specify those characteristics demonstrably connected with success (or failure) in the job

Independent—overlapping elements should be avoided

Assessable—list only the attributes that can be assessed with the selection tools available—(usually application form and interview).

The only practical way of consolidating the mass of data gathered during the job analysis is to incorporate it into a simple specification or plan which can be referred to at any time during the subsequent selection procedure. A plan helps avoid forgetting the small but often vital details which may render an otherwise good candidate unacceptable. Is a clean driving licence essential, or a minimum age necessary for insurance purposes, or accurate colour vision required? Avoid stating vague characteristics like 'bags of initiative'.

There are two plans in common use; the first and most popular is the seven point plan developed by Professor Rodger (1952); the second is the five point plan developed by Munro Fraser (1972).

Figure 3
The seven and five point plans

Seven point plan	Five point plan
Physical make-up	Impact
Attainments	Qualifications
General intelligence	Brains and abilities
Special aptitudes	Motivation
Interests	Adjustment
Disposition	
Circumstances	

Both the seven and five point plans have survived the test of time and will work satisfactorily. The secret is to get to know a plan thoroughly and stick with it. The headings used, provided they conform to the three above criteria, are not so important.

Alec Rodger's plan was devised in the 1930s primarily for vocational guidance, but it has a sound psychological basis and is now used widely for selection purposes. However, the meaning of some headings is not immediately apparent to busy managers and they, above all, must fully understand and work with any plan. Munro Fraser's plan is admirably brief, perhaps bordering on the cryptic and emphasizes the importance of assessing motivation in the selection process. In practice, a plan which is readily understood and accepted by most managers comprises eight headings drawn from both the seven and five point plans.

Figure 4
The eight point person specification

First impressions
Education and qualifications
General intelligence and special aptitude
Personal circumstances
Experience
Interests
Personality
Motivation

An explanation of each heading follows:

First impressions
This heading includes appearance, bearing, speech and manner. First impressions can have an important bearing on job success and if this is the case, as for example it may be in selling, then the appropriate elements should be specified.

This heading is used to draw a distinction between the 'surface attributes' described here and those aspects of personality which require far greater probing and which are described under a separate heading. Also, we all tend to rely too heavily on first impressions when making an assessment; this heading recognizes that fact and to some extent isolates and contains first impressions under one heading.

Education and qualifications
Avoid the temptation of making excessive requirements. It is a common fault amongst managers to demand higher levels of education of their subordinates than is realistic. 'Over-qualified' candidates may quickly become disillusioned with the job and its lack of prospects.

General intelligence and special aptitudes
Equal opportunities legislation reinforces the point that it is dangerous to play the amateur psychologist where testing is concerned. Levels of general intelligence should not be specified unless there is good evidence that the requirements are valid. Take a common sense approach to this subject particularly when specifying skills or special aptitudes. Use evidence from the job analysis, particularly answers to questions concerned with the most difficult aspects of the work. Holdsworth (1972) provides a comprehensive examination of tests and their value.

Personal circumstances
This is designed to take into account such personal factors as age and health in addition to the broader based domestic circumstances such as mobility, family and local ties. Often small but vital details are specified here. Do domestic circumstances make it impossible for the candidate to be sent away from home for long periods? Is there an age limit below which the candidate cannot be insured for certain driving jobs? Is good colour vision essential to the job?

Experience
This, in practice, is probably the most important heading. Consider previous job holders; was there any pattern of work experience associated with successful or unsuccessful job holders? Try to distil those elements

critical to success and then determine those jobs or patterns of jobs most likely to contain those elements. Do not consider only full-time work, much relevant experience may be gained in part-time or vacation jobs, a particularly fruitful source of evidence among younger age groups. Aim to think flexibly about specifying work experience since seemingly dissimilar jobs may contain substantial almost identical elements.

Interests

A person's interests tell us what they do from choice and give us an insight into personality and motivation, arguably the two most difficult factors to specify and assess. In some jobs leisure interests will have little bearing on successful performance, in others leisure interests could play a critical part. Alec Rodger provided a good structure when he specified five categories: intellectual, practical-constructional, physically-active, social and artistic.

Consider the recruitment of expatriate staff. Here, physically active outdoor interests will generally be the best fit for the expected life-style. The avid theatre-goer, with no other interests to fall back on, would be a risky proposition.

Interests may also indicate potential skills and abilities not revealed elsewhere in a candidate's career history. An interest in car maintenance may indicate mechanical comprehension; leadership of a group may indicate management ability; participation in intellectual pursuits may indicate an active mind capable of further development or re-training particularly in an older worker who might otherwise be 'written off' as untrainable.

Personality

Called 'adjustment' by Munro Fraser and 'disposition' by Alec Rodger, the list of qualities that could be specified is endless and the temptation to demand everything from a candidate should be avoided.

The best fit of personality to job is hard to specify and even harder to assess. Rely on common sense and describe requirements in terms that can be understood and recognized in candidates. The following checklist, based on one by Alec Rodger, is a useful starting point.

Acceptability—Does the job holder have to exhibit unusually high qualities in this area. If so, under what conditions?

Perseverance—Does the job put heavy demands on an individual in this area? Have previous job holders failed through lack of 'staying power'?

75

Stability—Does the job contain stressful, unpredictable elements that demand greater than usual stability in order to cope? Candidates low on stability may have shown a history of erratic job changes or inability to cope when faced with demanding circumstances.

Self-reliance—Does the job require independence of action with perhaps minimal supervision? Be cautious of candidates who have no positive aims or ambitions and of people who prefer to be led rather than take an active role in work or leisure activities.

Flexibility—Does the job impose frequently changing situations and problems on the job holder? If so, check the candidate's career history for unwillingness to change either personal circumstances or job when this could reasonably be expected. Other signs are an inability to cope when faced with new or unexpected problems.

Avoid making generalizations by using terms such as 'leadership'; although an undeniably important quality, it is too vague and open to misinterpretation left to itself.

Motivation
Even the best qualified candidates will not work to their fullest potential unless motivated to do so.

Try to assess those elements of the work that may act as a motivator or demotivator to prospective employees. Present and past job-holders' likes and dislikes should give useful clues. Remember too that what may motivate one candidate may demotivate another. For example, overseas travel may be an exciting adventure to some but a horrifying prospect to others. Under these circumstances your job would be to decide whether the candidate really is as excited by the prospect of travel as he might claim to be. Find out how long he has had this inclination and whether the applicant has shown any inclination to travel in the past.

The eight points so far described are summarized in figure 5 on page 77.

STAGE 2—RECRUITMENT

Recruitment is the process of contacting the public and encouraging suitable candidates to come forward for final selection. There are three ways in which this can be accomplished, namely casual application, agencies and advertising. Each of these methods implies that external

Figure 5
A summary of the eight point plan

First impressions
  appearance
  bearing
  speech
  manner

Are first impressions important eg in selling?

**Personal
circumstances**
  age
  mobility
  health
  location

Are there any circumstances that would prevent success—age, inability or unwillingness to travel, poor health?

**Education and
qualifications**

Avoid over-stating educational requirements

**Intelligence and
special aptitudes**
  verbal
  numerical
  clerical
  mechanical

What were previous job holders' weaknesses? Were they lacking a particular skill or aptitude not previously considered important? Factors under this heading can be assessed by achievements in school, college, work and leisure, in addition to tests.

Experience

An important category. Be realistic in your expectations.

Interests
  intellectual
  practical
  constructional
  physically active
  social
  artistic

Interests may have an indirect but important bearing on job success.

Personality
  acceptability
  persuasiveness
  perseverance
  stability
  self-reliance

Resist the temptation to specify every quality. Pick out one or two key personal attributes that could be critical.

Motivation
  money
  security
  status
  recognition
  achievement

What motivators (or demotivators) does the job contain? These can be matched with candidates' ambitions, likes and dislikes during the interview?

candidates will be sought. However, before resorting to external recruitment it is usually desirable to ensure that all possible internal candidates have been given consideration.

CASUAL APPLICATIONS

This is an unreliable method but occasionally good applicants will write 'out of the blue' saving the time and money involved in a full-scale recruitment campaign. This is more likely to happen in periods of high unemployment during which those out of work resort to a variety of approaches in the search for a job. This method usually works best for local staff in factories, offices and services and where skill levels are fairly low. Some companies rely on recommendations from their existing staff and occasionally offer incentive schemes for successful introductions. Any such payment should only be made after an agreed period of satisfactory performance from the new employee introduced by this method.

AGENCIES

There are three main types of agency:

1 Government-run agencies which include 'job shops' for blue collar and clerical staff and the professional and executive register (PER) which caters for management and professional staff.
2 Privately-run agencies which provide a shortlist of candidates and expect payment only after employment of a successful candidate.
3 A number of agencies now operate through a register system. In this case an agency holds a register of candidates and the client pays in advance to gain access to the register. This requires an act of faith on the client's part but the fee payable for such a register is considerably less than on a payment by results basis.

Private agencies usually specialize in separate market sectors such as clerical and secretarial, accounting or computing. Many provide such an efficient service, particularly in high demand areas such as London, that they are the most cost effective source of obtaining good candidates.

The overriding advantage of the payment by results agency is that no financial commitment is involved until the campaign has resulted successfully in a new employee joining the company. To survive, therefore, agencies have to provide good candidates quickly. Their interviewers have some expertise and probably specialist knowledge and there is no doubt that using an agency can considerably ease the load off a personnel department.

The danger is that their clients will spend many wasted hours interviewing candidates falling below the required standards. It is essential, for this reason, that employers take pains to brief agencies and encourage the good ones whilst ruthlessly discarding agencies that seem unable to provide good material. There is always the hope that one day a poor agency may produce the right person but in practice they never seem to manage.

The agency world is a highly competitive one and using a good agency is usually a cost effective means of recruitment. Fees vary but are usually in the region of 15 per cent of starting salary, payable when the successful candidate begins employment. Beware of agencies stipulating that a fee is payable when the offer of employment is accepted by the candidate; this is not the same thing at all since that candidate may well fail the medical, obtain poor references, or pull out at the last minute.

ADVERTISING

The advertisement is the most fragile contact between people in the marketplace and the potential employer; each advertisement competes with many others for attention and at best can expect a few seconds' scan from the reader. Although recruitment advertisements lack the glamour of their more colourful cousins in the world of consumer goods, they are probably more difficult to do well. After all, they are in black and white, they are competing with many advertisements on one page and there is little real difference between different house styles.

Marketing people have a simple but effective four-stage guide for creating good advertisements.

attract the readers' attention

generate interest in the vacancy

create desire for the job

stimulate the reader to take action.

First of all, however, ensure the advertisement is placed in the right medium, usually newspapers and professional journals, but it is worth considering television, radio and the Prestel service. The aim is to reach maximum members of your target audience as cheaply as possible.

The bible for advertising agencies is British Rate and Data, called BRAD for short, which contains all the information you need to know about newspapers, journals and magazines with details of costs and readership figures.

For a comprehensive guide to recruitment advertising see Ray (1980).

Figure 6
A classic example of 'up-market' advertising

Commercial Director

CIVIL ENGINEERING

for a major public group which is successful and expanding as a leader in this field.

• RESPONSIBILITY is for all Quantity Surveying services, managing claims and arbitration and joint venture Agreements.

• THE ROLE involves participation in commercial policy and new business development.

• THE REQUIREMENT is for a Quantity Surveyor with a relevant record of success, and holding a Chartered or equivalent qualification.

• AGE: unlikely to be under 35. Salary negotiable to about £18,500 plus profits bonus and other benefits.

Write in complete confidence
to A. Longland as adviser to the company.

TYZACK & PARTNERS LTD

MANAGEMENT CONSULTANTS

10 HALLAM STREET	and	LONDON W1N 6DJ
21 AINSLIE PLACE		EDINBURGH EH3 6AJ

By courtesy of Everetts

Attracting attention

There are a number of factors that will help gain attention:

position on the page

white space; the Tyzack advertisement (*see* figure 6 on page 80) illustrates the effective use of white space.

border and graphics; the Eagle Star advertisement (*see* figure 7 on page 82) illustrates how a border can be used to gain attention.

the headline.

The skilled designer will use these elements in combination to achieve the best effect for the least cost.

Generating interest

The key to this is the subheading, which provides the 'link' between headline and main body of the text. It is valuable for elaborating the headline or mentioning a second item of major interest, as for example the subheading 'civil engineering' in the Tyzack advertisement shown on page 80.

Salary is often quoted as subheading. This is usually important since salary is one of the few objective criteria against which the reader can assess the job. Provided it meets the reader's expectations, knowledge of salary will confirm and strengthen his interest in the vacancy. Remember the salary levels of existing job holders in similar positions in your company!

Creating desire for the job

Every company has some selling point to stress; it may be the biggest or fastest growing in its field or it may have an interesting or successful product. Selling the company both interests the reader and, just as important, lifts morale of the company's own staff.

Moving on to the job itself, it is necessary to extract from the job analysis features likely to be attractive to the reader. Eagle Star chose to emphasize the friendly working environment, pleasant surroundings and modern equipment. BAT (*see* figure 8 on page 83) emphasized that the Audit Manager reported at Board level and that the scope of the job went far beyond that of normal audit work. Other benefits worth emphasizing are training programmes, career prospects and advantageous remuneration packages. Selling the benefits applies at any level from free transport for shopfloor staff to the chief executive's Jaguar.

At this stage the advertisement moves from selling to informing and filtering. Too many applicants cause work and are *not* an indication of a

Figure 7
An advertisement with high visual impact

By courtesy of Riley Advertising

Figure 8
An elegant advertisement which portrays a 'blue-chip' company image

International
Audit Management

c.£20,000

B.A.T Industries is a British owned international group of companies with interests in Tobacco, Retailing, Paper, Cosmetics and Packaging. Current turnover is in excess of £7,000 millions.

The Group Internal Auditor, reporting at Main Board level, has scope extending beyond the conventional accounting field into the application and monitoring of business control systems throughout our worldwide sphere of operations.

The man or woman able to develop and implement our comprehensive control and audit philosophy will have had line management responsibility for a profit centre in addition to systems and audit management experience. Applicants should be aged over 35 with a degree and an accounting qualification or M.B.A.

Salary is negotiable and unlikely to be a limiting factor.

For further information please write to Andrew West, Recruitment and Selection Adviser, or ring 01-222 2610 and listen for details.

B.A.T Industries Limited, Windsor House
50 Victoria Street, London SW1H 0NL

B·A·T INDUSTRIES
——————— LIMITED ———————

By courtesy L.B.W.

83

good advertisement. The general economic climate will, of course, have a pronounced effect on response rate regardless of an advertisement's quality.

The skilful copywriter can 'distil' the essential ingredients of the job into a few highly meaningful words. A similar approach is taken in describing the person. The screening process will be more effective if quantifiable elements, such as age, experience and qualifications, are mentioned. Descriptions such as 'good leadership potential' or 'high motivation' are too vague to be of any use as filters.

Stimulating action
The last part of the advertisement, how to make contact with the advertiser, is one of the critical areas and yet often is regarded as a mere formality. No matter how 'attention-getting' the headline may be or how good the company and job may appear the advertisement will have failed if the appropriate readers do not make contact.

Companies frequently appear to go out of their way to seem unfriendly. Copy such as: 'Write to the Area Personnel Manager stating reasons why you should be considered for this vacancy', is common. It imposes maximum effort from the applicant with the minimum of encouragement.

Although administratively less convenient, asking applicants to telephone will almost certainly increase response rate and is particularly useful for such groups as salesmen and 'blue collar' workers. Rapport is quickly established and effective screening can also be carried out.

The BAT advertisement (figure 8) p 83 gives applicants the option of ringing an answerphone where they can listen to further information and, if they wish, leave their name and address on tape. This is a good compromise between the written application and the 'live' telephone call.

STAGE 3—SCREENING THROUGH TELEPHONE AND APPLICATION FORM

Before detailed selection can take place, it is necessary to reduce the field of applicants to manageable proportions. There are two methods available. The first, and less common method is to speak to applicants direct over the telephone. The second method is to screen from letters, *curricula vitae* or application forms. The former method is quick, and establishes rapport immediately whereas the latter method is usually easier to administer, but keeps good candidates 'at a distance' for longer.

Telephone screening

Telephone screening can considerably shorten the time of a selection assignment since applicants who are requested to ring rather than write can often be selected for interview on the basis of the telephone conversation alone. Interview dates can be arranged immediately and the delay between an enquiry and first interview can be cut down to days rather than weeks. Such a system requires considerable flexibility and skill from selection staff. The telephone must always be manned, and staff must be knowledgeable about the job and person specification. It is useful to prepare a short introductory script and a checklist of questions. Keep to quantifiable aspects such as:

name, age, location, present earnings

education and training

experience

other essential points such as clean driving licence.

Avoid making judgements on less tangible evidence such as accent or fluency unless the job to be filled requires this skill.

Good applicants can be offered an interview immediately, poor ones can be rejected immediately and those falling just short of requirements can be kept on file and interviewed later.

Screening by letter, curriculum vitae (CV) or application form

Initial screening is usually based on information gathered from a letter, cv or application form or a combination of these. The process is administratively convenient, but takes longer than screening by telephone. The information required for screening can be obtained by any of the three methods; in the case of the letter or cv, applicants tell you what they think you want to know, whereas the application form will provide you with uniform and precise information about each candidate.

The most appropriate screening method will depend on the type of job to be filled and seniority of the likely applicants. Senior managers are generally reticent to complete application forms and will probably have a cv available. Application forms should vary in their design according to level of the job; clearly, it would embarrass a shopfloor worker to be asked to list postgraduate training!

Application forms are to be preferred for screening wherever possible since they provide all the necessary information in a uniform way enabling quick and accurate comparison to be made between individual applicants. cvs are notoriously frustrating to work with since they invariably have different layouts and omit vital pieces of information should the applicants consider them damaging to their cause. Rather like estate agents' descriptions of property, cvs are as important for what they fail to say as for the information they contain.

Application forms are not a formality but a valuable source of data. They help the selector eliminate applicants failing to meet quantifiable standards and can give insights into personality and motivation which can be followed up at the interview.

Application forms are for data gathering only; they are not test instruments in themselves and it is unwise to assess applicants, for example, on the quality of their handwriting or creativity of their replies. The information contained in an application may have to be taken on trust at the screening stage, but inconsistent or ambiguous information should be checked during the interview or later on through references.

APPLICATION FORM DESIGN

Many application forms appear so complex that applicants refuse to complete them. It is always a good idea to accompany the form with further information about the job, prospects and conditions of employment in the hope of overcoming any initial resistance to the form. Another useful gambit is to send two forms, making it clear that one is for the candidate to keep and the other is to be returned.

Design points to bear in mind are:

ask only as many questions as are absolutely necessary

make the form look uncluttered and easy to complete; avoid excessive numbers of lines, boxes and grids

give respondents sufficient room to write their answers

avoid excessively large blank areas requesting applicants to 'write anything else that may be of interest'.

The last point is worth further consideration since there is no doubt that some useful information can be gained from this sort of question. On balance there is more against it than for it since applicants will spend hours worrying about what is really required and may be put off completing the form altogether. There is also the problem that each applicant's statement will be different, making comparisons between applicants impossible. A better approach would be to restructure the page

Figure 9
This part of the application form with its career record in chronological order can be used as a basis for a subsequent interview.

CAREER RECORD - IN CHRONOLOGICAL ORDER PLEASE

COMPANY NAME	STARTING & LEAVING DATES	STARTING & LEAVING SALARIES	POSITIONS HELD & KEY RESPONSIBILITIES	MAJOR ACHIEVEMENTS	REASONS FOR LEAVING

PRESENT (OR MOST RECENT) EMPLOYMENT

COMPANY NAME:	KEY RESPONSIBILITIES:	MAJOR ACHIEVEMENTS:
LOCATION:		
JOB TITLE:		
STARTING (AND LEAVING) DATE:	ORGANISATION STRUCTURE SURROUNDING PRESENT JOB:	WHY ARE YOU SEEKING A CHANGE IN EMPLOYMENT?
PRESENT REMUNERATION:		
NOTICE REQUIRED:		

87

under various headings as: 'What attracts you to this vacancy?' 'How relevant is your experience?' 'What are your present leisure interests?' 'What do you regard as your major strengths?' and so on.

The well designed application form should play a major part during the interview. Figure 9 on page 87 is the centre page of a simple but effective two page (A4 size each) application form. It has a clear, uncluttered appearance which should minimize any resistance to completing it.

It asks for career information in chronological order, which is less confusing both for the applicant and interviewer than the more usual reverse chronological order. This enables the form to be used as an effective interviewing aid since the interviewer can see the applicant's career history at a glance and is well placed to ask questions about major achievements and reasons for leaving. A good form should help the interviewer, particularly the unskilled line manager, to follow up useful clues and conduct a more penetrating interview.

INTERPRETATION OF THE APPLICATION FORM

The application form contains a wealth of information which, if interpreted correctly, will significantly reduce the number of applicants required for interview. The two primary purposes of the application form are to eliminate applicants failing to meet minimum quantifiable requirements and, for applicants that remain, to formulate hypotheses about their personality and motivation to be explored at the interview.

Try using the following checklist when interpreting information from an application form:

Assess quantifiable factors
Check factual data from the application form against the minimum acceptable requirements set out in the person specification. Such facts as age, education, qualifications and experience need to be checked. This is the most straightforward use of the application form and should result in reduction of at least 70 to 80 per cent of initial applicants. If a reduction of say 50 applications down to 10 is not possible then either the specification is insufficiently precise or the present application form is in need of revision.

Check for consistency
Skilled selectors soon develop a 'feel' about good applicants based on the consistency of the data contained in their application forms. Does the

applicant's date of birth tally with examination dates taken at 'O' level, 'A' level and university? Are there any gaps between school and higher education and if so what happened during this time? Does the career record contain a series of jobs running consecutively one to the next or are there periods unaccounted for?

Many months can be hidden by using dates vaguely. Check the form in this way for concealed or ambiguous information and follow this up at the interview stage.

LOOK AT BEHAVIOUR PATTERNS FOR INSIGHTS INTO MOTIVATION AND PERSONALITY

A good application form will ask questions about applicants' reasons for leaving previous jobs, achievements, reasons for applying for the present vacancy and future aspirations. Answers to these questions should give us an insight into applicants' motivation and personality. Some answers will be unreliable, particularly those relating to reasons for leaving. Usually, the truth will show through even if in the form of a broad hint, such as 'disagreement with my boss'.

One of the principles underlying selection is that past patterns of human behaviour are the best predictors we have of future behaviour. It follows that the younger an applicant is the more difficult it will be to assess behaviour patterns and therefore make predictions about future performance. Senior managers have track records which literally 'speak for themselves'.

Try to avoid jumping to conclusions or eliminating candidates entirely on the basis of single occurrences; everyone should be allowed one or two genuine mistakes in their career, and redundancy no longer carries the stigma it once did. In looking at behaviour problems the following make useful clues:

Job changes

Has the applicant moved from one job to the next gaining in responsibility each time, or have there been odd changes in direction? Though small clues in themselves these need following up at the interview. For example a change from teaching into selling may indicate a change in circumstances and an increased need for more money. A move from a management position in the private sector to a substantially less well paid job in local government may indicate redundancy or an inability to cope under pressure.

Time spent in the job
Examine the length of stay in any one job. There can be no specific guidelines for the right length of time per job since this will vary with job type and speed of career progression. A rapid succession of jobs each lasting six months may indicate instability and the pattern may be repeated at your expense.

Leisure interests
Leisure interests may appear irrelevant to predicting job success; in practice useful insights into personality can often be gained through careful examination of this area since this tells us what the applicant *chooses* to do with his time, not what he *has* to do with it as at work. Are interests in general 'group' interests or 'loner' ones? Does the applicant prefer active/outdoor interests or more academic indoor ones? Does the applicant play an organizing role or is he more of a follower?

Assess these factors against the person specification whilst remembering that they are tentative clues only and need to be followed up during the interview.

STAGE 4—THE SELECTION INTERVIEW

INTRODUCTION

For many managers the selection process begins and ends with the interview. The selection interview is most effective as part of a systematic process; it follows screening by telephone or application form and should in turn be followed by reference checking.

There are three broad objectives to be achieved at the interview:

1 to confirm existing information about candidates and expand on it where necessary
2 to assess candidates' personality and motivation
3 to ensure applicants have a reasonable knowledge of the job and the organization which they may join.

It is easy to forget that applicants need to make up their own minds about the job; the selection interview is a two-way process. The 'better' the applicant, the more fussy he or she is likely to be and the more important it is for the interviewer to create a favourable impression by conducting a competent interview.

Interviewees will be under considerable pressure at this time and first impressions, however atypical, will carry undue weight.

Interviewing is principally a means of information gathering; quantifiable data from the application form is verified as far as possible and the applicant's personality and motivation is explored through following up past patterns of behaviour. The interview is not a test in itself and test elements should not be built into the interviewing procedure. Many untrained interviewers seem to rely on one 'infallible question' the answer to which is used to the exclusion of all other evidence. Putting an applicant 'under pressure' is another favourite device of the untrained interviewer. It is unlikely however that the interviewee will react to pressure under interview conditions in the same way as he will react under pressure on a day to day basis; the two pressures are not comparable and the technique therefore not valid.

Interviewing is a skill for which training is the only means of gaining competence. Unfortunately, like driving, no one likes to believe they are bad at it. In consequence few new managers like to ask for training and are left to gradually develop bad habits as they grow older. The evidence is overwhelming that untrained interviewers make poor selection decisions; frequently they do no better than could be achieved through selecting candidates by chance!

A good interviewer should not only be able to select the 'best fit' of candidate to job, but also understand that person's strengths and weaknesses, be able to prescribe future training and development needs and arrive at an informed opinion as to their future potential.

In contrast a poor interviewer tends to be unduly swayed by inconsequential evidence, fails to listen, jumps to conclusions too quickly and fails to assess the interviewee against the person specification.

Above all, the interview is part of a sequence of steps in the selection process, not an end in itself. For a further discussion on interviewing see Higham (1979).

PREPARATION AND TIMING

A smoothly run interviewing programme will make all the difference in attracting really good candidates. Little things, peripheral to the interview, such as a friendly welcome at reception, the offer of a cup of tea or coffee and prompt payment of travel expenses may seem trivial to the interviewer but assume great importance to the interviewee. Other points to check are that you have a free office and that the telephone is blocked.

Most managers are over-optimistic when it comes to scheduling their days interviewing. The time allowed per interview will depend on the vacancy to be filled but it will rarely be less than 30 minutes or longer than one hour. Quite apart from the interview itself, time must be allowed for reading the application form beforehand, answering candidates questions and writing up conclusions, making a 30 minute minimum seem very short.

At the other end of the timescale interviews lasting much over one hour bring with them fatigue to both parties and a law of diminishing returns sets in. Two shorter complimentary interviews would be more effective than one longer one.

A polished introduction always helps to get the interview off to a good start. It helps to plan an introduction in advance by covering such topics as travel expenses, the purpose and length of the interview and a few brief details about the vacancy.

TYPES OF INTERVIEW

There can be many possible permutations of selection interview and most can be made to work provided interviewers are properly trained and briefed beforehand. The usual problem is to decide whether to use a 'one to one' or 'panel' interview. Both have advantages and can be used exclusively or in combination under the right circumstances.

The 'one to one' interview is frequently used but needs a skilled interviewer for best results. Given sufficient skill, the interviewer can quickly establish good rapport and conduct an interview of astonishing penetration in a relatively short period of time. However, the pressures imposed on the interviewer under these circumstances are enormous as he or she will have to follow the application form, ask the right questions, listen to the answers and take notes all at the same time. This can be done with practise but the manager conducting only the occasional interview is in danger of losing control and allowing the interview to degenerate into a simple chat.

Panel interviews at their best contain around three members who work together probing previously allocated topics under a chairman's guidance. Such a system is well suited to the less skilled interviewer as it removes the pressure from any one individual by spreading the workload. It will be more likely that all relevant information is gathered, that notes are taken and that the interview is kept under control.

Drawbacks to the panel interview method are greater difficulty in reaching rapport with interviewees and the danger of uncoordinated and therefore less penetrating questions. With large panels, each interviewer will have very little time and may resort to asking one or two 'pet' questions at every interview, regardless of their suitability. Under these circumstances the panel interview tends to become nothing more than a superficial vetting procedure.

CONTROLLING THE INTERVIEW

The interview, unlike day to day conversation, requires the exchange of accurate and relevant information within tight time limits. Controlling this process demands considerable skill from the interviewer; a skill quite different from any other likely to be found in the busy manager's armoury. The interviewer must above all listen and observe. He must subjugate his own personality and allow that of the interviewee to flourish. He must avoid arguments, maintain a polite but businesslike atmosphere and exert firm control through the application of his interpersonal skills rather than the sheer force of authority. In addition, the interview must be structured so as to cover only relevant issues, the questions must be correctly phrased and notes, however cryptic, must be made. This section is concerned with the control of the interview and factors which can help or hinder the process.

Rapport
The first requirement of any interview is the willingness of the candidate to co-operate by answering questions. Younger interviewees in particular may be nervous and unable to formulate their replies as lucidly as usual. Establishing rapport means developing an atmosphere of mutual trust and relaxation between both parties. This fulfils two objectives; to get the candidate talking and to encourage candidates to behave more as they would under normal circumstances. Quiet candidates will still be quiet and garrulous ones will still never stop talking; the point is that the interview should modify their behaviour as little as possible.

Methods of establishing rapport will vary depending on the personal style of both interviewer and interviewee and it is impossible to prescribe the universal correct approach. The best guide is to put yourself into the position of the interviewee and try to assess how things must seem from his point of view.

Long delays and poor administration occurring before the interview will almost certainly create difficulties, whereas a good opening introduction stating the length, purpose and structure of the interview will begin to put the interviewee at ease.

It is important to appear attentive. This is easier said than done and many potential interviewers, whilst concentrating very hard, give the appearance of being disinterested or even hostile. Only a colleague sitting in on the interview, or use of a video camera, can give adequate feedback. Points to check are frequency of eye contact and signs of interest such as nods of the head and the occasional verbal interjection such as 'aha'. Try to avoid words of encouragement that have a double meaning or slightly menacing undertones such as 'I see'.

Try to convey the impression of neutrality. The interviewee should feel free to say what he likes without any hints, however subtle, from the interviewer indicating approval or disapproval. Imagine a scale ranging from outright hostility to ingratiating friendliness. The interviewer should pitch the tone of the interview just on the friendly side of the neutral centre.

Once the interviewer's opening remarks have been completed it is important that the interviewee hears the sound of his own voice as soon as possible. Nothing settles candidates down faster than being allowed, without interruption, to answer a straightforward question at reasonable length as early as possible in the interview. This should set the pattern for the whole interview; the interviewee talking and the interviewer listening!

Environment

Environmental factors are frequently under-estimated in their impact on the interview. Offices are arranged for the comfort of the occupant which can occasionally be to the detriment of the interviewee. The most common example is for the user to sit with his back to the window so that daylight falls over his shoulder on to the desk in front of him. Interviewees then sit opposite the interviewer and, in order to maintain eye contact, are forced to stare into bright light from the window. This can on occasions cause acute discomfort to the interviewee but go completely unnoticed by the interviewer. Temperature and noise levels should also be kept within reasonable levels. Comfort in itself will not induce greater rapport but discomfort will almost certainly inhibit it.

Room layout itself can also exert a psychological impact on interviews. A large desk, causing greater physical separation, appears to inhibit rapport more so than a small one. It is hardly a coincidence that, in general, the more senior the manager the larger is his office and desk. The size of desk reinforces the 'bosses' status and increases the psychological distance between him and his subordinate. This is exactly the opposite of what is required in the interview.

Interviewing across a desk is the most formal and common layout for interviewing. A less formal approach is to interview across one corner of the desk; the interviewer retains a working surface for application form and notes but the physical barrier is kept to a minimum. Experienced interviewers, consultants in particular, usually prefer the most informal layout possible which is two armchairs with perhaps a small coffee table for notes. Although simple and informal, this layout demands great skill of the interviewer if he is to keep the interview under control.

Silence

It is easy for managers to forget that their job in the interview is to listen. About 80 per cent of the talking should come from the interviewee and yet, paradoxically, interviewers tend to believe that the more talking they have done the better the interview is. Listening for such a large proportion of the time does not come naturally to most people! It is a skill which must be learnt and practised. The skilled interviewer should use silence to his advantage by asking one question and then keeping quiet.

QUESTIONS

Nothing will affect the interview more than the quality and phrasing of the questions. The difference between a well phrased and badly phrased question can be so subtle that it would go unnoticed by untrained interviewers, yet such small differences in phrasing could completely alter the outcome of an interview. The 'good' question should force the candidate to think and then reply in his own way, free from any bias the interviewer might inadvertently introduce.

Leading questions

It is perhaps easier to make the point by illustrating what not to do. Good interviewing style is, in many ways, the exact opposite of what is required for polite everyday conversation. For example the question 'Presumably you found working overseas a fascinating and challenging experience?' would be a perfectly acceptable remark to make in any social setting. It implies interest and even admiration from the questioner, just the thing to maintain a conversation at the dinner table. In fact, everyday conversation is usually made with the purpose of supporting and building up relationships whether socially or at work. Conversation is not usually carried out with the intention of forcing one's friends to think hard before answering questions and then to have their answers received in a non-committal, neutral way.

Interviewing demands precisely this approach; this is why people seldom make good natural interviewers without training. The above question, for example, leads the interviewee to agree with the questioner since it is far easier to answer in the affirmative to such an overwhelmingly one-sided question. Not only is the question 'leading' but it also betrays the questioner's attitude to the topic under discussion.

Similarly a question such as 'I see you were in sales for three years; I suppose you found it tough but rewarding?' is fine as a conversational opening gambit, but useless as an interview question. The obvious non-leading form of the question would be 'How did you find your three years in sales?' The interviewee may have found it easy or boring or highly stressful; the only way to find out is to put the question in a 'non-leading' way. The most common leading question is the 'Did you enjoy ...?' variety, taken directly from our day to day conversations. Typical examples are 'Did you enjoy working for the Civil Service/free enterprise/ with a woman boss/on night shift?' The better phrasing for interview purposes would be 'How did you feel about ...?'

Leading questions bias information received in two ways. Inexperienced or timid candidates tend to follow the path of least resistance by agreeing with the questioner's implied correct answer. More skilful candidates will feed back answers they think the interviewer wants to hear. In either case, the information gained will be useless.

Closed questions

A further question type to be avoided is the closed question. Again, this occurs naturally in everyday conversation, but its use should be avoided during the interview. A closed question prevents interviewees answering questions as fully as they might wish, usually permitting only a yes or no answer. The following are common examples: 'Did you pass 'A' level maths at school?' or 'Did you go straight from school to university?'

Closed questions do not, as a rule, bias the interviewee's response (unless they are leading) but they do damage rapport. Nothing damps down an interview faster than a series of closed questions followed by yes or no answers. Interviewers can soon find themselves talking 80 per cent of the time, a pattern once established that is exceedingly difficult to reverse. Closed questions can be used to establish matters of fact but their use under these circumstances should be kept to a minimum.

Probing

Inexperienced interviewers are reluctant to follow-up or probe answers to their opening question. In the majority of cases probing is necessary, either to clarify answers or to gain more information.

Avoid the temptation of accepting answers at face value; if the answer is inadequate or throws up an interesting line of investigation then follow it up. A dialogue might go as follows:

Interviewer:	'How do you feel about that job?'
Candidate:	'I didn't really enjoy it very much!'
Interviewer probes:	'Why not?'
OR	'Tell me more about it?'
	'What was it that you didn't enjoy?'

Contrasting questions

Interviewees frequently need help in putting their answers into words. A useful technique is to structure some questions so as to encourage candidates to contrast one topic with another. The most common example is 'likes and dislikes', a theme which can be applied to almost any subject usually with successful results. These 'contrast' questions usually run something like this:

'What do you like most about ...?'
'What do you like least about ...?'

OR

'What was your most successful job?'
'What was your least successful job?'

Questions such as these (likes/dislikes, easy/difficult, best/worst, most enjoyable/least enjoyable) produce a substantial amount of useful data from which inferences can be drawn about interviewees' personality and motivation.

Critical questions

It is worth adding a note about questions implying criticism. The job of the interviewer is to gather accurate data, but there is a risk that data will be biased if the interviewer becomes involved in arguments with the candidate, or implies criticism even though none is intended. Examples are:

'Why did you *only* manage to get two 'A' levels?'
'Why did it take you *so long* to gain promotion?'

Once recognized, such questions can usually be rephrased in a less critical way.

Using examples of behaviour

A useful approach is to ask interviewees to give examples from their own experience: A nervous interviewee may have difficulty in recalling his spare time activities, in which case he could be asked 'Tell me what you did last weekend?' Such questions draw the interviewee's attention away from generalities to specifics.

We can explore an interviewee's ability to copy under pressure in much the same way. If, for example, we were to ask a salesman 'How do you cope with difficult customers?' we would be given a predictable and socially acceptable answer. If, on the other hand, we were more specific and said 'Tell me about your most difficult client?' followed by 'How did you cope with him?' the answer would be more accurate. There are many variations of this type of question. We might ask a general manager 'Which is the most difficult industrial relations incident you have had to face?' Follow-up questions would include 'What do you think caused this incident?' 'How did you tackle the problem?' and 'Would you tackle it the same way again?'

STRUCTURING THE INTERVIEW

It is advisable to follow a structure when interviewing, if for no reason other than to ensure that no vital questions are omitted. The easiest approach is to start with the interviewee's childhood and work through to the present time. Some interviewers prefer to begin with the inter-viewee's present job, which is freshest in his mind, and work backwards. The structure you use is not really important; what is important is that having found a suitable structure you stay with it.

The structure you use and the questions you ask will, of course, depend on the vacancy to be filled and the age and experience of the applicant. A common preference is to use a 'biographical' approach based on the following structure:

Home background
To find out the level at which the candidate starts off in life, ie was it tough or soft, encouraging or discouraging?

School and further education
To assess the candidate's early academic ability and the first opportunity we have of judging his motivation and personality.

Work history
Probably the most important part of the interview where we concentrate on matching the candidate's skills and experience to those required for the job. We should also look for patterns of behaviour that were repeated

throughout the candidate's work experience, to enable us to predict future behaviour.

Leisure activities
Important because this tells us what the candidate prefers to do rather than what he has to do at work.

Present circumstances
Do the candidate's domestic circumstances, ability to travel and health allow him to carry out the work required?

The advantage of the biographical interview is that is enables us to trace the candidate's life and experiences in their correct sequence, making it far easier to assess behaviour patterns. For example, the interviewee might have a history of leaving his job suddenly after a disagreement with his boss or he may be continually attracted to new and more exciting jobs only to become quickly bored.

Each interview will tell a different story but almost all will show some trends from which predictions of future behaviour can be made.

STAGE 5—TAKING REFERENCES AND MAKING THE SELECTION DECISION

REFERENCES

The reference check is usually the last stage in the selection process. Good referees are almost certain to know more about the applicant than the selector and it would be foolish not to seek their advice or treat the reference check as a mere formality. A reference should give us more than a single yes or no answer as regards applicant's suitability for employment; it should provide information on strengths and weaknesses, training needs and potential for future development.

Telephone or written reference?
It is undoubtedly easier for the hard pressed personnel department to issue a standard letter requesting a reference. The disadvantages are that it imposes a considerable workload on the referee who may in any case be reluctant to commit damaging evidence to paper. As a result written references tend to become a formality rather than an invaluable source of further information on which to base a selection decision.

Using the telephone as a means of gaining a reference is time-consuming and inconvenient, but once contact is made, a short semi-structured conversation will provide infinitely better and more accurate information. As with any reference check, referees should be contacted only after permission has been given by the applicant. Many companies forbid their personnel departments to give references by telephone, and for good reasons, but it is not the personnel department whom we would ideally contact for a reference.

Who to ask?

Applicants' present employers are usually contacted only after an offer of employment is made. Where possible, previous employers should be asked for references before an offer is made. Most experienced selection practitioners prefer to speak direct to an applicant's previous manager rather than the personnel department, since the manager is in the best position to know the candidate really well. Managers are usually willing to talk over the telephone provided you have permission to approach them and that you introduce yourself. Occasionally, a manager will take the sensible precaution of ringing you back in order to check your identity.

Character references from relatives or people in authority are seldom used now and have limited usefulness in industry.

How far back should reference go?

A useful general rule is to go back five years or two previous jobs. The obvious exception is when a candidate has worked for his present company for longer than five years in which case you may have to go back further in time or rely on a reference from the present employer after the job offer is made. Always try for references from at least two people or more if contradicting evidence emerges.

It is worthwhile raising the question of referees at the interview. Some episode may need further checking and you can ask for a referee there and then.

What questions should we ask?

Not only do we wish to know that the candidate has performed satisfactorily in past jobs but also something about his development potential, personality and motivation. A semi-structured questionnaire (whether for written or oral reference checks) ensures the fullest possible assessment. The following sequence of questions is useful:

Introduction: introduce yourself, give reasons for calling and say you have permission.

Factual information: start with early factual questions such as dates of joining and leaving and final salary.

Performance data: how well did he perform? What was his attendance record? Was he closely supervised? How well did he get on with other people? These sort of questions are a little more subjective but straightforward nevertheless.

Key questions: key questions should be kept until rapport has been sufficiently built up.

Would you re-employ him?

What are his major strengths?

What are his weaknesses?

Does he have any domestic or financial problems?

Development potential: finally describe the job to the referee and ask if the applicant would be able to cope. Discuss the applicant's aspirations and abilities in general in order to formulate a development programme.

Naturally, the effort expended in the reference checking stage will depend on the type of vacancy involved. But even an elaborate telephone check is likely to take only a tiny proportion of the total time involved in the selection process and will yield information of value out of all proportion to the time invested.

THE SELECTION DECISION

In practice the final decision will probably be between three or four candidates, since most will have been eliminated during the earlier selection stages. Most applicants will be eliminated at the application form stage, through failing to meet the quantitative requirements. The rest will be eliminated after the interview, again on the quantitative evidence or through failure to meet requirements based on personality or motivation.

It is unlikely that any of the three or four remaining applicants will meet the person specification in every way. The personnel specialist together with line management will now have to weigh up the strengths and weaknesses of each candidate. One may have more experience but another greater development potential and so on.

There are no shortcuts; reaching a decision is difficult and taxing. Easy systems based on numerical ratings can prove to be a delusion; it is not possible to compare on a points basis, for example, experience against motivation. Such systems give managers an easy way out by encouraging them not to sift properly through all the evidence.

In the end making the right decision depends on management judgement; the evidence must be assessed and the best match made of person to specification, whilst taking into account the present and future demands of the job.

OTHER ISSUES IN SELECTION

CONSULTANTS AND EXECUTIVE SEARCH

Selection consultants are specialists who usually recruit through advertisements, conduct screening interviews and present clients with a shortlist of three to six candidates. They charge a fee of between 15 and 20 per cent of starting salary excluding advertising costs and other expenses.

In return for their fee, consultants should provide a skilled and speedy service since they do the job full-time. They are geared up to deal with advertising agencies and all the other services concerned with recruitment. For example, an unduly heavy response to your advertisement could mean that you are under-equipped to reply quickly, thus running the risk of losing good candidates and also spoiling your company's image. Consultants are equipped to avoid these problems and present a professional front to your prospective employees.

Consultants will never pretend to replace the in-company personnel professional, but they can save his or her time and provide an up to date knowledge of salary levels, details of media and the likelihood of attracting good candidates at the right price. They are particularly useful to managers of smaller companies with limited facilities and expertise who need to make important senior management appointments and cannot afford to get them wrong.

The executive search approach is to pinpoint a small target group of individuals, who are felt to be suitable candidates for the job in question. Prospective applicants are approached direct by the consultants and the possibilities of a move tactfully explored.

Very few vacancies merit this highly specialized and individual attention but there are occasions when it is advisable. It is regarded as undignified, for example, for jobs at the very highest level to be advertised in the national press. It is generally felt, possibly incorrectly, that managers above a certain salary level will refuse to respond to an advertisement. Nonetheless, there are certainly cases when a direct approach needs to be made and it is then that the 'head hunter's' services are used.

By its very nature, head hunting is an expensive business. Each consultant must be able to call on extensive research facilities including libraries and research assistants. The consultant will conduct many more face to face meetings and travel extensively and there will be less opportunity for 'streamlining' procedures. For this reason fees usually begin at around 30 per cent of starting salary (which is usually a large one) and expenses can easily amount to half as much again. For that sort of money you should expect a fast and discrete service with candidates of a uniformly high calibre from which to choose.

PSYCHOLOGICAL TESTS

Psychological tests are regarded by some as having almost magical properties and they can easily be misused and misinterpreted by untrained people. Tests tend to be used as an easy option in the decision making process with managers becoming over-dependent on test results. Tests are simply one selection tool amongst many and should complement manager's judgement not supplant it.

Good tests are useful in the right circumstances because they can provide an objective measure of peoples' abilities. However, because they are precise objective measuring instruments they tend to be very specific in what they measure. For example, a test of general intelligence which is objective in itself may nevertheless be very limited in predicting a candidate's success in a job. Tests therefore should be validated, that is proved to predict future performance, before they are used in the selection process. This is important because tests may unfairly discriminate against certain groups of the population. All this makes testing an expensive business and it is better not to test at all than to test badly.

Tests fall into a number of categories, the most common and possibly most useful are tests of ability and aptitude.

Ability and aptitude
Mental ability is synonymous with the term general intelligence and is probably the best researched area in testing. There are also a number of

specific abilities such as verbal, numerical, spatial, clerical and mechanical for which there is clearly an application in selection.

Tests of general intelligence and specific ability are often used in selection; they are convenient to use and most may be administered by personnel managers after one week's intensive training. They can be applied from the shopfloor for mechanic or apprentice selection through to senior management appointments.

Attainment

Aptitude and ability tests are useful in predicting future performance on the job. Attainment tests, on the other hand, are designed to assess a present level of achievement. Tests of typing, product knowledge and driving fall into this category.

Interests and personality inventories

Since there can be no right or wrong answer in assessments of interests and personality the term, test, cannot strictly speaking be used. These inventories are more easy to 'fake good' than tests of ability; applicants may try to give answers they think the selectors are seeking. Inventories are most useful in careers guidance where candidates will willingly co-operate; they should only be used in selection under skilled supervision, usually that of a psychologist.

Perceptual motor tests

Perceptual motor tests assess combinations of sensory and muscular abilities. The most commonly quoted example is manual dexterity but there are many more. Application of these tests is widespread on the shopfloor for selection of general operatives, apprentices and mechanics.

Trainability tests

This is a new approach to testing devised in the UK by the Industrial Training Research Unit. It is similar in approach to the assessment centre in that applicants are asked to carry out a series of tasks representative of the job for which they are being selected. Unlike perceptual-motor tests which measure very specific abilities, the trainability test can assess the complete range of skills required for the successful performance of one job. Typical applications are in the selection of trainee drivers of forklift trucks and heavy goods vehicles, mechanics, electricians, fitters and plumbers. However, trainability tests must be designed and validated for each job and they take longer to give than other types of test.

In summary, tests can form part of the selection procedure but only if they are correctly constructed, administered and validated. Reputable tests are restricted to trained and registered test users. Two agencies, amongst others, who provide tests and give training in their use are the NFER and Saville and Holdsworth.

THE ASSESSMENT CENTRE

This is becoming a fashionable technique but one, in fact, that has been in use for many years, ie the War Office and Civil Service Selection Boards were early examples. The principle behind this technique is to break down the major components of a job into short, manageable exercises which candidates are then asked to perform. The assumption made is that candidates' behaviour on the exercises is a good prediction of their future performance on the job.

The advantage of this type of approach is that it enables selectors to assess skills and personal characteristics by direct observation. The interview, in contrast, allows selectors only to draw inferences based on past behaviour reported 'second-hand' through the interviewees themselves.

Assessment centres are normally associated with management selection. They can however be used advantageously for selection or promotion at almost any level within an organization and furthermore are increasingly used for career development purposes. Their primary use lies in selection for jobs demanding different sets of skills from those previously used by the candidates. Examples include assessing shop-floor workers for supervisory posts, salesmen for sales managers, graduates for management trainees and functional specialists for general management.

A typical programme will last one to two days and include individual exercises such as the 'in-tray' and presentation, group exercises such as a leaderless group discussion, possibly psychological tests and interviews. In addition to formal exercises, candidates can be shown the factory or office premises, be given a presentation on the company and be involved in a question and answer session about the job. All this helps establish greater rapport between the management team and candidates generally resulting in good candidates being more likely to accept an employment offer.

Disadvantages are the high accommodation costs and the greatly increased commitment of management time. These are generally far outweighed by improved selection decisions (in which line management play an active part) and a more accurate prediction of the future potential of the successful candidates. For an excellent, clearly written book on the subject see Andrew and Valerie Stewart (1981).

LEGAL CONSIDERATIONS

In the selection context the most common cause for concern is racial and sexual discrimination. Selection by definition is a method of discrimination but any discrimination must be based on valid job-related criteria. The Sex Discrimination Act 1975 and the Race Relations Act 1976 make it unlawful to discriminate on the grounds of sex, marital status, colour, race, nationality and ethnic or national origins. It is only within the scope of this section to create an awareness of the problem; for a useful booklet on this subject see Pearn *et al* (1980) and Lewis (1983).

Overt racial or sexual discrimination is now relatively uncommon; more insidious however is discrimination which occurs when the selector applies criteria that indirectly discriminate on the basis of sex or race. Indirect discrimination is often unintentional, occurring as a result of long established patterns of behaviour. Even the use of the innocent sounding term 'man-profile' can imply sexual discrimination where none may be intended.

Indirect discrimination can occur throughout the selection process:

Person specification: demanding unrealistic levels of skill for the job in question eg requiring reading ability out of all proportion to the job requirement.

Advertising: placing the advertisement where only one ethnic group is likely to read it: implying a sexual preference by using terms like waitress or barman: illustrating advertisements with pictures exclusively of one sex or race.

Application form: asking for a photograph may indicate an intention to discriminate: asking for marital status or number of children.

Interview: using untrained and subjective interviewers. The problem can be minimized by interview training and through the use of well designed selection systems.

Testing: using tests not validated for the job in question. Tests can be 'culturally biased' by using language unfamiliar to certain ethnic groups.

106

These examples, whilst not illegal in themselves could indicate an intention to unfairly discriminate. Whilst this looks like a formidable list of 'DON'TS', the chances of unintentional indirect discrimination are minimized if systematic and objective selection procedures are followed.

MANAGING THE SELECTION PROCEDURE

The decision to recruit is usually made by line management, sometimes without consulting the personnel department, who are normally expected to manage the operation. This can cause problems for the recruitment specialist who will need to establish answers to the following questions as soon as possible:

Is recruitment really necessary?

Can the job be filled internally?

Will the job change in future making it necessary to recruit someone with potential to cope with the change?

Which method of recruitment and selection is most appropriate?

Is the time-scale allowed realistic?

Who will be involved in the final selection decision?

Realistic timing is a particularly important consideration and very easy, even for an experienced selector, to under-estimate. The time-scale will vary with the type of job and method of recruitment and selection. Blue collar vacancies can take around four weeks to fill whereas senior management posts can take six months or more. The first thing the selector must do is to plan a timetable. The following illustration is of a middle management vacancy requiring an advertisement, first and second interviews.

Week 1   Decide to recruit.
           Prepare person specification.
           Prepare advertisement or brief agency.
           Book interview times for line management.

Weeks 2/3 Advertisement appears (avoid holiday periods and allow more time for monthly publications).

Weeks 4/5 Application forms are sent, returned and screened.

Weeks 6/7 First interviews held with personnel department and line management. Shortlist prepared.

Weeks 8/9   Second interview(s) or special selection procedure such as assessment centre.

Week 10   Make selection decision and take up references and medical. Make an offer.

This time-scale assumes ideal circumstances; but there can be many delays such as advertisements appearing late due to strike action, interviewers or interviewees unable to attend and refereees being unobtainable for several weeks.

Using agencies or consultants can reduce the time taken, but not by much. The most significant saving in time is possible through using the telephone for initial screening and arranging all appointments.

Remember also to add the successful candidate's notice period to your time-scale. This can range from one week to three months (even more with some senior managers) making the total time taken to recruit and engage a new employee almost six months. For this reason it pays the personnel recruitment specialist to liaise as closely as possible with line management in order to become part of the decision making process rather than a recipient of it. Resist management pressure to recruit within unrealistic deadlines because it is far better to wait a few weeks and make the right decision. The old adage 'act in haste, repent at leisure' was never more true than in recruitment and selection.

Finally, the relationship between the personnel function and line management demands careful consideration. It is natural for line management to wish to be involved in decisions concerning selection of their subordinates; the line management will also possess expertise which can help in determining the suitability of candidates, particularly where technical knowledge and experience is important. The personnel department, however, should possess the knowledge and experience in the recruitment and selection process to be able to manage the process as a whole. This requires good relations between personnel and line managers and an understanding of what each can contribute. One pattern is for the line management to be involved in the initial decision to recruit and the final choice of candidate; with the personnel department doing the rest of the work. In practice, where the personnel department can demonstrate its competence, line management will probably seek its involvement in all stages of the process.

REFERENCES

HIGHAM, Martin (1979). *The ABC of Interviewing*. London, Institute of Personnel Management.

HOLDSWORTH, Roger (1972). *Personnel Selection Testing—A guide for Managers*. London, British Institute of Management.

LEWIS, David (1983). *Essentials of Employment Law*. London, IPM.

MUNRO FRASER, John (1978). *Employment Interviewing*. 5th ed. London, MacDonald and Evans.

PEARN, Michael *et al* (1980). *Discriminating Fairly: A Guide to Fair Selection*. Leicester, British Psychological Society/Runnymede Trust.

RAY, Maurice (1980). *Recruitment Advertising*. London, Institute of Personnel Management.

RODGER, Alec (1952). *The Seven Point Plan*. London, National Institute of Industrial Psychology. (Now available through the NFER (National Foundation for Educational Research)).

STEWART, Andrew *and* Valerie (1981). *Tomorrow's Managers Today*. London, Institute of Personnel Management.

FURTHER READING

GENERAL BOOKS ON RECRUITMENT AND SELECTION

ARMSTRONG,Michael *and* HACKETT, Penny (1979). *Recruitment Handbook*. London, Kogan Page.

PLUMBLEY, Philip (1976). *Recruitment and Selection*. London, Institute of Personnel Management.

PLUMBLEY, Philip *and* WILLIAMS, Roger (1981). *The Person for the Job*. London, Kogan Page.

UNGERSON, Bernard (ed) (1983). *A Recruitment Handbook*. 3rd ed Farnborough, Hants, Gower.

FURTHER READING ON INTERVIEWING

ARGYLE, Michael (ed) (1975). *Bodily Communication*. Harmondsworth, Middx., Penguin.

Argyle, Michael (ed) (1981). *Social Skills and Work*. London, Methuen.

Goodale JG (1982). *The Fine Art of Interviewing*. London, Prentice-Hall.

Keenan A *and* Wedderburn A (1980). 'Putting the boot on the other foot: candidates' descriptions of interviews.' *Journal of Occupational Psychology*. Vol. 53.

Torrington, Derek (1982). *Face to Face in Management*. London, Prentice-Hall.

Further reading on testing and assessment

Guion R (1965). *Personnel Testing*. London, McGraw Hill.

Mackenzie, Davey D *and* Harris, Marjorie (1982). *A Guide to Orthodox and Unorthodox Methods of Assessment*. London, McGraw Hill.

Miller KM (ed) (1975). *Psychological Testing in Personnel Assessment*. Farnborough, Hants, Gower.

Moses JL *and* Byham WC (eds) (1977). *Applying the Assessment Centre Method*. Oxford, Pergamon.

Pearn, Michael (1979). *The Fair Use of Tests*. Slough, NFER.

Warren, Anne *and* Downs, Sylvia (1978). *Trainability Tests—A Practitioners Guide*. Cambridge, Industrial Training Research Unit.

Chapter five

Performance appraisal

INTRODUCTION: THE PURPOSES OF APPRAISAL

In any kind of organization where people co-operate in working towards some goal, the appraisal of an individual's performance, by himself, by his peers, or by his superiors, is a more or less inescapable fact of life. Much of it goes on informally, as part of people's everyday practice of forming impressions of others, but the process has been enshrined in systematic appraisal schemes by organizations going back at least as far as the first World War. These schemes consist typically in modern times of a report form which contains an assessment of an individual's perform-ance written by one of his superiors and, in most cases, an appraisal interview as well, in which manager and subordinate discuss the latter's job performance and various other topics.

The purposes of appraisal schemes vary considerably, but the following list contains those most frequently encountered:

motivating staff and thus improving performance

providing a fair and rational basis for making individual decisions on promotion, training, transfer and dismissal

acting as one of the criteria for merit pay awards

collecting information that facilitates manpower planning and de-velopment

improving manager-subordinate communication.

These are primarily organizational goals; they meet the needs of the organization. But the individual who is appraised has needs too, and whilst he may in varying degrees identify with the organizational goals, he is often more concerned to use appraisal for the following reasons:

obtaining feedback on performance. Uncertainty is a state most human beings find difficult to tolerate, yet by its nature much managerial and administrative work in large organizations provides little direct feedback as to how satisfactorily it has been performed. Feedback from appraisers reduces uncertainty, and where the work has been done well, is rewarding in itself

influencing promotion and career prospects and obtaining an adequate merit pay award. This means presenting himself in as favourable a light as possible which may involve arguing with the appraiser to justify his performance level and rejecting feedback given, if it suggests a poorer level of achievement than the individual thinks is a fair reflection of the truth. The appraisee may find a conflict of interests, ie he wants feedback, but sometimes finds the content of it prejudicial to his other needs

seeking advice and guidance on performance and career matters. In this respect, the appraisal is an opportunity for counselling.

Clearly, there is no shortage of functions for appraisal, and appraisal schemes often give the appearance of trying to be all things to all men. The problems that arise when this happens are well documented (McGregor 1957; Meyer, Kay and French 1965; Burke 1972; Pym 1973). A key problem is that the different aims of appraisal frequently clash. The main conflict is between the assessment and reward aspects on the one hand and the motivating and counselling aspects on the other; it centres on the appraiser's difficulty in reconciling the roles of judge and of helper. This point will feature in the present chapter on a number of occasions, and the implications of it for the type of scheme adopted will be dealt with later when the general strategy of designing and introducing appraisal schemes is discussed. First, however, the actual techniques used in appraisal need to be described, and, in the manner of many appraisals themselves, their strengths and weaknesses discussed. The distinction must be drawn here between appraising *performance* and appraising *potential*, two related but quite different activities. Accordingly, they will be dealt with separately.

METHODS OF APPRAISING PERFORMANCE

The central question, the answer to which markedly influences the technique employed, is *what* to appraise: job related abilities, personality or results? Early appraisal systems stressed the assessment of personality traits, but these kind of judgements are more difficult than most to make and lay behind the appraisers' dislike of 'playing God' that McGregor (1957) noted. Appraisals based on personality are frequently difficult to relate in any very direct or constructive way to the job itself. Also, by their nature, they are apt to elicit defensive reactions on the part of subordinates who, not surprisingly, take such direct criticism rather personally. For these reasons there was a swing in the 1960s towards appraising job-related behaviour and abilities only, or simply to assessing outcomes, that is, results achieved. Nonetheless, Gill (1977) notes that incorporating personality ratings in appraisal may be staging something of a comeback in the UK, whilst Williams (1980) reports that this element of appraisal is 'as strong as ever' in America. Perhaps this reflects the fact that, whatever the difficulties it has as a vehicle for appraisal, personality has a strong influence on many aspects of performance at work (interpersonal relations, motivation, reactions to stress and so on) and many organizations feel that this has to be represented somewhere, somehow in their assessments. This issue will be encountered at various stages through this chapter, but for the moment we will move on to look in turn at the four main techniques of appraising performance—rating scales, results-oriented approaches, essay methods and the critical incidents approach.

RATING METHODS

Rating scales are the traditional and best-known method of appraisal. Their development involves two types of decision; first the decision about what aspects of personality and performance to rate and secondly the decision about how to rate, that is, what type of rating scale to use.

Methods of determining what to rate

The aim is to identify those attributes that are crucial to effective performance in the job and which can discriminate between people who show varying levels of success in the job. There are a variety of techniques for doing this, which will only be mentioned briefly here; for a further description, *see* Stewart and Stewart (1977):

> The committee method is probably still one of the most widely used approaches. A group of senior managers including some from the personnel department get together and decide what they think are the most important qualities that should be assessed. This is a rather unsystematic and haphazard technique, which is often not backed up

113

by any hard evidence that qualities chosen really do relate to the jobs in question—an important legal point as will be seen later.

A proper **job analysis** can be carried out, and the main elements of a job incorporated into the appraisal form.

The critical **incidents** technique can be employed to obtain in detail specific instances of good and bad performance (or performers) and this information then used to identify the qualities and abilities that seem to differentiate the two.

The **repertory grid,** a specialized technique devised by Kelly (1955) and developed by Bannister and Mair (1968) can be used. It is a procedure which can, when used skilfully, discover the chief ways in which managers see effective and ineffective performers as differing from one another.

The **performance questionnaire** technique, advocated by Stewart and Stewart (1976, 1977) produces information similar in some respects to that of the repertory grid.

All, apart from the first of these methods, are systematic in approach, take time to complete, and have the implication that different qualities may be identified for different jobs or groups of jobs, probably necessitating a different set of ratings for each.

Methods of obtaining ratings
Having identified the criteria to be rated there are numerous types of rating scale to choose from, the four main ones being:

1 *Scales with verbally-described intervals:* These can be illustrated by the following:
Overall performance

Outstanding	Very good	Good	Fair	Not quite adequate	Unsatisfactory
☐	☐	☐	☐	☐	☐

2 *Numerical (or alphabetical) ratings:* The individual is rated on a number of criteria using a scale ranging from best to worst, with a number or letter given to each interval point. For example:

	High				Low
Effectiveness with people	1	2	3	4	5

3 Graphic rating scales: These generally dispense with formal interval points apart from the two extremes and the middle, but define in some detail the behaviour associated with the quality being rated. For example:

Dependability is evidenced by the following behaviours (1) follows instructions (2) completes work on time (3) is punctual and regular in attendance (4) does not require excessive supervision.

HIGH ├────────────────────────┼────────────────────────┤LOW

4 Comparative scales: The individual is rated on some quality in terms of his standing relative to others of his level. For example:

Initiative

A Not as good as the great majority

B OK, but many I have known have been better

C Typical of the middle group

D Better than most, though I have known better

E One of the best I have known

There are other variations on these themes; some refinements will be mentioned below, and a comprehensive survey will be found in Whisler and Harper (1962). One matter that should be mentioned here is the range of rating scale interval points. Although some people would have you believe otherwise, research shows that people have difficulty in handling much more than seven discrete categories, and any rating scale with defined interval points should not have more than seven under normal circumstances.

Advantages and disadvantages of rating methods

The advantages

One of the foremost reasons for adopting rating scales, indeed for doing appraisal at all, is to facilitate comparisons between staff when making decisions on pay or promotion. Most organizations seem to find some grading procedure of this kind essential in generating reward policies that seek to be fair and equitable. This is often reflected by the inclusion of overall performance rating scales in appraisal forms that do not otherwise use the rating method.

Rating scales encourage an analytical approach to considering subordinates' performance, rather than just judging them on the basis of results; in other words, it looks at *how* goals are achieved rather than simply *what* was achieved.

The technique is potentially flexible in that rating scales can be devised and tailored to suit the appraisal of a wide range of jobs. In fact, if they are to be at all appropriate, they must be tailored to the specific job.

These, then, are some of the advantages of rating methods, providing they are used properly. However, this condition is seldom met, and there are substantial problems with rating scales as listed below.

The disadvantages

The major difficulty centres around the problem of subjectivity. Whilst there is a subjective element in all techniques of performance appraisal, it seems particularly evident in the use of ratings. There are two aspects of it. First, the rater often makes assessments on scales that are too impressionistic and insufficiently tied to evidence; it is almost too 'easy' to give a rating. One then gets phenomena like the 'halo' effect; where one quality of an individual is judged very favourably and is allowed to colour the assessor's ratings of other qualities. Secondly, quite apart from subjective biases of this kind, the scales themselves are open to differing interpretations. This is often the result of inadequate definition of the scale end points or interval points, but to some extent is inherent in the technique, which imposes the dimensions of assessment upon the rater rather than letting him use his own. The ratings he is asked to use may not represent the way he thinks about an individual's performance at all, or may be interpreted quite differently by different assessors (try getting different people to define 'drive', 'integrity', 'maturity' and 'determination' and you will frequently get quite significantly different concepts emerging). All this has the inevitable consequences of variable standards of assessment being operated, which undermines the comparability function of many rating scales.

One of the aims of rating scales is to achieve a useful discrimination of varying levels of performance amongst staff. Unfortunately, it is very common to find that appraisers do not distribute their ratings very widely or evenly. All too often they show either a central tendency (putting most people in the middle of the scale) or a positively skewed rating (almost everyone rated very favourably). For example, in one organization the overall performance ratings were distributed like this (*See* Anstey, Fletcher and Walker 1976):

116

Outstanding	Very good	Good	Fair	Not quite adequate	Unsatis- factory
4%	50.5%	39%	6.5%	0.5%	0%

Two possible reasons for this come to mind. One is that appraisers are reluctant to appraise (Rowe 1964) and thus mark subordinates rather favourably in order to avoid conflict with them. The other is that in most organizations, unsatisfactory employees are dismissed or leave of their own accord fairly quickly and the rest of the workforce do a good job in general, and this is reflected in their assessments. Probably both of these factors contribute to the kind of rating distributions we see, but nonetheless the effect is to reduce the value of rating scales as a means of differentiating performance levels.

Rating scales often do not reflect the attributes necessary for effective performance in a particular job. Indeed the variation in the content of jobs and in the criteria for effective performance imply that different rating scales be used for different jobs. But for the sake of comparability, and perhaps for simplicity, organizations often apply the same scales to large numbers of people doing quite different work. Sometimes they use methods to try to get round the disadvantages of this, such as leaving some additional blank rating scales for appraisers to fill in their own dimensions, or getting the appraiser to indicate whether each quality rated is of high, medium or low relevance to the job concerned. However these are usually only partial solutions to the basic problems of conducting ratings on inappropriate criteria. This is, of course, a problem in the improper *use* of scales rather than of the method as such, but even where scales are properly tailored to the particular job it could be argued that they never adequately reflect the complex behaviour required to fill the managerial role effectively.

Some approaches to improving rating methods
If an organization feels that establishing some system of comparing individuals is a prime function of its appraisal scheme, can it do anything to overcome the problems of rating scales? Several things have been tried, some affecting the type of scales themselves and some the way they are used. For example, the use of a forced distribution of ratings is not uncommon; the appraiser might be asked to allocate his subordinates ratings in such a way as to approximate to a normal distribution, with perhaps 10 per cent at the top level, 20 per cent in the next, 40 per cent in the middle, 20 per cent next to lowest and 10 per cent at the bottom level. The idea is to prevent the problem outlined above concerning the

117

'bunching' of ratings at the top or middle of the scale. But this is an unsatisfactory solution as it takes no account of the fact that one appraiser may indeed have many very good or many very poor people and should therefore show a skewed distribution of ratings. Also, some appraisers just do not have enough subordinates to make this approach feasible in their case. One small step that can be taken to help on this problem is present the rater with a forced-choice; that is, to ensure that the rating scale has an even number of points (say, 6) so that there is no middle point as such, forcing the appraiser to make a basic choice between one side of the scale or the other.

An altogether more sophisticated and well thought-out improvement on the rating method is the behaviourally-anchored rating scale (BARS). This consists of a scale whose points are defined very precisely in terms of the behaviour that characterizes them. The process by which such scales are developed is too complex to describe here, and the reader is referred to Campbell, Dunnette, Arvey and Hellervik (1973) or Campbell *et al* (1970). Such an approach attempts to reduce the subjective element in ratings and to increase their relevance to actual job behaviours important for effective performance; in doing so, it casts the appraiser more in the role of an observer than that of a judge. However, BARS are not easy or quick to develop and the research findings to date are not entirely convincing that the effort in developing them is worthwhile (Schwab, Heneman and De Cotiis, 1975).

A quite different approach is to bring about a change in the people who actually do the ratings, rather than change the scales themselves. Greater objectivity can be achieved by increasing the number of people involved in the appraisal process, such as having 'father' and 'grand-father' complete separate ratings, or obtaining ratings from individuals' peers, or by getting the individual to do some self assessment (Basset and Meyer 1968; Margerison 1976). A cynic might observe that all this does is to multiply the subjective element, but discrepant ratings might well be useful in indicating areas of doubt. Indeed, it could be suggested that one might formalize the extent of such differences into measures of uncertainty of the assessment of the individual. Another strategy, as far as the raters are concerned, is to train them properly in the use of rating scales (*see* Lodge 1973 for one unusual approach to appraisal training) and then later to monitor the ratings and their distribution.

Conclusion
Clearly, there are serious difficulties associated with rating methods. However as we shall see, the other approaches to appraisal have their

problems too, and rating scales are still widely used in the UK (Gill 1977). But many organizations confine themselves to using only one or two broad scales on performance or promotability to meet their needs for comparability, whilst preferring to adopt alternative methods to achieve the other aims of appraisal.

RESULTS-ORIENTED APPRAISAL

This approach derives from Drucker's (1955) management by objectives (MBO). The general idea is that the manager and his subordinate together agree on specific work objectives or goals for the period ahead and on how the achievement of these objectives is to be measured. As part of the same appraisal session, they will review performance over the last year (assuming yearly appraisal) against the targets set 12 months ago.

Such an approach has a drastic effect on appraisal forms. Most of the paraphernalia associated with rating scales disappears and in its place one tends to find a few headings only followed by large spaces for the appraisers to write in their reports. For example, one organization gives the appraiser half a side to write his comments under the following heading:

Assessment of performance. Review performance in key areas of the job and achievement in relation to any targets and objectives previously agreed, and to any constraints. Comment in particular on the individual's strengths and weaknesses.

Another section of the form has this heading:

Agreed shorter term targets, longer term objectives and key areas of performance improvement. List the agreed items for assessing performance during the next 12 months.

Advantages and disadvantages of results—orientated appraisal
The practice of appraising people in terms of outcomes, of ends rather than means, was a marked trend throughout the 1960s and 1970s both in the UK and abroad and is still increasing in popularity here (Gill, 1977). The reasons for this are not hard to find.

The chief advantages attributed to results-oriented appraisal are as follows:

It offers a more objective yardstick by which an individual's performance can be measured. Goals are clear-cut and whether they have

119

been achieved or not is readily assessed. Thus there is greater reliability and validity in this kind of performance measure.

Goal-setting sessions are effective motivators and engender less defensiveness on the part of the appraisee. This is due to three things. First, the discussion is kept task-oriented and does not stray into the area of personality. Secondly, as already noted, it is a more objective performance measure. Thirdly, goal setting and review usually involve the participation of the appraisee to a greater extent, and it is argued that self-assessment and participation reduce negative reactions to appraisal.

This approach is, by its nature, job-related. Thus, one of the main legal requirements of appraisal systems is met; that concerning equal opportunities legislation (Holley & Field, 1975).

Setting and reviewing objectives makes a review of the job and its priorities inevitable; something which might otherwise be overlooked. Since the individual's objectives to some extent have to agree with his superior's, it widens the former's perspective on the work.

On the face of it, the results-oriented approach to appraisal is very attractive and overcomes many of the problems of rating methods. However, this technique is not quite as easy to operate as it might appear, and has drawbacks of its own:

By itself, it offers no scope for making quantifiable comparisons between employees for use in reward decisions.

Not all aspects of a job can be described in terms of objectives, indeed, sometimes very little is. Even where this does not rule out appraising the job in this way, concentrating solely on those elements that can be cast in terms of targets may lead to the neglect of other important elements, and thus to an unduly pragmatic emphasis on ends rather than means.

Sometimes circumstances change quickly and make goals out of date or inappropriate before the time comes to review them (though this can be offset by holding more frequent review sessions).

The individual may not have sufficient control over his environment to be sure that achievement of goals is dependant purely on his own performance. In fact, this is almost always the case in large, complex organizations. Some schemes try to build in a recognition of this (as in the reference to 'any constraints' in the example cited earlier). Whilst this helps, it does not overcome the problem of trying to assess someone in terms of achieving objectives that are not entirely within his control; the extent to which other factors have influenced performance and whether the individual could really have controlled them brings the discussion firmly back into the subjective realm.

The goals to be achieved can vary in standard of difficulty from appraisee to appraisee. Setting goals is a collaborative effort between appraiser and appraisee. It is not unknown for goals simply to become euphemisms for minimum standards of performance: appraisees do not often want to commit themselves to achieving difficult targets and appraisers sometimes collude with them in setting objectives that are too easily achieved so as to avoid any difficulties that may arise from discussing the failure to achieve them. So, the standards against which people are assessed may vary considerably, and sometimes the standards are not as high as might reasonably be expected.

Goal setting does not necessarily fulfil one of the appraisee's needs from appraisal, namely that of obtaining feedback. Indeed, this is claimed as one of its strengths insofar as it does not elicit defensive reactions. However, it is not quite as black and white as this; if the individual has not achieved his goals fully, some discussion of the reason why should take place and this inevitably leads one into the contentious area of critical feedback (again, in this context, *see* the example given earlier, where explicit reference is made to strengths and weaknesses).

Any detailed examination of results-oriented approaches quickly brings to light elements of subjectivity that are sometimes played down by advocates of this kind of appraisal. However, it does offer a quite different technique to rating methods and has its own marked advantages.

ESSAY OR FREE-WRITTEN METHODS

In their 'purest' form, these methods simply require the appraiser to produce a pen-picture of the appraisee. Sometimes, further guidance is given in the form of a checklist of personal or performance qualities that are to be commented on in the narrative, or at least kept in mind when writing it. In a sense, the results-oriented approach to appraisal is a special kind of essay method, though it is not generally thought of in this way.

As Gill (1977) notes, this approach is rarely used alone. However, one commonly finds some section or other of a report that is largely free-written. For example, one large public sector organization requests the appraisee to complete a job description and then commences the assessment section by giving the appraiser half a side to answer the following question:

How effective is he/she in the duties set out?

Essay methods seem more popular for appraisal at very senior levels and where the 'boss', two levels up, is required to add his report to the immediate superior's. In this context, the 'grandfather' is frequently left with an unstructured report form. The virtues of this kind of appraisal are that it is essentially simple, and that it does not constrain the assessor to the dimensions the personnel department thinks are important, but lets him say what he wants to and thinks is important. Whilst this is laudable, there are obvious disadvantages:

It is almost impossible to compare pen-pictures (not least because different assessors will chose to comment on different performance criteria, some or all of which may not be clearly job related).

It depends considerably on the appraiser's ability to express himself on paper, an ability that varies greatly.

It is highly subjective and not always very informative. As Rowe (1964) found, 'glib, generalized, enigmatic statements abound'.

An interesting aspect of this approach is that it can act as a projective device (ie the appraiser 'projects' himself, or at least his own implicit theory of personality and ideas of what is important to comment on, into the assessment). So it may end up telling you as much about him as about the individual reported on! More seriously, free-written sections in appraisal forms do have their place, if only to cater for the fact that while forms may be standard, people are not and some flexibility is a good thing in any appraisal. But relying exclusively on free-written appraisal is generally unwise.

CRITICAL INCIDENTS METHOD

This technique (Flanagan, 1954; Flanagan and Burns, 1957) was referred to earlier as a way of deriving performance criteria for rating scales, but it can be used as the core of appraisal in its own right. The appraiser is asked to record specific important ('critical') incidents of good and poor performance (often the two are given separate sections of the form) on the part of the subordinate during the period under review. The incidents may sometimes be classified to show consistent patterns that the individual demonstrates in his work. This aproach may be little used, but it certainly has its advocates (eg Levinson, 1976). By basing itself very solidly on work behaviour it is clearly relevant to the job and perhaps has more objectivity that rating methods. It can encompass both how the job is done and the objectives achieved. On the negative side, critical incidents appraisal is of little use for comparative purposes and for the subordinate it may appear a little similar to 'anything you say/do may be taken down and used in evidence against you', although it is only a more systematic approach to what most competent managers do for appraisal anyway, that is, to use specific examples of job behaviour to illustrate the points they wish to make about performance during the appraisal interview. As a vehicle for giving feedback on performance it is quite good, since it allows the subordinate to come to grips with concrete examples of the kind of behaviour that influence his manager's opinion of him. There is still scope for disagreement, of course, as the appraiser's historical account of the incidents may vary greatly from the subordinate's (though this in itself can be illuminating) and as the appraiser is unlikely to be able to record every incident over the period, his sampling of them may be biased or at least open to dispute.

METHODS OF APPRAISAL: CONCLUDING COMMENTS

It will be immediately and easily apparent even from this brief survey that there are no easy or neat solutions in the field of performance appraisal. Some organizations have developed extremely statistically sophisticated, even machiavellian, schemes to overcome the difficulties (eg Handyside, 1973). But no amount of quantification or ingenious manipulation of ratings by central personnel departments (quite apart from the alienating effects such antics have on line managers), and no amount of targets being set, can hide the essentially subjective nature of appraisal. There is certainly nothing wrong in trying to minimize the subjective component, but appraisals that seek to appear totally objective are not quite believable. The methods used to appraise performance are imperfect, but each has its own strengths and weaknesses. The choice made between them will reflect the purposes and priorities of the appraisal scheme in that organization. It is not surprising that many appraisal schemes incorporate several different approaches to try to balance the advantages and disadvantages. Despite the danger of falling between several stools, this intuitively makes some sense. However, the methods themselves are relatively insignificant compared to the way they and the appraisal scheme as a whole is introduced and operated. We will discuss that after the next section, on appraising potential.

APPRAISAL OF POTENTIAL

Gill (1977) reports that 87 per cent of the participants in a survey of UK organizations included the assessment of potential or promotability as one of the purposes of appraisal. One should immediately draw the distinction (though many appraisal schemes do not) between promotion, which usually relates to the next level up, and potential, which implies longer term development capacity and the likelihood of the individual being promoted through several levels. The production of criteria on which to base such assessments is difficult and in practice most companies use one criterion only which is past performance. Hence the role of performance appraisal in this respect.

The actual method of assessment is similar to that of performance assessments, with rating scales and free-written reports very prominent, along with all their attendant pros and cons. The following two examples are fairly typical.

Example A
Estimate of potential

Please assess irrespective of probable opportunities or competition, but should these appear to be serious constraints please mention the fact in the space below the boxes. Mark the box(es) as appropriate and suggest any other departments, sections, functions or jobs in which the assessed could make a contribution or which would at some stage contribute useful career development, indicating when such a move would be desirable.

Could go well above present level ie to	Ready for promotion in same or another field ie	Ready for sideways transfer ie to	Ready for advancement within present job	Suitable for advancement but not yet ready	Unlikely to go further
....	....	....			

124

He/she is at present:

well fitted   for promotion

to

☐

fitted

☐

not fitted

☐

Comment on your recommendations

Long term potential

He/she seems at present:

Unlikely to progress further

☐ 1

or

to have potential to rise about
one grade but probably no further

☐ 2

or

to have potential to rise two or
three grades

☐ 3

or

to have exceptional potential

☐ 4

There are two fundamental problems encountered when appraisal of potential is tied in with appraisal of performance.

THE CRITERION PROBLEM

Are past and present performance a valid indicator of an individual's ability to perform at higher levels? And even if it does have some predictive value, can you really rely on track record alone? There are serious doubts as to whether a manager can effectively assess the potential of a subordinate to perform at a level the manager himself has not experienced. This is especially the case when training or guidance on such judgements is so seldom given (*see* Gill *et al* 1973, page 38, for one example of a more thorough approach). The judgements made seem to be more speculative the more one projects beyond immediate promotability and into the future. The criteria on which long-term potential assessments should be made is a subject in itself, and the reader is referred to Stewart and Stewart (1976) and Dunnette (1976) for further consideration. For the moment, it should be noted that the simple assessments coming out of appraisal reports do not look at all convincing for this purpose.

PROMOTION AS PART OF THE REWARD SYSTEM

Promotion is more often than not part of the reward system, and it was pointed out earlier that mixing together a constructive review of past performance and the more emotive matters of pay and promotion may not be wise. If the individual is not considered promotable at the present time, this approach may have a demotivating effect and elicit defensive reactions which block contructive responses to appraisal. Some appraisers avoid this by not being entirely frank about promotion ratings, giving the appraisee too rosy an impression of his prospects (Anstey *et al* 1976). Not surprisingly, a number of authorities have taken the line advocated by Randell *et al* (1974), which suggests that reviews of performance, of potential and of rewards 'should be kept separate not only in time but also in paperwork, procedure and responsibility'. Not many companies seem to have taken this advice (Gill, 1977), perhaps because of the increased cost and complexity of the procedures that would result.

More positively, performance in the present job clearly does sometimes have prognostic significance and cannot be ignored when assessing potential. Also, some line management involvement in identifying potential is desirable in itself. The trouble is, very few organizations bother to use more systematic procedures such as tests and exercises for assessing potential (Holdsworth 1975). When it comes to promotion to the next level, appraisal forms are often used to arrive at a short list, but the final decision then rests on the appraisal data and on interviews, the validity of which is questionable to say the least (Schmidt 1976).

ASSESSMENT CENTRES

For longer term potential, there has been increasing interest in the use of assessment centres. These consist of groups of assessment procedures, usually including psychological tests, simulation exercises, (in-tray, committees, business games and so on) and interviews, that are combined together in a programme typically lasting two to three days. The individuals assessed are young managers in the main, and the assessors are groups of senior managers (trained in making such assessments) and psychological consultants. At the end of the programme, the assessors meet and pull together all the information obtained on each candidate, resulting generally in a profile of strengths and weaknesses and an overall

126

rating of potential in each case. Such procedures can be used for a variety of other purposes besides identification of potential. In one form or another they have been used for selection and have a proven ability in terms of predicting future career success (Anstey 1977). They can also be used for career counselling and development purposes. For a full account of the assessment centre technique, the reader can consult Finkle (1976), Stewart and Stewart (1981) and Byham (1977).

Not all assessment centres will be aimed at assessing the same dimensions of ability. The point is that they should have been so devised as to tap the qualities that have been found to be necessary for effective performance at higher levels, which of course implies that careful development work has been done. This immediately gives a clue to the main problem of the approach: it is costly in time and money. Another difficulty is the 'crown prince' syndrome, the tendency for the very fact that an individual has done well at an assessment centre to lead to his being given special treatment that more or less ensures he subsequently does well, or at least is seen to because it is expected of him. This kind of thing is a fairly general human phenomenon which can work in both directions, with people being prematurely 'written-off'. Despite these problems the research shows that this approach has considerable promise (Howard 1974). This may be so particularly with young staff who, at an early stage of their career, are something of an unknown quantity and also with technical staff who have little managerial experience. As time goes by and knowledge of an individual's capacities increases it may be possible to develop more systematic procedures for using the evidence already obtained, for example an appraisal, to do the same job at rather less expense.

DESIGNING, IMPLEMENTING AND MAINTAINING APPRAISAL SYSTEMS

Whilst a consideration of the relative merits of different approaches to appraisal is a useful starting point, the eventual choice made will depend on other factors as well. Factors such as who is to be appraised, the amount of training to be given to appraisers, the other personnel management systems that are operating and so on. Here we are dealing with the general strategy of developing appraisal schemes and looking at it in the context of the organization as a whole. Some of the issues that arise are dealt with below and for a detailed case history of an appraisal scheme the reader is referred to Anstey et al (1976). Two brief case studies of appraisal systems are included at the end of this chapter, in appendices A and B on pages 135-38, to give a wider impression of what an appraisal scheme looks like once it is set up and of the problems it can run into.

THE DESIGN OF AN APPRAISAL SYSTEM

First the purpose of the exercise must be decided, ie what are the objectives of the scheme to be? Is it to provide assessment and feedback; motivation and performance improvement or comparability and an equitable reward system? Is it to be biased towards the needs of the organization or will it also try to meet the needs of the individual? If it ignores the latter totally it is unlikely that the prognosis will be good, so some effort at finding out what the needs of the individual are, is worthwhile. This will involve consultation at an early stage with trade unions or staff associations (who have become increasingly interested in appraisals) and, ideally, some more systematic attempt at gathering information on employees' needs, such as a questionnaire survey. It may well be that different groups, for example professional compared with managerial, or levels of employees have quite different needs in this respect. Consultation with the managers who will be doing the appraisals (or their representatives) is also important. The success of the scheme depends on them and also on commitment from the top of the organization, and their ideas on the objectives and techniques should be noted. A feeling of identification with the scheme is likely to increase their commitment to it, a vital factor that cannot be over-emphasized.

The influence of objectives on the design of an appraisal scheme
In the process of defining objectives, three particular issues often arise. The first might be termed 'feedback versus motivation', the second 'open versus closed' and the third 'comparability versus job relatedness'. Each is discussed below.

Feedback versus motivation: The potential conflict between feedback and motivational functions has already been alluded to. However, there is now enough evidence available to conclude that feedback need not generate defensive behaviour and block the motivating effects of appraisal sessions (Fletcher 1973; Fletcher and Williams 1976), and that a combination of feedback and goal setting is the most effective approach to appraisal (Nemeroff and Consentino 1979). This should not be surprising since it incorporates a basic psychological principle that knowledge of results is a necessary condition for effective learning; you cannot improve performance if you do not know where you are going wrong in the first place. Much depends on the amount of feedback conveyed and the style in which it is given (*see* Fletcher and Williams, 1976, for a further discussion of this).

Open versus closed appraisal: The second issue, related to the first one, concerns the decision of whether or not the individual is to be allowed to see his appraisal form. Open appraisal, where the individual sees his report, is obviously a provision of feedback, which we have just observed is a good thing. However, there is a danger that open reporting will lead to a deterioration in reporting standards, with appraisers not being sufficiently frank in their comments for fear of adverse reactions by the appraisers; this can have an important and detrimental effect on the organization's promotion system if it is based to any extent on written appraisals. The trend is definitely towards open appraisal both in the UK and abroad (Gill, 1977, Williams, Walker and Fletcher 1977), and there are good reasons for it. All that will be said here is that if open appraisal is opted for, it is advisable to combine it with a results-oriented or possibly a critical-incidents approach (a large series of rating scales tends to give scope for fruitless discussion and disagreement) and to separate appraisal of performance from appraisal of potential. For a wider review of the openness issue, *see* Walker, Fletcher, Williams and Taylor (1977).

Comparability versus job relatedness: The third issue essentially comes down to the question of whether ratings or a results-oriented approach is to be chosen. If comparability is a primary objective in the appraisal, then at very least an overall rating will be needed. However, unless a good deal of time and resources are devoted to developing them, any further sets of scales are likely to be of dubious relevance to the job (particularly in organizations where there is a wide range of jobs). This has now become a legal issue, as any measure of job performance used in personnel decisions potentially comes under the race relations and equal opportunities legislation. An individual who was to feel that the appraisal procedure discriminated unfairly against him or her could bring a legal action. If there were any grounds for accepting the claim of 'adverse impact', that is, that the system did in some way seem to produce unfavourable results for some minority group, the burden of proof would switch to the organization to show that its procedures were (a) job-related; (b) a valid measure of performance. This is difficult to establish with rating scales but by their nature results-oriented approaches (and perhaps critical incidents technique too) fit the requirement of (a) and very possibly of

(b) as well. This is an important issue, already affecting American practice (Holley and Field, 1975) and showing signs of increasing influence here (Pearn, 1979). But of course, results-oriented approaches are not applicable to all types of work and so other techniques have to be used in such a way as to meet the requirements of employment legislation.

The influence of contextual factors on the design of appraisal schemes

So far, the design of appraisal systems has been looked at in terms of defining objectives and of some of the wider issues which relate to that and which have implications for the type of appraisal used. Now attention can be turned briefly to the other factors that need reviewing when deciding on the length, content and flexibility of the report form, the timing of the appraisals, who does them, and the degree of central or local control of the system.

The organizational style: It has been argued (Handy 1975), with some justification, that different styles of appraisal are needed for organizations of varying types. Thus, the heavily bureaucratic, stable organization might reasonably adopt a relatively formal appraisal scheme incorporating detailed appraisal forms, regular yearly appraisal and a considerable degree of central control. On the other hand, an organization operating in a fast-changing area like high technology might itself undergo rapid changes in the development of staff and in its internal structure. Here appraisal would need to be more flexible, both in content and timing, and be more subject to local (line management) control. The emphasis might be more on development than on assessment.

The management structure: This helps determine who does the appraisal and when. A 'flattened pyramid' structure will mean that towards the lower end of the scale each manager will have a large number of subordinates, so appraisal almost inevitably falls on the first-line supervisor (father). Even then, the numbers involved may be such that the appraisals have to be staggered over the whole year, or even given less often than annually. When there are variations in management structure, different levels of appraiser or different periodicity may be needed to keep the whole thing manageable. However, the question might also be asked whether an individual who has so many subordinates as to be unable to appraise them over a six-week period can in fact be in any position to manage them properly on a day to day basis anyway.

Geographical spread: The amount of contact managers have with subordinates based elsewhere inevitably effects appraisal. Sometimes separation

130

makes the appraisal all the more necessary, but the situation should always be looked at to see whether any superior on the spot who sees the individual's performance more regularly might not be at least partly involved in the appraisal. Also, the frequency of appraisal might be increased in these circumstances. One of the most repeated claims one hears on appraisal training courses is that if we had managers who communicated with staff frequently, appraisal would be unnecessary. This is just not the case; it is precisely those managers who have the most communication with staff who do the best appraisal interviews (Fletcher 1978).

Participation: The staff levels involved and the existing climate of the organization need to be kept in mind when looking at the degree of participation the appraisee has in the appraisal process. Participation in appraisal seems to be increasing (Gill 1977). This can take the form of writing comments on the report, or using an appraisal interview preparation form, right through to self appraisal. The research findings suggest that participation is a healthy influence, certainly as far as the appraisal interview is concerned (Solem 1960; Basset and Meyer 1968; Fletcher 1973; Burke, Weitzel and Weir 1978). However, with younger and inexperienced staff, a highly participative approach does not always work best (Maier 1958). As far as the appraisees are concerned, the amount of participation they are normally used to does not seem to affect the extent to which they benefit from participation in appraisal (Wexley *et al* 1973), although it is extremely difficult for managers who are not used to a participative style of leadership to switch to one in an interview of this kind.

The level of the appraisees: Some organizations involve only certain management groups in appraisal. Experience suggests that appraisal can work well with all sorts of groups, ie telephonists, nurses, secretaries, policemen and not just managers. However, the appraisal may meet different needs both for the organization and for the individual at different levels. For example, routine low-level clerical jobs scarcely require a complex appraisal form. This does not, however, mean that they are not worth appraising. But the content, style and frequency may be different. Age too, is a relevant factor here; younger staff with potential may need more frequent appraisal, while staff nearer retirement may have much less wish and need to be appraised.

Other personnel management systems: The appraisal must complement the promotion, training and career development systems of the organization, and in some cases the financial reward system too (though the less the connection with the latter, the better). It should be designed with these considerations in mind, and preferably in such a way as not to overload the central personnel management resources.

IMPLEMENTING THE SCHEME

Having devised the scheme, you are ready to introduce it. Again, consultation with the interested parties is important. But at this stage the motive behind consultation will be more to gain understanding and acceptance than to get fresh ideas. The scheme has to be publicized in some manner for both appraisers and appraisees. Apart from written materials explaining the purpose and the procedure, which are often used and probably often lost or forgotten by the recipients, it is not easy to see other methods for achieving this. At senior management levels, oral presentation can be used (indeed, should be). Something similar could be done lower down, but the cost in time is rather heavy. Whatever method is used, it is wise to stress the consultative aspects of the scheme's development and not to present it as an 'ivory-tower' personnel exercise.

TRAINING FOR APPRAISAL

As far as the appraisers are concerned, the best way to introduce them to the scheme is in the form of a structured training course. Such a course should cover both the appraisal form and the appraisal interview (assuming one is given). Written instructions are seldom enough by themselves; case studies involving the writing of reports on pen-picture characters are better, especially when the results are discussed with others. Even more difficult than the written appraisal is the skill required to conduct effective appraisal interviews. The best approach is to develop training courses that incorporate at least two practice interviews under guidance. This will involve having a group of tutors available, either staff already trained to a reasonable degree or occupational psychologists, and the cost and difficulty entailed in this sometimes persuades organizations to send their people on standard courses. Whilst this is better than no training at all, it is preferable to have courses specifically tailored for the needs of the individual company. For a detailed account of training in appraisal interview skills, *see* Stewart and Stewart (1977), Randell *et al* (1974) or Anstey *et al* (1976). A useful approach to interview training in general is described by Lewis *et al* (1977). Appraisal interview training does work, as evidence shows (Allinson 1977; Anstey *et al* 1976). Where managers

132

have not been used to carrying out such interviews, this training is most essential, reducing much of the anxiety they feel over conducting the interviews and improving their handling of them.

If you are training people for appraisal, where do you start? The advice given is, usually, 'at the top'. And with good reason: if top management is not seen to be involved and committed, nobody else is likely to take it seriously either. Appraisal is not something that should be seen as 'good for *other* people'. Starting at the top and working down, even if done only in one section of the organization at a time, also lets subordinates know what it is like to be on the receiving side of appraisal, an insight which may help when they in turn do their appraisals.

STORAGE OF INFORMATION AND FOLLOW-UP PROCEDURES

Another point that needs close attention during the implementation stage is the follow-up procedure. Some kind of mechanism whereby action recommendations coming out of the appraisal that are beyond the scope of the appraiser's authority are noted and rapidly dealt with is essential. This has to be organized from the start and will usually take the form of a procedure operated by personnel and/or senior management. However, it needs to be kept as simple as possible, with a minimum of paper work (in fact, minimizing paper work should be a consistent aim generally, as more than one appraisal scheme has collapsed under the weight of its own 'bumpf'). The way in which appraisal information is stored, as well as questions of access and retrieval depend upon the method of appraisal and the other personnel systems in operation. For example it is relatively straightforward to store numerical ratings on a computer, but less so with other methods of appraisal. Whatever the procedure, care must be taken to ensure confidentiality.

MAINTAINING THE SCHEME

Once it is 'off the ground and going', even the best system needs much care and attention. This is particularly so in the early stages, for if anything goes wrong, it needs to be spotted quickly before the whole scheme is brought into disfavour. Two ways to ensure this are to monitor reporting standards and to do a questionnaire survey of appraisers and appraisees. The reporting standards might be looked at in terms of the distribution of ratings (if used), ie are they excessively skewed, or bunched together at the centre, or do they differ wildly from one section of the company to another? The quality of the written comments can also be

133

gauged in terms of their relevance to the aims of appraisal and the degree of information they actually impart. The monitoring of written appraisals can be done by personnel and to some extent by senior managers, who should be encouraged to take a keen interest in their subordinates' reporting standards. The questionnaire survey could cover appraisal interviews (have they taken place?), their content (did they cover what they were supposed to?), the style (participative or authoritarian?), the assessment conveyed (accuracy and perceived fairness) and the outcome as seen by both sides (eg in terms of motivating effects and subsequent performance). Much of this information can be employed in an adaptation of Group Feedback Analysis (Heller 1969), with groups of 10-12 appraisers being presented with the more important findings from the monitoring exercise and asked to discuss them. This not only gives more information, albeit of a different kind, on the scheme, which might be useful in indicating any modifications needed, but it also helps keep interest in it strong. Considerable effort goes into starting appraisal schemes, and the impetus has to be kept up, otherwise there is considerable danger that the whole thing becomes ritualized and taken for granted. A lowering of its effectiveness then generally follows in close order.

Another vital element in the maintenance of appraisal is the following up of action recommendations arising out of the interviews. The necessity for a system to do this was noted above, and the smooth running of that requires monitoring too. There is probably no quicker way for an appraisal scheme to be discredited, than for it to generate recommendations on training transfer and so on which are not acted on as soon as is appropriate. Regular checks are needed to see that recommendations have been carried out, and if they have proved impossible to achieve, that the individual concerned has been told why.

Where deficiencies are noted, remedial action can be taken; for example where appraisers are not completing forms satisfactorily, some further training may be desirable. Sometimes this action will amount to little more than tinkering with the system. Later, it may involve a more fundamental review of the system: circumstances and organizations change, and so if they are to keep their relevance appraisal systems too must change. This might be seen as a potentially expensive process, but not as expensive as failing to maintain adequate performance standards, or failing to motivate staff, or failing to develop employees in the appropriate ways at the right time. In the long run, however, perhaps the best way of ensuring that appraisal is done well and conscientiously is to make it one of the tasks that a manager is himself formally assessed on.

Too often appraisal is treated as a minor, unrewarded task. The amount of time and effort spent on it, the effect it has on the appraisees and their careers and its potential contribution to the organization all indicate that appraisal should be regarded as one of the most vital and direct contributions a manager can make, and should be assessed as such.

APPENDIX A

This case concerns a public sector organization employing about 4,500 people, mostly in the London area. The previous history of appraisal in this organization was very sketchy; indeed, one of the greatest problems was that the managers involved simply did not think of themselves as managers of staff. It was therefore one of the basic aims of the new appraisal system to try to make them face up to their responsibilities in this direction. Other, more 'public' aims were to assess performance, give feedback and improve performance in the year ahead.

An appraisal form was first designed by a committee; it bore the hallmarks of this in that it looked rather like a long-winded compromise document, though this was partly a consequence of the decision to make the same form standard for all but the most junior levels (who had a simplified version). Therefore comparability and uniformity were put ahead of job relevance to some extent. The form contained pre-written sections for comments on performance of duties, general remarks and 'grandfather's' comments; it had overall performance, promotion and potential ratings, and numerous ratings on aspects of performance. Further sections on biographical details, job description and recommendations for training or transfer made up this eight-page blockbuster. However, it was introduced with some care, with case study material completed by all managers in consultation with their seniors, having worked through a programmed learning text on it. This process was started at the top level of the organization, as was the associated appraisal interview system. The idea was that 'father' completed the report, discussed it with 'grandfather' who then conducted the interview and finally completed his section of the report. The option of two-up appraisal interviewing was chosen because of the desirability of increasing the contact of senior managers with staff. This made senior managers more aware of their responsibilities and 'got them more involved'. The interview was intended to convey the gist of the report (which was closed) in the process of identifying areas for performance improvement, and to facilitate superior subordinate communication generally. All interviewers were sent on a two-day in-house training course where they carried out practice interviews under guidance. A problem-solving approach (Maier, 1958) was advocated as the best style for the interview, combined with a balanced review of performance. The scheme also included a preparation form for the appraisees, which encouraged a degree of self-appraisal, and a simple action sheet to record action points jointly agreed by the two parties in the interview (copies held by both and also sent to personnel division as a record that the interview had taken place and to note any recommendations for central action).

The scheme was subject to a questionnaire survey after its first 18 months operation. The results indicated that on the whole it was working well and was achieving some considerable gains in the eyes of both managers and subordinates. Staff clearly wanted feedback on perform-ance, and those interviews where this was given were very successful. However, there were still too many interviews (about 25 per cent), where feedback was very inadequate. Discussion of promotion was unsatisfac-tory since it appeared that appraisers were not being sufficiently clear or, in some cases, honest about this. Use of the report form was generally satisfactory, but the overall performance rating was positively skewed, hardly anyone being rated as less than 'good'. Results of the study were fed back to senior managers in discussion groups, chaired by the chief personnel executive or by one of top management. The results were also described in staff association journals which definitely helped keep the momentum of the scheme going.

The appraisal system continued well, but despite the fact that with successive appraisal interviews people gained a more accurate idea of how they stood (on performance, not promotion), the pressures for open reporting grew. Eventually the organization concerned 'grafted' an ele-ment of open reporting onto the existing appraisal scheme. This was probably a mistake, since 'grandfather' is now having to reveal and discuss parts of a report written by father when the latter is not present; in the circumstances, it would, perhaps, have been better to redesign the report form (reducing the number of ratings and perhaps separating the potential element into another form) and to bring 'father' in as the appraisal interviewer. This illustrates one of the problems of very organ-ized, bureaucratic appraisal systems that are introduced in a thorough fashion. They have a degree of inertia built-in to them, in that having made this investment there is a tendency for organizations to be reluctant to contemplate changing them, other than marginally to keep abreast of changing circumstances.

Appendix B

This second case study concerns a large commercial concern which has annual reports and appraisal interviews that cover essentially all supervisory and management staff (a total of about 3,500). The many clerical and sub-clerical staff employed are not subject to formal appraisal except when recommended for promotion.

All appraising officers receive at least 16 hours training in appraisal. Normally, a manager appraises his immediate subordinates, having first consulted with his own immediate superior (who later countersigns the report). No manager should need to appraise more than 10 people, as to do so would be placing an 'unreasonable burden' on him in the company's view.

Staff are encouraged to participate in the appraisal process through the completion in advance of a Preparation for Appraisal form though they do not actually contribute to the writing of the Performance Appraisal form itself. The latter is filled out by the manager either before, during or after the interview. Most managers opt to complete it during or after the appraisal discussion, though they will have frequently pencilled-in their comments beforehand. So what tends to happen is that both parties will go through the subordinate's comments on the preparation form; with the interviewer being particularly careful to note any discrepancies between his assessments and the individual's own views on how he has been getting on. In the light of this discussion, the Performance Appraisal form is finally completed by the manager and sent to the subordinate for him to read and sign (this form is quite short, essentially only three pages covering strengths and weaknesses in performance, performance characteristics, foresight, adaptability, etc, the overall rating and action plans). One other piece of paper is involved in the appraisal interview, the Agreed Targets form. This is given to the subordinate at the end of the interview and is completed by him during the next week; it simply lists the targets to be achieved in various areas of work over the next 12 months and leaves space for the progress in meeting these to be reviewed at a later stage. The subordinate discusses the targets he has set for himself with the interviewer in a separate session about one week after the formal appraisal. The manager may, of course, alter these targets if he feels it is necessary.

From what has been said, it will be appreciated that there is ample opportunity for dissent to be expressed by the subordinate if he disagrees with or objects to the assessment given. However, taking one typical year as an example, no formal appeals were made but about a dozen cases of unresolved disagreements did come to the notice of the Management Development department (which scrutinizes all reports and tries to sort out any problems of this kind that may arise).

The annual potential review is done after the appraisal and is closed. It involves the completion by senior managers of a 'management inventory' which is used in career planning. Managers are encouraged to give staff career interviews in which future prospects may be discussed, and current performance is seen as a good indicator of future potential. The Performance Appraisal form plays a considerable but still insufficient part in the promotion procedure, and the company feels that the biggest weakness in the system at present is the utilization of staff reports to the extent that they merit. Assessment centre techniques are now being increasingly used by this company, both in selection and in assessing potential.

The present appraisal scheme has been in operation for a few years. Previously, the individual saw what was written about him but could not comment and contribute as he can now. When the new scheme was introduced, ratings of overall performance were skewed towards the positive end of the scale. Now, the majority (60 to 65 per cent) fall around the middle of the scale and the company aims at something like a 'normal distribution' of ratings, which are linked directly with merit pay increases. The new scheme is seen as having brought about an improvement in the quality of reporting, and the training given to reporting officers is seen as being a key factor in this. It is worth noting that half the company's top management were consulted in the process of devising the scheme.

Subsequent evaluation of the scheme showed that most people got the performance ratings they expected, and that a high level of feedback was given in the interviews. Some deficiencies were noted in the follow-up of action plans. However, the majority of appraisers and appraisees regarded the scheme and its success favourably.

REFERENCES

ALLINSON CW (1977). 'Training in performance appraisal interviewing: an evaluation study'. *The Journal of Management Studies*, 14, 179–191.

ANSTEY E (1977). 'A thirty year follow-up of the CSSB procedure, with lessons for the future'. *Journal of Occupational Psychology*, 50, 149–159.

ANSTEY E, FLETCHER C and WALKER J (1976). *Staff Appraisal and Development*. London, George Allen and Unwin.

Bannister D and Mair JMM (1968). *The Evaluation of Personal Constructs*. London, Academic Press.

Bassett GA and Meyer HH (1968). 'Performance appraisal based on self-review'. *Personnel Psychology*, 21, 421-30.

Burke RJ (1972). 'Why performance appraisal systems fail'. *Personnel Administration*, (May-June), 32-40.

Burke RJ, Weitzel W and Weir T (1978). 'Characteristics of effective employee performance review and development interviews: replication and extension'. *Personnel-Psychology*, 31, 903-19.

Byham WC (1977). 'Applications of the Assessment Center method' in J.L. Moses and W.C. Byham (Eds.) *Applying the Assessment Center Method*. New York, Pergamon.

Campbell JP, Dunnette MD, Lawler EE iii and Weick KE jr (1970). *Managerial Behaviour, Performance and Effectiveness*. New York, McGraw-Hill.

Campbell JP, Dunnette MD, Arvey RD and Hellervik LW (1973). 'The development and evaluation of behaviourally based rating scales'. *Journal of Applied Psychology*, 57, 15-22.

Drucker PF (1955). *The Practice of Management*. London, Heinemann.

Dunnette MD (ed) (1976). *Handbook of Industrial and Organizational Psychology*. Chicago, Rand McNally.

Finkle RB (1976). 'Managerial Assessment Centres' in M.D. Dunnette Ed. *Handbook of Industrial and Organizational Psychology*. Chicago, Rand McNally.

Flanagan JC (1954). 'The critical incident technique'. *Psychological Bulletin*, 51, 237-58.

Flanagan JC and Burns RK (1962). 'The employee performance record: a new appraisal and development tool'. In TL Whisler and SF Harper eds. *Performance Appraisal: Research and Practice*. New York, Holt, Rhinehart and Winston.

Fletcher CA (1973). 'Interview style and the effectiveness of appraisal'. *Occupational Psychology*, 47, 225-30.

Fletcher CA and Williams RS (1976). 'The influence of performance feedback in appraisal interviews'. *Journal of Occupational Psychology*, 49, 75-83.

Fletcher CA (1978). 'Manager/Subordinate communication and leadership style: a field study of their relationship to perceived outcomes of appraisal interviews'. *Personnel Review*, 7, 59-62.

GILL D, UNGERSON B *and* THAKUR M (1973). *Performance Appraisal in Perspective.* IPM Information Report No. 14. London, Institute of Personnel Management.

GILL D (1977). *Appraising Performance: Present Trends and the Next Decade.* IPM Information Report No. 25. London, Institute of Personnel Management.

HANDY C (1975). 'Organisation behaviour: organisational influences on appraisal'. *Industrial and Commercial Training*, 7, 326-30.

HANDYSIDE JD (1973). 'Some contributions to the technology of staff performance appraisal'. Paper read to the Brighton and Sussex Branch of the Institute of Personnel Management, 24th April 1973.

HELLER FA (1969). 'Group feedback analysis: a method of field research'. *Psychology Bulletin*, 72, 108-17.

HOLDSWORTH RF (1975). *Identifying Managerial Potential.* BIM Management Survey Report 27, London, British Institute of Management.

HOLLEY WH *and* FIELD HS (1975). 'Performance appraisal and the Law'. *Labour Law Journal*, 26, 423-30.

HOWARD A (1974). 'An assessment of assessment centres' *Academy of Management Journal*, 17, 115-34.

KELLY GA (1955). *The Psychology of Personal Constructs.* Vols. I & II, New York, Norton.

LEVINSON H (1976). 'Appraisal of *what* performance?' *Harvard Business Review*, July-August, 30-44.

LEWIS C, EDGERTON N *and* PARKINSON R (1976). 'Interview training: finding the facts and minding the feelings'. *Personnel Management*, 8, May, 29-33.

MAIER NRF (1958). 'Three types of appraisal interview'. *Personnel*, March-April, 27-40.

MARGERISON C (1976). 'A constructive approach to appraisal'. *Personnel Management*, 8, 30-34.

McGREGOR D (1957). 'An uneasy look at performance appraisal'. *Harvard Business Review*, 35, 89-94.

MEYER HH, KAY E *and* FRENCH JRP Jr (1965). 'Split roles in performance appraisal'. *Harvard Business Review*, 43, 123-9.

NEMEROFF WF *and* CONSENTINO J (1979). 'Utilizing feedback and goal setting to increase performance appraisal interviewer skills of managers'. *Academy of Management Journal*, 22, 566-576.

PEARN MA (1979). 'Towards fairer selection: Selection Tests—uses and abuses'. Paper given at the IPM National Conference, Harrogate.

Pym D (1973). 'The politics and rituals of appraisals'. *Occupational Psychology*, 47, 231–235.

Randell GA, Packard PMA, Shaw RL and Slater AJ (1974). *Staff Appraisal.* London, Institute of Personnel Management.

Rowe KH (1964). 'An appraisal of appraisals'. *Journal of Management Studies*, 1, 1–25.

Schmitt N (1976). 'Social and situational determinants of interview decisions: implications for the employment interview'. *Personnel Psychology*, 29, 79–101.

Schwab DP, Heneman HG iii and De Cotiis TA (1975). 'Behaviourally anchored rating scales: a review of the literature'. *Personnel Psychology*, 28, 549–62.

Solem AR (1960). 'Some supervising problems in appraisal interviewing'. *Personnel Administration*, 23, 27–35.

Stewart A and Stewart V (1976). *Tomorrow's Men Today.* London, Institute of Personnel Management.

Stewart V and Stewart A (1977). *Practical Performance Appraisal.* Farnborough, Hants., Gower.

Walker J, Fletcher C, Williams R and Taylor K (1977). 'Performance appraisal: an open or shut case?' *Personnel Review*, 6, 38–42.

Wexley KN, Singh JP and Yukl GA (1973). 'Subordinate personality as a moderator of the effects of participation in three types of appraisal interviews'. *Journal of Applied Psychology*, 58, 54–59.

Whisler TL and Harper SF (1962). *Performance Appraisal: Research and Practice.* New York, Holt, Rhinehart and Winston.

Williams R, Walker J and Fletcher C (1977). 'International review of staff appraisal practices: current trends and issues'. *Public Personnel Management*, January–February, 5–12.

Williams R (1980). *A Study of Career Development Practices in Some North American Organizations.* London, HMSO.

FURTHER READING

It will be apparent from this chapter that a considerable body of research, development and description of appraisal systems has been published. Throughout the chapter the reader is referred to particular books or articles for more detail on specific topics.

For a detailed account of the development, operation and evaluation of an

141

appraisal scheme, see Anstey E, Fletcher C and Walker J (1976) *Staff Appraisal and Development*. London, George Allen and Unwin.

For a review of organizational practice, see Gill D (1977) *Appraising Performance: Present Trends and the Next Decade*, IPM Information Report Number 25, London, Institute of Personnel Management.

For a detailed outline of a particular approach, see Stewart V and Stewart A (1977) *Practical Performance Appraisal*, Farnborough, Hants., Gower Press.

For a recent review of American practice on appraisal and career development, see Williams R (1980) *A Study of Career Development Practices in Some North American Organizations*, London, HMSO.

Chapter six

Manpower planning

INTRODUCTION

Manpower planning is an effort to integrate, through personnel policies and planning, the various personnel activities such as recruitment, training, management development, payment and industrial relations. Personnel managers have been criticized for taking too short a view of the timescale of personnel events; for recruiting the employees they need today and training those in need of training now with little or no thought for tomorrow's needs. These points have been emphasized by Drucker (1961) who criticized personnel professionals for being firefighters with too little concern for the future development and problems of the organization. Manpower planning is an attempt to overcome this type of criticism.

Manpower planning also provides an opportunity to integrate a concern for manpower and human resources into more general corporate planning and policy development by providing an input from a personnel perspective. Manpower planning should ideally be an integral part of corporate planning. At the same time planning should not be divorced from operational activities since they are different sides of the same coin, not different coins.

Manpower planning began to be widely adopted in large organizations in the 1960s. A number of external factors were increasing the complexity of management and the need for planning. The need for manpower planning was particularly influenced by the changing social and political environment which limited managements freedom of action, by technological change and its impact on the type of manpower required and by the unpredictable economic environment. A significant problem in the 1960s was shortages of key manpower. More recently the problem has been the need to cut manpower and it seems likely that those organizations that planned prudently are able to cope with this more easily.

Inevitably, like all new approaches, manpower planning was initially oversold and despite its potential and some clear benefits, it has attracted considerable scepticism. This has been fuelled by a tendency to collect masses of information and not use it; by the use of complex, sophisticated planning techniques which were insufficiently understood by senior managers; and by the divorce of planning from operational issues and concerns. Therefore while the need for manpower planning is accepted, organizations face some difficult choices about its form and complexity.

The practice of management implies an ability to identify and select goals and means to achieve the overall objectives of the organization. Decisions which affect the future are made, whether or not planning takes place. The choice is whether to be systematic in making decisions about the future or to be swept along by events. This holds true whatever the size of the organization. Yet there is unlikely to be a need for small organizations to undertake complex manpower planning. The choice, whatever the size of the organization, revolves around three general areas:

1 what sort of information about the internal and external environment to collect
2 the uses to which information should be put, particularly with respect to planning
3 what techniques and methods of manpower planning should be utilized.

These three issues will provide the focus for this chapter. The relevance of these three issues can be seen in the framework for manpower planning presented in figure 1 on page 145. As a first stage in manpower planning in any organization, it is important to establish a conceptual framework that allows consideration of each part separately. A word of caution is necessary for it is unlikely that the process presented in the framework can be easily applied in any given organization. Diagrams tend to suggest a beginning and an end, but of course manpower planning is not like that.

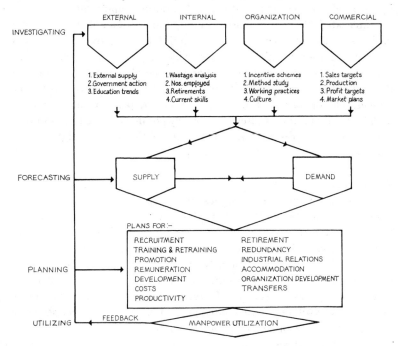

Figure 1
A framework for manpower planning

	EXTERNAL	INTERNAL	ORGANIZATION	COMMERCIAL
INVESTIGATING	1. External supply 2. Government action 3. Education trends	1. Wastage analysis 2. Nos. employed 3. Retirements 4. Current skills	1. Incentive schemes 2. Method study 3. Working practices 4. Culture	1. Sales targets 2. Production 3. Profit targets 4. Market plans

FORECASTING — SUPPLY — DEMAND

PLANS FOR :—

PLANNING

RECRUITMENT	RETIREMENT
TRAINING & RETRAINING	REDUNDANCY
PROMOTION	INDUSTRIAL RELATIONS
REMUNERATION	ACCOMMODATION
DEVELOPMENT	ORGANIZATION DEVELOPMENT
COSTS	TRANSFERS
PRODUCTIVITY	

UTILIZING — FEEDBACK — MANPOWER UTILIZATION

Source: Bramham J. *Practical Manpower Planning.* London, PM, 1982.

COLLECTING INFORMATION: THE INVESTIGATION STAGE

1 THE TYPE OF INFORMATION REQUIRED

Information is the very 'stuff' of planning and before one can begin to make any forecasts, any plans or policies or make any comment on the organization and its manpower, a clear picture of the current position is required. As indicated in the framework diagram figure 1 above, there are a number of aspects to be considered.

Business plans
If manpower is to be effective it must be part of the total business planning of the company or organization to which it relates. For instance, the organization's financial or sales targets will influence the need for

145

manpower. It will not only give an indication of the numbers of employees that can be afforded but it must also give an indication of the skills that will be required. It is important that business and manpower plans are integrated. Previously managers might have been able to determine business plans and expect manpower to adjust accordingly either through recruitment from the labour market or by reducing manpower through redundancy. However because of changes in employment legislation and the increasing time-scale for training for jobs this situation no longer applies. The operation of many firms is now dependent on supplies of highly skilled manpower often in a few key positions. If the right number of suitable employees are not available the business plans might not be fulfilled.

Organization

It is important to be able to diagnose the adequacy of current features of organization, to identify those in need of change and to anticipate future changes. There are, for example, obvious manpower implications in any policy for greater centralization or decentralization, or for changes in organizational structure. Similarly a change in reward systems may influence other control systems such as supervision and the number and quality of supervisors required. In relation to organization, manpower planning activity therefore contributes to diagnosis of the need for change, to the development of policy and to plans for the implementation of anticipated changes.

The external environment

The third area to consider is the external environment and its effects on the business itself. The manager will be most interested in those aspects of the external environment that directly affect him. Any changes in legislation will have to be taken into account as they may involve quite substantial changes in practice in his own company. More obviously he will need to know about the supply of labour on the labour market. This might take a number of forms such as the employees available for recruitment from other companies, from the unemployed, from training centres or of course directly from schools and colleges in the form of output from the education system. It is important that we deal not only with quantity but also with quality.

Internal manpower

It is important to analyse and study the current employment position in the organization. In general terms the purpose is to highlight current

146

opportunities and problems. The manager will be searching for areas of under-utilization and/or high cost or high labour turnover, or for instance where technology has overtaken the available skills of the employees or where one departmental activity has declined but the employees working in it have remained stable.

In addition to general structural problems, it is necessary for the manager to look at the characteristics of employees (of groups rather than individuals). For example the manager will need to know about the age distribution of his employees; whether they are predominantly young with consequent problems of promotion, lack of experience or increased wastage; or whether the workforce is ageing which might indicate an increase in retirement and sickness. Past wastage rates and length of service patterns could give an indication of future wastage while analysis of skills and qualifications held by employees could enable the manager to take stock of his manpower.

HOW THE INFORMATION CAN BE COLLECTED

Knowing what information is required is one thing; being able to collect and assemble it in a useful form is quite another. Before investing what might be quite considerable resources of time, effort and money, it is important to know why you want the information and what you are going to do with it. This includes how precise the information should be and what form it should come in. Only when you have a clear idea of the type of information required and the uses to which it will be put can sensible decisions be made about the way in which the information can be collected.

Information on business plans

Ideally some sort of corporate plan and longer term strategic plan will exist and manpower planning will already have provided an input. The formulation of such plans should be a continuing interactive process between top management and the planners from different departments or occasionally within the same planning department. For the manpower planner, relevant information will be derived mainly from interviews with key planners and policy-makers. Ideally these interviews will be part of a continuing dialogue leading to a corporate plan. Short-term manpower policy decisions (for example, on the number of graduate recruits or the desirability of retraining older employees) may be made partly with reference to this plan.

147

Information on organization

Interviews with key personnel involved in both policy development and day to day operations will provide a major input into organizational diagnosis. So, too will performance records. In certain circumstances, where the views of staff are of particular importance, opinion surveys may be valuable. They may, for example, help in the diagnosis of organization 'climate' or in assessing the feasibility of relocation plans.

A key type of organizational information for planning purposes is data on productivity and effectiveness. It is not possible to go through all the aspects of productivity that are important in assessing manpower requirements and determining policy. However it is perhaps worth noting that since the time and motion studies of the 1920s there has been an assumption that the secret to increased production lies in individual effort which is often based on the belief that employees are lazy and need incentives to work. A study in Tyneside Shipbuilders in 1979 shown in table 1 below is worthy of note.

Table 1
Measuring productivity

Unproductive time per man per day (8 hour day)

Morning and afternoon breaks	23 minutes
Late start/Early finish	47
Idle time under employees control	31
Travelling time	26
Waiting time	21
Bad weather	17
Errors and others	20
	185

What this shows is that about 40 per cent of hours available are lost. Curiously when measured in the remaining hours individual productivity is quite high. The waste is in the organization and integration of the work of different departments. It is perhaps in this area not in studying individuals that large increases in production can be found. Care must therefore be taken to ensure that the production data collected is of a type relevant for diagnosis and planning.

The external environment for manpower planning can be extraordinarily complex. Ideally it requires constant monitoring and information gathering. National statistics, including national manpower forecasts are provided on a regular basis by the government and its agencies. *The Department of Employment Gazette*, other information from the Department and a variety of analyses from the Manpower Services Commission,

148

including its corporate plan, provide an initial data base. Reports on specific sectors of industry, containing general economic analyses with varying degrees of manpower information, are produced from time to time by the sector working parties of NEDO and by City institutions. Increasing amounts of information on local labour markets are also available through the regional offices of the Department of Employment and Manpower Services Commission. A key issue with much of this information lies in determining how relevant it is to the concerns of a particular organization. However even where there are doubts about this, an informed appreciation of national manpower trends is likely to be valuable input into corporate manpower planning and policy development.

Internal manpower
The quality of internal manpower information depends upon the nature of existing manpower information systems. The subject of personnel information was discussed in some detail in chapter three, which should be referred to for a fuller idea of what to collect and how to collect it. For manpower planning purposes it is worth emphasizing the importance of collecting reliable information over a sufficient time to analyse trends. It is also essential to ensure that the information is collected, analysed and presented in a suitable form for planning purposes, bearing in mind that it is probably collected for a variety of uses.

UTILIZING THE INFORMATION

This section will deal with the heart of manpower planning. The first part deals with methods of forecasting manpower requirements, the second examines manpower supply and the third focuses on policy formulation around a notional manpower plan.

FORECASTING MANPOWER REQUIREMENTS

A number of techniques and approaches have been used to forecast the requirements for manpower. Before considering these there are a number of points that should be made.

First in considering manpower requirements management need to know about type and quality as well as quantity. It is tempting to forecast numbers of employees without knowing enough about the skills, training and experience that will be expected.

149

Secondly it has to be acknowledged that forecasts beyond the short term will be subject to extreme variation and may be of little practical value. Consequently beyond two to three years there is little practical value in detailed forecasts. In respect of the longer term the manager should concentrate on indicative planning; that is setting general objectives and deciding overall principles consistent with achieving them.

Thirdly the matter of timescale is important not only in respect of the type of policy and decision that can be adopted. This point is set out in table 2 below.

Table 2
Timescale of forecasts and plans

	Basis of requirement	Basis of availability	Possible actions
0–6 months	Current budget	Current manpower	Contractors overtime recruitment redundancy
6–18 months	Forward budget	Current manpower less projected leavers	Promotion transfer recruitment
18 months 5 years	Forward budgets and plans	Projected current manpower plus those completing training	Recruitment planned rundown training programmes
more than 5 years	Predicted market and technological changes	Expected labour market and education system supplies	Organization development and job restructuring management development programmes

The amount of time available to a company varies in relation to the situation it is in and its objectives. If the objective is the salvage of a company in trouble management may only have a period of months to resolve problems. Consequently forecasting and planning will be limited by that time horizon. This in turn restricts the range of options open to the manager: over such a short time scale there is no possibility for fundamental restructuring and long-term training to have any effect. The manager is limited to those personnel policies which can have an immediate effect such as the recruitment of 'ready-made' people on the open labour market, the use of overtime and contractors to increase output (or the cutting of them if a reduction in output is needed) and so on.

As the time horizon lengthens so the range of options increase. Wider use of training and development or retirement policies become possible while over a longer period still management can hope to effect fundamental changes in how the organization is controlled and how effective it is.

Returning to the first point, forecasting manpower requirements consists of two main steps, namely forecasting workloads and then, on the basis of this, forecasting the quality and quantity of manpower needed to cope with the workload. Although this may often be a rather static exercise, working from a set of given parameters, in practice it may be possible to feed manpower assumptions into the parameters. For example, there is often choice of technology and therefore job design. This in turn can affect both workloads and the quality of manpower required.

In many respects, forecasting the workload is the more difficult task; once this has been achieved, the manpower required to achieve the workload may be relatively easy to specify. This section will therefore concentrate on methods of forecasting the workload.

The workload method

A method of forecasting workload which has been used widely is simply called the 'workload method'. It consists of separating work to be done into its constituent parts usually by work study methods. The time each unit of work takes is measured and these units are themselves forecast using either time series or ratios. An example of the use of this method is shown in table 3 on page 152.

It has been used with success where work is amenable to being broken down in this form. Consequently it has been found helpful in forecasting workload in respect of installing and maintaining gas appliances in peoples' homes.

There are problems with this approach: a main one being that it is not always possible to update work study times to take account of new working methods, either because of the effort involved where the environment is continually changing or because of trade union difficulties.

Time series

This approach consists of analysing past events and projecting them into the future either by 'eye' or by using a statistical method such as regression analysis. Of course in using such a method one has to be cautious about the likelihood of the past being repeated. As time progresses this is less likely to be the case.

To some extent it is possible for the manager to analyse the position he is in and make an assessment where an event has or is likely to occur that will affect past trends. In some cases the events are easily identifiable

Table 3
Using the workload method

(i) Classify work

Meters	hours per job = 0.5
Installation	= 2.2
Maintenance	= 1.6
Emergency	= 1.1

(ii) Forecast work in jobs 000s

	1983	1984	1985
Meters	12	13	10
Installation	95	104	123
Maintenance	29	34	38
Emergency	8	6	5

(iii) Convert into man hours 000s

	1983	1984	1985
Meters	6	7	5
Installation	209	229	271
Maintenance	46	54	61
Emergency	9	7	6
Total	270	297	343

(iv) Convert into employees required assuming 1,800 hours/employee

	1983	1984	1985
Employees	150	165	191

(Figures are examples only.)

such as the UK entering the EEC or a rise in oil prices; though the effect on any given company might be more difficult to assess. Figure 2 on page 153 illustrates various types of time series and demonstrates the importance of ensuring a sufficient time period is used.

Forecasting using ratios

A common method of forecasting workload is by relating work or employees required to some known factor. Figure 3 on page 154 shows a method used where work to be done is assessed against the number of appliances in use in customers' homes. The assumption is that within a reasonable margin of error the number of jobs to be completed depends on appliances in use. The 'appliance production' as it is called is measured by Market Research Surveys.

Figure 2
Time series

a.

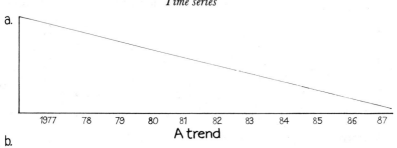

A trend

b.

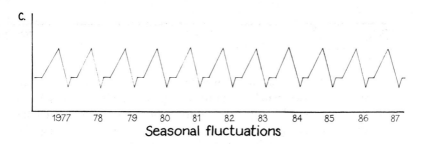

Cycles

c.

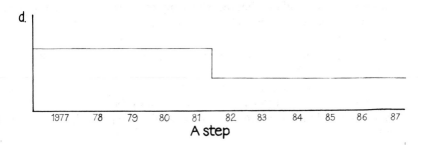

Seasonal fluctuations

d.

A step

153

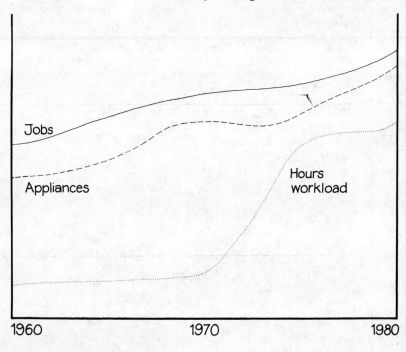

Figure 3
Workload forecasting

Jobs

Appliances

Hours
workload

1960 1970 1980

As figure 3 shows, this worked well for some time. However gradually the relationship began to break down and the forecast became unreliable. What had happened was that the nature of the appliance population had changed through the greater use of whole house central heating. The installation of such a unit was counted as one job along with the installation of cookers and fires but the work content varied from around three to five days for central heating to an hour or two for other work. The result of this increase in central heating sales had been to disturb a previously reliable relationship between appliance and population, jobs and hours of work.

This example is not intended to discredit the ratio method but to demonstrate the need to analyse constantly work being done as well as how work is done to ensure that changes are being properly accounted for.

Manpower requirements

Once the workload requirements have been estimated, it is relatively straightforward, using standard assumptions about experienced worker performance standards, to make some estimates about the quantity and quality of manpower required. In practice these estimates may be based on assumptions about the nature of workers and their motivation. This will be particularly apparent in estimating for supervisory and control activities. It may be helpful to make these assumptions explicit.

Problems in demand forecasting

This brief overview has acknowledged the limitations in methods of forecasting workload and therefore the demand side of manpower planning. The main shortcomings can be summarized as follows:

uncertainty about the future

relying on the past through uncritical extrapolation

lack of data on past and present workload

difficulties in making assumptions

lack of integration with corporate planning

over-reliance on statistical techniques

too time consuming.

These shortcomings should be taken into account before embarking on any major analysis of workload. In practice, very general estimates may suffice, particularly where financial considerations and considerable uncertainties about even the short-term economic future may render even the most sophisticated analysis and planning redundant.

FORECASTING THE SUPPLY OF MANPOWER

In the face of a difficulty in forecasting the need for manpower it is important to retain as much flexibility as possible concerning supply.

A great deal of management's freedom in this area has been curtailed by government legislation, trade union power and social pressure. The manager is no longer free to recruit and dispense with employees at will. Any attempt to do so is likely to prove expensive.

Current employees

At least in the short term, the most likely source of future employees is existing employees. Consequently a first step in manpower planning is to count and classify manpower in terms that are relevant to training,

155

recruitment, management development and so on. The major analyses to be prepared cover such items as age, skills, sex, qualifications, promotion rates, productivity, labour turnover and so on. Most managers will appreciate an annual manpower report setting out various analyses of main employment categories. The report should be presented with good quality, easily understood visuals. These reports should be prepared prior to the preparation of financial and manpower budgets and forecasts. A danger in such reports is a tendency to include too much detail and too many figures; it is better to highlight and present a few key issues otherwise the document will have no impact.

Analysis of leaving rates

The second important consideration in forecasting future manpower available is to analyse the rates at which people are leaving the organization. Leaving can be taken to include voluntary resignation (usually the most important factor), redundancy, retirement, dismissal and death. It would not be normal to include internal transfers within a company from one department to another. However, such movement requires measurement as the manager whose staff leave to move to another department may well consider the distinction between promotion and wastage somewhat academic and the impact on his own department is pretty much the same.

It is important to have an understanding of leaving rates because a great deal of recruitment, training, development and promotions in a company take place because people leave. It should also be said that wastage is not necessarily a bad thing. Undoubtedly high rates leading to unstable, untrained employees unable to perform satisfactorily are a problem. However wastage results in staff movements and an opportunity to recruit fresh minds and prevent the organization going stale. In addition if new technology, for example, leads to a need for fewer people the company might be glad that employees will leave voluntarily to lessen the likelihood of redundancy.

The process of leaving employment after recruitment has been found to follow well-defined patterns. In figure 4 on page 157 a typical pattern is shown:
This has been found to occur in a variety of occupations and many companies though the time scales of leaving vary.

The phases are described as:

the **induction crisis:** new employees do not settle down and leave
quickly

156

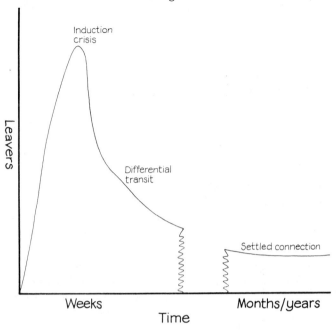

Figure 4
Wastage curve

differential transit: when employees give their new job a chance but
   find it unacceptable and leave
settled connection: employees settle down for longer service.

The importance of this analysis is that if a manager wishes to solve
problems of high wastage different solutions will be necessary if the
problem is among new recruits or in long stayers. The first may be solved
by better recruitment or induction training while the latter may require
more fundamental methods. Some information on the reasons for leaving
can be gleaned from exit interviews. However these should be carefully
handled and the information obtained from them used with caution
because many people will be reluctant to give their real reasons for going.

Forecasting wastage
One common method of measuring wastage is the labour turnover index.
This is:

$$\frac{\text{Numbers of employees leaving in a period} \times 100}{\text{average employees in the period}}$$

The problem with this method is that is can be an extremely unreliable indicator of present patterns and of future trends. An example is given in table 4.

Table 4

Labour turnover

Department	A	B
Average employed	1,117	382
Leavers	98	65
Index of turnover (wastage)	8.8%	17.3%
Average service	5 yrs	7 yrs

Using the labour turnover index it seems a greater percentage of people will leave department B than department A but the average service in B is greater than in A.

This paradox arises because wastage is strongly related to length of service. The reason wastage is high in department B is because they have more employees with short service. It does not mean that the department is inherently less stable or that the existing labour turnover index can be used as an indicator of future leaving. Consequently any consideration of a wastage forecast has to be done by reference to length of service as well as occupational group. One simple if cumbersome method which is the basis of others is 'cohort analysis'.

This consists of taking groups of employees in similar occupations recruited at similar times. As already mentioned it has been found that leaving rates follow the pattern shown in figure 4. This curve is known as a 'log normal' curve and follows a set statistical pattern. Because this is so, the phenomenon can be used as a basis to forecast wastage. Indeed if the information in figure 4 is plotted on a special 'log graph' paper the curve becomes a straight line as shown in figure 5 below.

The advantage is that the line can be forecast and thus an assessment of future wastage gained. A further useful concept arises from this—the 'half life'. This is the time it takes half of an occupational group of employees recruited at a given time to leave. It has for example been used in determining graduate and apprentice recruitment levels. For example if 20 gas fitters are required in 4 years time and the half life of apprentices during training is 4 years we need to recruit between 35–45 apprentices now and not 20 or 25 or some other number.

Using the kind of approaches outlined above, it becomes possible to obtain some estimate of the likely supply of labour. However in making any forecasts, care must be taken to separate out the various reasons for

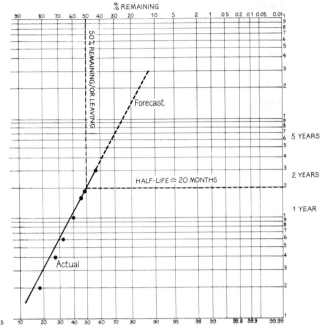

Figure 5

Leaving curve plotted on log paper

leaving. In particular voluntary labour turnover should be distinguished from any management inspired redundancy programme. It may also be helpful to separate those who leave because of retirement, illness and dismissal.

In this chapter it is only possible to review wastage forecasting briefly. Though for the interested it should be noted that computer packages capable of doing the mathematics are available for hire from the Institute of Manpower Studies. Suffice it to say that when analysing and forecasting turnover, length of service is usually the most important factor in determining the propensity to leave. For simplicity, with good results it is possible to divide service into less than one year (where high turnover tends to occur) and over one year. Finally the manager has to keep an eye open for possible changes in the company or the environment which might affect the relationship between labour turnover and length of service.

GENERAL INPUT INTO PLANNING AND POLICY FORMULATION

The process of trying to reconcile the need for manpower with the supply will lead to plans covering a variety of personnel areas.

Recruitment

A knowledge of future requirements and internal supply of labour is a pre-requisite to setting plans for recruitment. This is particularly directed at recruitment effort in respect of key occupations in the company and where expensive and lengthy training and development is involved such as for graduates, engineers, computer scientists and apprentices.

Training

A knowledge of manpower intentions will enable the organization to determine the requirement for training. They might be new employees coming into the organization or retraining existing employees whose jobs have changed.

Management and employee development

Managers will get some indication from their plans of the likely need for managers of various skills and the problems that might exist in respect of promotion and development.

Manpower costs

Manpower planning should enable more realistic costing of manpower to be made for inclusion in financial plans; at least financial and personnel budgets should be drawn up using the same figures.

Remuneration

Analysis of the current manpower may help to identify where problems exist in payments and the sort of pay policy to be adopted. It may help in any attempt to plan and manage the make up of total pay, including the impact of manpower levels on overtime. Other possible questions concern incremental scales and the number of steps that may be desirable when there are various levels of internal labour mobility.

Finally the effect of bonus and overtime earnings on mobility of labour and attitudes of staff must be considered, particularly when supervisors and junior managers do not receive them and those who may be promoted into these grades risk financial losses.

Industrial relations

The negotiator is invariably in a much stronger position if he possesses good manpower data and forecasts. Effective planning (for example to avoid redundancies) is also likely to facilitate good industrial relations. A further important consideration is how far manpower information and plans should be disclosed to trade unions and how far they should be encouraged to participate in aspects of manpower planning. In many organizations this is already an area of consultation. In others, the link between manpower planning and industrial relations has hardly been recognized.

MANAGEMENT DEVELOPMENT AND CAREER PLANNING

To illustrate the ways in which manpower planning can help to indicate future requirements and highlight policy options, the area of management development has been selected for more detailed examination.

The basic manpower theme, outlined at the start of the chapter, can be adapted for the purposes of management planning:

Figure 6
Planning for management development

Policy		Operations
Career development		Succession planning
What kind of person?		Which person?

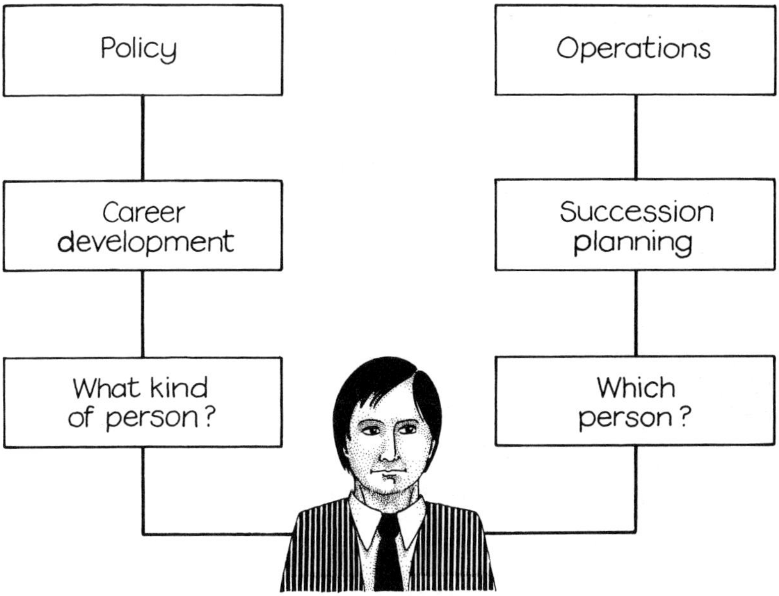

Manpower planning and succession planning
The idea that careers can be managed does not come easily. We have to steer a careful course between direction on the part of a company while still allowing the individual to mould his development as he thinks fit.

161

Consequently it is perhaps best to plan for groups rather than individuals. This is the implication of figure 6 on page 161. One is therefore concerned with questions such as whether there are sufficient engineers and whether so many accountants are required. In terms of personnel activity such as recruitment and training the effect is that instead of asking which person should be recruited or should go on this course, the query is what sort of people should be recruited and what type of training they should be given: that is career planning. Many companies have emphasized more individual, short-term planning, relying heavily on what are called succession charts. The purpose of these charts is to highlight short-term recruitment and training problems. The age of employees is indicated as well as those nearing retirement. Immediate possible successors are also listed.

Assessing potential for manpower planning

A second requirement for management manpower planning is the need to develop some estimate of the potential of existing management. One possible technique that might be used in forecasting potential is given in figure 7 below.

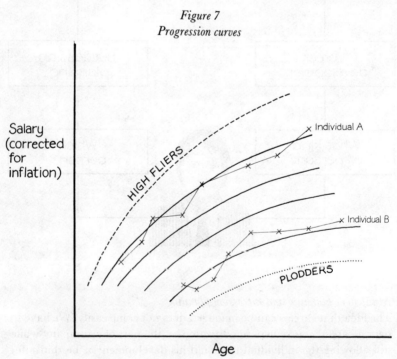

Figure 7
Progression curves

Elliott Jaques in his work on salary administration found that there was a useful relationship between age and salary and that salary when corrected for inflation tended to follow a set pattern throughout an employee's career. This method has been used with success in a number of companies. The implication is that by following an employee's progress in his early career an indication can be given of future development. There are risks. It can be self-fulfilling (high fliers are promoted quickly—which proves they are high fliers and so they are promoted quickly). In addition where changes in company structure have taken place (say through mergers) the information may be misleading. Also the problems of currency conversion and standards of living may make comparisons for multinational companies difficult.

However subjective methods are not without weakness and this sort of technique taken together with succession charts and assessment centres might provide a useful combination of approaches for cross referencing in assessing potential. Also although information relates to individuals it can more safely be used in aggregate form for manpower planning.

Career planning

Manpower planning also requires a method of looking at career progression so that one can ascertain at what rate employees progress, whether factors such as the age-spread will lead to promotion blockages or the over-promotion of inexperienced employees. One method is the 'career progression diagram' shown in figure 8 on p 164.

This diagram shows the percentage of employees at any given age in any managerial grouping.

In the example above few managers in their late 20s have moved into middle management jobs, while by 35 more than half have done so. It also suggests that managers who are still in junior posts in their 40s are likely to stay there.

This technique can be developed as shown in figure 9 on p 164.

Here there is a noticeable kink in the chart and what can be diagnosed is that around age 40 a group of middle managers are not obtaining the promotion they might expect resulting in a promotion blockage.

With this knowledge the company can respond with some remedial action, (eg retirement or cross division moves) if considered appropriate in the context of other factors. More valuably the manager can build in certain assumptions about recruitment, training and wastage and see what the future charts will be like. It might show the situation is getting worse or perhaps that managers are being promoted younger with consequent problems of a lack of experience in the company. Diagrams for

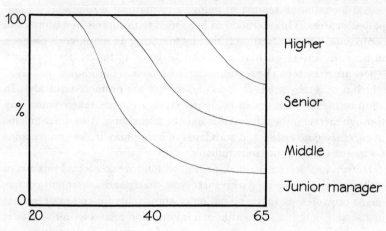

Figure 8
Progression diagram

Higher

Senior

Middle

Junior manager

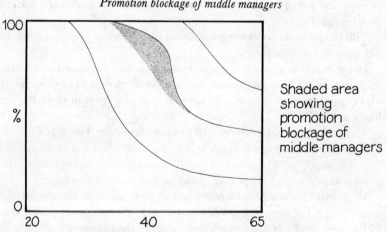

Figure 9
Promotion blockage of middle managers

Shaded area
showing
promotion
blockage of
middle managers

different functions, divisions, or companies can be prepared to assess whether promotion prospects differ and an assessment made of the importance of this. This is an area that has not always been fully explored and understood. There are now computer programs which make its use considerably simpler and allow forecasts and inter-department comparisons to be made.

It is probably of more value in larger companies with a degree of hierarchy and it is probably more useful for considering groups of managers rather than individuals, although a computer model simulating individual progression is available. The main advantage of using groups is any individual managers progression may well not follow a particular pattern and trends are more likely to be discernible when groups of managers are considered.

EVALUATING UTILIZATION

A final step, and one which in some respects completes the circle, concerns evaluation. There is no point in developing manpower plans if they are not implemented or if they do not result in better utilization of manpower.

Measures of utilization
There are a number of possible ways of measuring utilization. One may be reduced manpower costs; indeed in difficult economic times it may seem particularly attractive. However reduced costs may not be the sole objective if they result in a poorer service to the customer and therefore a loss of customers. An alternative, linking in to measures of labour demand, is to use indices of productivity and output.

Measures of manpower flows
Part of the aim of manpower planning is to improve the flow of manpower within the organization. Measures of labour turnover, recruitment, promotions and promotion blockages may therefore provide a more specific indication of the extent to which plans have been implemented. Employee opinion surveys may also be used to provide a more subjective form of feedback.

Cost-benefit analysis
Some attempt must be made to cost manpower planning. Indeed various attempts have been made to cost the computerization of personnel records. Inevitably however such costings are somewhat arbitrary.

165

Attempts to assess benefits in financial terms run into even more difficulties and the questionable assumptions about cause and effect that are inevitably required raise doubts about the value of any attempt at detailed cost-benefit analysis.

Human resource accounting

Human resource, or human asset accounting, is an attempt to put a price on human resources and therefore on personnel policies and practices which invest in effective utilization of these resources. Much of its value lies in encouraging managers to think of employees as resources rather than costs and it can therefore help to put a rather different perspective on a number of personnel activities including manpower planning. However, despite attracting attention in the mid-1970s, it has not proved possible to put a price on human resources in a wholly convincing way. Its value, therefore, lies in encouraging managers to consider investment in manpower planning in a more positive way.

Whatever method is used, it is essential that criteria for success are established and monitored to ensure that manpower plans are acted upon and manpower goals are achieved. Without this there is the risk that manpower planning may be no more than an expensive exercise.

COMPUTERS AND MODELS

The use of computers and models has been an important stimulant to the quantitative aspects of manpower planning. Companies with large numbers of employees would find it difficult to analyse and review their manpower using manual methods.

It is possible to establish a separate computerized information system but probably the ideal solution is a common data base from which payroll and personnel matters can be worked. This reduces waste from duplicated procedures and increases the accuracy of both systems. Of course the organizational situation may prevent this ideal from occurring but it should be the target. In addition in data-based applications, more than where personnel systems are separate, due consideration must be given to the security of confidential personnel information.

An important development in manpower planning is the facility for using models to represent the organizations manpower system. The development of computer-based manpower models requires skills which few personnel managers will possess. Organizations such as the Institute of Manpower Studies have a number of ready-made models which can be adapted to meet specific organizational requirements. An example of a manpower system is given in figure 10 below.

In this example it is relatively simple to 'model' the system by allocating a variable to each factor—an equation of the movements in and out can easily be constructed.

Figure 10
A simple manpower system

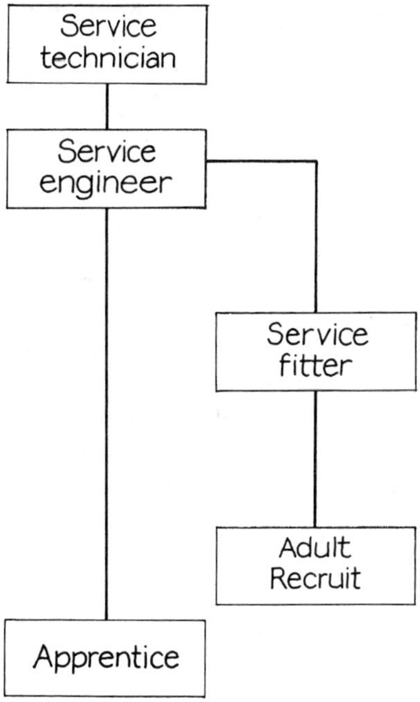

This figure shows a typical structure of manual employees. By estimating wastage and analysing current employees it is possible to estimate training and recruitment requirements. An advantage of a model is the facility it gives to make changes in assumptions so that the effect of say a cut in the recruitment rate or an increase in wastage can be assessed. One result of using models is to draw out the key decisions management has to make. It can be customary for managers to argue at some length over marginal changes in recruitment but the most important single factor in determining future levels of craftsmen is often not recruitment but levels of wastage. It is in that area where effort should be concentrated. Although it can result in much internal dispute the argument about whether to recruit 45 or 50 apprentices can be of limited consequence in the longer term.

In using computers and models it is important to avoid the tendency to an over reliance on statistics. There is a natural tendency to see order in things where none exists. Figure 11 on page 169 gives an example.

In 1965 there was a major and prolonged power failure in New York. Between 240–313 days later the birth rate increased. This piece of information was seized upon when it was pointed out that the gestation period for a human baby is 276 days varying between 240–313 days. Suddenly the great New Yorkers' question 'what were you doing when the lights went out' was answered—Or was it?

A psychologist with a passion directed at research looked back at the birth rate statistics. He discovered what is shown in figure 11. There had been increases in the birth rate at exactly the same period over the previous few years. Whatever it was that led to this event it was not increased human activity rates during the Great East Coast Blackout.

How boring the truth so often is and not surprisingly people choose to ignore it. As managers though, the lesson is salutary; do not be lured by the magic of computers, models and statistics into subverting human judgement. It may be clothed in an alluring numerical form but much of manpower planning is substantially subjective and liable to immense variation. The manager should always exercise his judgement even in the face of the 'facts', and of course be willing to accept the consequences.

CONCLUSION

This chapter has outlined the basic steps in manpower planning and described a number of the techniques available. Of course such is the variety of likely future events in a volatile economic, social and political environment that forecasting and deterministic planning for other than a short period seems unwise. No manpower or corporate plan will stay relevant for very long.

Consequently the manager should establish systems of responsive and adaptive planning able to handle the unforeseen and meet change. This means the manager should have a keen, sensitive and accurate picture of the present environment.

For manpower planning is, at the level of the manager and director anyway, less a set of techniques and more an approach to managing people at work. Its key aspects are its integrative and comprehensive

Figure 11
New York birth rates

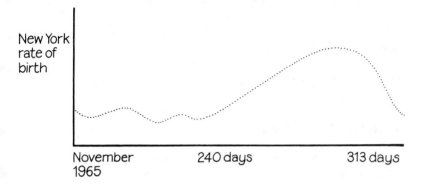

New York
rate of
birth

November   240 days   313 days
1965

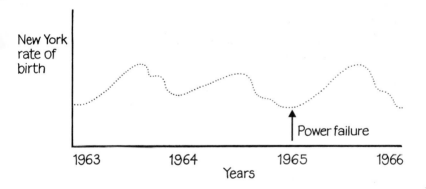

New York
rate of
birth

Power failure

1963   1964   1965   1966
                  Years

nature supported where appropriate by quantification. This is the 'manpower' element of personnel resource management which provides the sound base for management to handle the challenge of social change within an adequate knowledge of employee expectations.

REFERENCES

DRUCKER P (1961). *The Practice of Management*. London, Mercury Books.

FURTHER READING

Much of the material for this chapter is distilled from BRAMHAM J (1982) *Practical Manpower Planning*. Institute of Personnel Management, London, 3rd edition, and the reader who is interested in looking further into the subject is referred to that text.

BELL DJ (1974). *Planning corporate manpower*. London, Longman.

HMSO (1974). *Company Manpower Planning*. London, HMSO.

Manpower Society Reports (nos 1–6) Manpower Society.

HMSO (1970). CAS *Occasional Paper* No 15 'Some Statistical Techniques of Manpower Planning', London.

PURKISS CJ (1976). 'Manpower Planning Literature' in *Department of Employment Gazette*, July and November 1976.

All these texts, particularly Purkiss, list further areas of study and research to which the attention of the interested reader is directed.

Section Four

The three chapters in this section cover the central features of training in industry, namely analysing training needs, devising and implementing training programmes and evaluating the results of training. The chapters are concerned with the types of approach available and the criteria that influence the decision about which to select. They therefore do not deal with specific types of trainee or general categories of training, such as operator or management training. On the other hand the type of trainee and category of training will inevitably be factors which help to influence the choice of, for example, method and media. The aim in each chapter is therefore to present a set of approaches which are relevant to all types of training.

By selecting as the focus of the three chapters the subjects of analysis of training needs, choice of methods and media and evaluation, the general framework is implicitly that of the systematic approach to training (*see* Davies, 1971). This suggests that training should consist of a series of logical steps, starting with analysis of the job and ending with evaluation. The logic and inclusiveness of this approach make it attractive as a framework for organizing writing on training. However it is important to recognize that in practice not all training follows this pattern. For example the training of personnel managers, within the Institute of Personnel Management's educational system, reflects a professional model in which general assumptions about common knowledge and skill requirements are made. In other words, whatever the diversity of jobs that newly qualified personnel officers undertake, they are all expected to start with the same professional core of knowledge and skills. By implication this core is transferable from one type of personnel job to another. Another different view of training is the kind of problem-centred approach advocated, for example by Thurley and Wirdenius (1973) for supervisory development. The starting point is the development of an approach to analyse and resolve performance problems and the training consists largely of the involvement of supervisors (and managers) in the process of problem analysis and resolution. Despite the variations in approach, it can be argued that training will seldom be effective if it fails at some point to consider the three elements covered by the three chapters in this section.

Chapter 7, by Bev Walters, outlines what is involved in the analysis of training needs. The initial analysis can be considered at two levels, the first being whether or not a training solution is appropriate. The second assumes training is appropriate and therefore attempts to identify the nature of the training need. Many methods can be used to analyse training needs and the trainers will benefit from a set of criteria to aid them in determining both the choice of method and the depth of analysis. In the chapter, Bev Walters has adopted a style of presentation designed to aid the trainer who wants to identify the pros and cons of each approach quickly and make a sensible assessment of their merits for a particular setting.

Chapter 8, by David Jenkins, deals with the planning and implementation of a training programme. This is a vast subject and David Jenkins starts by clarifying some conceptual issues. The chapter then identifies some of the main criteria that can be used in selecting an appropriate method of training, before outlining and briefly evaluating each method. The criteria help to emphasize the compromises that must be made in training, perhaps because of a lack of resources, and recognizes the need to make the best choice in the given circumstances.

Chapter 9, by Judith Davis, deals with evaluation of training. She outlines the main stages of evaluation and the choice of method available. In practice, a more or less formal evaluation of training will be undertaken by all those involved, directly or indirectly, in the training process. The chapter emphasizes the need for the training function to control evaluation and highlights some of the more sophisticated techniques that can be used to facilitate this. The emphasis on evaluation demonstrates how important it is to ensure that it is a central part of the training process. Careful evaluation should also help to ensure that training is not seen as an isolated one-off activity but as a central and continuing part of organizational life, with feedback through evaluation pointing to the benefits of further learning.

REFERENCES

DAVIES IK (1971) *The Management of Learning*. London, McGraw-Hill.

THURLEY K *and* WIRDENIUS H (1973) *Supervision: A Reappraisal*. London, Heinemann.

Chapter seven

Identifying training needs

INTRODUCTION

Learning goes on in every organization. Some of it, perhaps most of it, helps the organization to become more effective. Individuals learn new jobs or get better at existing ones. They learn to work together, to co-operate or compete, to help or hinder their colleagues, to forward the aims of the organization or impede its progress. They introduce change and learn to change or they may resist change. Much of this learning is inefficient, some of it is counter-productive, but it goes on. The job of the trainer is not to stop or even control this process. He must give it direction. He should be able to use his abilities, skills and techniques both to foster and support productive, and to inhibit wasteful, counter-productive, learning.

The ability to recognize learning needs is therefore the cornerstone of the trainer's art. Identifying areas in which training can make a real contribution, choosing between competing needs so as to get the maximum return for the organization from its investment and then clarifying those needs are particular skills he should offer.

The recognition and analysis of training needs can be looked at in four stages.

1 recognizing areas in which training needs are likely to exist and where intervention by the trainer will be both possible and productive

2 selecting an appropriate needs assessment strategy including the methods of data collection

3 collecting and analysing the needs data

4 formulating and presenting recommendations for action.

175

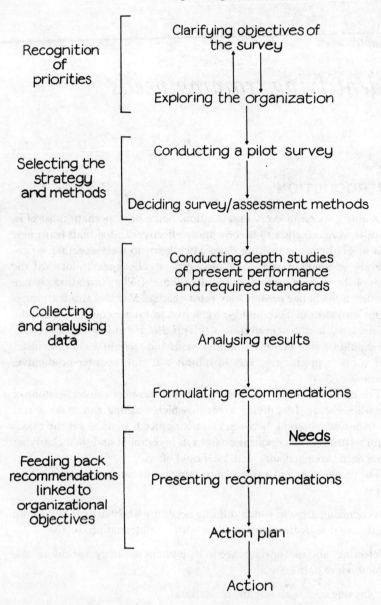

Figure 1
Assessing training needs

Recognition of priorities
- Clarifying objectives of the survey
- Exploring the organization

Selecting the strategy and methods
- Conducting a pilot survey
- Deciding survey/assessment methods

Collecting and analysing data
- Conducting depth studies of present performance and required standards
- Analysing results
- Formulating recommendations

Needs

Feeding back recommendations linked to organizational objectives
- Presenting recommendations
- Action plan

Action

This pattern as it can be applied to a 'one-off' training survey is set out in figure 1. A trainer who is enmeshed in the activities of his organization may not be operating on this 'one-off survey' basis. In a more integrated way he may be reanalysing and reusing his data to meet the changing demands of the business. The trainer is seeking out contexts in which to be catalyst, innovator and occasionally even inhibitor, and the more detailed explanation of the four stages of needs assessment which follows is done with his requirements in mind.

Before examining the four stages, a word of warning is necessary. The analysis of training needs has threatened to become a ritual. The powerful and important influence of McGehee and Thayer (1961) in the USA, and Meade and Greig (1966), Thurley and Hamblin (1963) and Boydell (1976) and a considerable range of 'How to' books produced by most Training Boards in the UK, established a systematic basis for the identification and analysis of training needs. In this country the Training Boards were able to thrust training forward by the financial pressures of their levy/grant schemes and the exemption alternatives. Unfortunately, along with the many striking advances in training, there came a need for training to be 'seen to be done'—a need for tidiness first, effectiveness sometimes second. 'The Systematic Approach to Training Need Identification' was applied unthinkingly and sometimes cynically within companies and organizations. It is legitimized training by providing a quasi-scientific, data-based justification for it. One of its uglier aspects was the emergence of training officers whose raison d'étre was the maintenance of relations with, and maximization of return from, training boards.

A framework which its originators intended as a means of highlighting priorities and helping development, was too often misused or badly applied. Properly used, however, it must still be the basis for identifying learning needs.

RECOGNIZING WHERE TRAINING NEEDS SHOULD BE INVESTIGATED

How should a personnel or training officer set about recognizing possible training needs? Which ones should be vigorously pursued, analysed and met, and which should be given a lesser priority? If there are scarce resources in terms of money, time and expertise, then where should they be concentrated? Initial recognition of training needs starts with an analysis of the organization and its environment. For the trainer this means analysis and investigation of the organization in which he works and of the aims and approach of the system of which he is part, whether it is a factory, hospital, office or large company.

At the grandest level organization analysis looks at the total enterprise and takes account of corporate plans, organizational objectives, manpower plans, organizational ideology and climate. Only an analytical strategy linked to the corporate plans of the organization can be fully successful and the trainer must get as near to this ideal as he can. What 'people skills' does it need now and will it need in the future? What sort of organization patterns will emerge? The best integrated training and development functions, working closely with senior management and corporate planners, will already have influenced the strategic plans so that they take account of the existing 'people' position and take advantage of the individual strengths available. An illustration of the link between training and the corporate plan is given in Case Study 1.

CASE STUDY 1: COMPANY POLICY AND TRAINING NEEDS

The five year corporate plan of an internationally operating construction company laid down that around 70 per cent of the company's work during that period would be outside the UK, much of it in the Middle East.
The training and development implications of this were:

An increased need to produce self-sufficient managers, engineers, accountants, surveyors and supervisors who could operate self-sufficiently without the back-up available in the UK.

An increased need to produce supervisors able to train and manage craftsmen and labourers who could not speak English.

A reduced need for apprentices and craftsmen in the UK, because the overseas work would be manned by local or expatriate non-British labour.

A need to develop skill—tests and ways of training non-British manual workers to an acceptable standard on site.

These needs were arrived at by:

Projections of the staffing and organization already developed on similar sites.

Surveys of training needs on existing overseas sites to provide predictive information on types, skills and numbers of staff.

Interviews and discussions with line management to clarify likely changes in work type, organization patterns and the sources of suitable manpower.

All trainers at all levels should see the operational plans of their part of the organization as the basis for all their actions. Whether the trainer works in a department, a small factory, a retail store or a building site he needs to ask similar questions. Different contexts may demand varying degrees of flexibility and longer or shorter time scales, but the operational plans and the place of people in them must form the basis for his decisions. His real success, and credibility will be a function of his ability to produce training plans which support and forward the central aims of the organization and its management at the level at which he reports. If the training programme is not co-ordinated with the goals and objectives of the organization, time and money will be wasted. The unnecessary use of expensive courses or hardware, training staff in skills they already possess, meeting the requirements of a training board even when these conflict with organizational priorities, and training for yesterday's company priorities, are recurring mishaps. Even where care is taken to avoid these mishaps, problems can arise because of a failure to understand or take sufficient account of complex factors like company culture and the kind of commitments that this attracts. An example of this kind of problem is presented in Case Study 2.

CASE STUDY 2: KNOW THE BACKGROUND

A new training officer with particular expertise in management and organization development joined the head office staff of a multi-national company. His first brief was to produce manager development courses that would be flexible enough to cope with the diverse nature of a company ranging from its original base in the food industry to electronics, supermarkets and pharmaceuticals. For 15 years the original food company had used a packaged American programme for its managers and had developed a considerable body of training expertise throughout the world. Most expatriate British managers in the early days, then later the indigenous managers who replaced them, were trained as 'package trainers' and ran the standard courses for managers in their territory. All managers in the food company took part in that course as an integral and expected part of their career development. They were pleased to have been on it and could discuss the approaches advocated on the course, but the training officer could detect no clear advantages flowing from the company's large and continuing investment.

The more recent members of the Group, the managers in electronics, pharmaceuticals and supermarkets, had not used the 'package' or any alternative. After a thorough investigation involving interviews with over 50 managers throughout the world and the completion of questionnaires by another 100, the trainer developed an original but soundly based course which would take advantage of developments in distance learning and self development techniques. A pilot run was greeted enthusiastically but proposals for full scale implementation were politely received but ignored. Meanwhile 'package' courses continued around the world for food company managers. Most of the directors of the holding company had worked overseas for the food company. They had been trained as 'package trainers' and a number of them, including the Chairman had been particularly committed to the approach.

The outcome was that the training officer's new courses were later offered to the 'non-food' parts of the Group as divisional courses. They were welcomed and judged by all involved to be successful. To date, however, the food company, with the background of its commitment to the package programme, has not been prepared to use them.

Table 1 on page 181 lists a number of approaches the trainer can use to find out more about the organization in which he works and to highlight the areas on which he should concentrate his efforts. Since the resources available for training are usually limited, priorities need to be established, deserving and attractive training needs may have to be passed over in favour of those areas where the trainer can make a more cost-effective contribution. Day by day the trainer, working closely with his management should be teasing the learning implications out of their decisions and concerns and then interpreting and meeting them.

CHOOSING WHICH TECHNIQUES TO USE TO IDENTIFY TRAINING NEEDS

This is the second stage in the process of recognizing and analysing training needs. Priority areas have been established. It is now clear that certain departments have to be looked at in more detail or that there is a shortfall in the skills of some craftsmen, or that planning and control procedures in a factory are not implemented. An investigation in sufficient depth and with appropriate investigatory methods must now be set up. Again the context in which the trainer operates will influence his choice of methods. A summary of 13 of the most useful methods with their characteristics, advantages and disadvantages follows. This in turn is followed by an outline of some of the criteria to take into account when deciding which method or combination of methods to use.

Table 1
Approaches to recognizing training priorities

Approach	Tells you
1 Organizational goals, Corporate plans.	The direction the organization is taking. What it values. Where there are new training requirements and where existing ones may be obsolete or need modifying.
2 Manpower planning, Succession planning.	The size and scope of training needs. Replacements to fill gaps left by retirement, leavers. The availability of skills and knowledge in the organization and some indication of its quantity, quality and appropriateness for the future.
3 Personnel statistics and indices. Labour turnover and stability, absenteeism, accidents, sickness, productivity, complaints and suggestions.	The size and scope of potential training needs. Provides a basis for separating training needs from other legitimate improvements which may require organizational or procedural solutions.
4 Exit interviews.	Where problem areas are, particularly management and supervisory training needs.
5 Key manager consultation and involvement.	What people with power and influence think and intend. The views which form the working climate of the organization.
6 Production and efficiency data. Information and indices from planning, production control cost control, Productivity services on labour, plant and material costs, quality, waste, distribution, etc.	The relationship between actual performance and required performance.
7 Plant or layout changes.	Training required on new equipment or new production lines. May have skills, knowledge and social implications.
8 Management requests.	One-sided but powerful perceptions of needs. The commitment may be useful in implementation. Subjective but often knowledgeable and committed. May be sought or unsolicited.
9 Management accounting, and financial plans.	What resources will be available. Where there are profitability or cash flow problems.

181

The methods

can be formal or casual, structured or unstructured, with open or closed questions.

may be used with a sample of a particular group of people, or conducted with everyone concerned.

can be done in person, by telephone, at the work place or away from it.

are an acquired social skill requiring a number of abilities and allowing for differences of approach to fit the personality of the interviewer as well as the requirements of the survey.

Advantages
are adept at revealing feelings, causes and possible solutions to problems which the employee is facing or expects to face.

provide maximum opportunity for the interviewee to present himself spontaneously on his own terms (especially when conducted in an open-ended, non-directive manner).

insights gained by the employee during an interview can result in be-haviour changes directly without need for further training.

are highly flexible, providing scope for immediate checking of under-standing, follow up of key issues and adjustment to the level of the interviewee.

Disadvantages
are usually time consuming and therefore costly.

can be difficult to analyse and quantify results (especially from unstruc-tured formats).

rely for success on a skilful interviewer who can collect data without making the interviewee feel self-conscious, suspicious, or defensive.

In a **structured interview**
the trainer prepares the questions in advance and interviews to a prede-termined plan.

182

Advantages
the set structure can compensate for unskilled interviewers.

answers are often more easily coded and analysed.

Disadvantages
the interviewee's responses have to follow the pattern of the questions.

the trainer must have thought up the right questions in advance.

In a **free or unstructured interview**
the trainer knows in advance the ideas he wants to examine and will prepare a list of topics to be covered rather than a formal set of questions.

the trainer encourages the interviewee to talk and follows up points raised and explores them if he thinks they have value.

Advantages
flexible and responsive to new data.

open ended.

Disadvantages
calls for greater interviewer skills.

takes time.

the data are often difficult to classify.

QUESTIONNAIRES

may take the form of a survey or poll of a random or stratified sample of respondents, or an entire population.

can use a variety of question formats: open-ended, forced-choice, priority-ranking, rating scales.

may be self-administered (at home or at work) or be completed, often in small groups, in the presence of an interviewer who is able to explain or ask supplementary questions.

Advantages
can reach a large number of people in a short time so is a quick way of getting data from a large sample.

useful for identifying the nature and extent of problem areas and issues within an organization.

gives chance to respond without fear or embarrassment.

can be used over and over once the questionnaire has been prepared.

responses can be subjected to statistical analyses.

some can be bought 'off-the-peg' and adapted to the organization's needs.

Disadvantages

makes little provision for the expressing of unanticipated responses.

good questionnaires are difficult to prepare while bad ones are written easily.

are of limited use in getting at causes of problems or possible solutions.

can suffer low return rates (by post) or grudging responses.

OBSERVATION

may be as unstructured as walking through an office.

can be as patterned as a work study or as behaviourally specific such as observing a carpenter at work or a manager interacting during a meeting.

can be used experimentally to examine effective and ineffective behaviours, organizational structures, etc.

Advantages

does not interrupt, though it may influence work routines or group activities.

focuses on job-related skills and behaviour rather than job knowledge or attitudes.

provides data on the context in which any knowledge or skills acquired through training will have to be applied.

can provide an important check (in conjunction with interviews) on the employee's own perception of his job and how he uses his time.

provides a basis for understanding *how* the job is done (ie process) for later comparison with a job description stating what the job involves (ie content).

useful where people find it difficult to describe the nature of their work.

Disadvantages
requires a highly skilled observer with an ability to order and analyse the data.

very time consuming and therefore expensive.

carries limitations arising from only being able to collect data that can be seen or heard. It can therefore be misunderstood or misinterpreted unless discussed with the employee later.

employees may see the observation activity as 'spying'.

GROUP DISCUSSIONS

can be focused on job (role) analysis, specific problems and their causes, group goal setting, or any number of group tasks or themes, for example, 'leadership training needs of project managers' or 'weekly planning and its training implications'.

can use one or several group techniques, such as brainstorming, force-field analysis, consensus ranking and goldfish bowls.

permits varying degrees of structure and control by the trainer.

Advantages
permits on-the-spot synthesis of different viewpoints. The ensuing consensus is a strong base for action.

builds support through involvement and builds joint responsibility for training decisions.

helps participants become better problem analysts and better listeners, and therefore is itself a training medium.

particularly useful for preliminary needs analysis to identify priority areas.

Disadvantages
it is time consuming.

185

can produce data that are difficult to synthesize and quantify (more a problem with the less structured approaches).

RECORDS, REPORTS

can consist of organization charts, planning documents, policy manuals, audits, budget reports, management information systems.

employee records (grievance, turnover, stability, accidents, leavers, age profiles, succession charts, career plans, etc).

minutes of meetings, weekly/monthly progress reports, memoranda.

Advantages
provide clues to trouble spots and therefore priorities.

provide objective evidence on the consequences of problems within the organization.

provide some 'process clues' on how the organization works, for example, who gets copies of what, who is consulted or approves action, etc.

can be collected with a minimum of effort and interruption since the information already exists.

can be supplemented by asking staff to keep 'daily diaries' for discussion.

Disadvantages
the information may reveal what the problem is but fail to explain its cause.

the information usually reflects the past problems rather than the present ones.

usually needs complementary techniques to fill out the picture.

need a skilled data analyst if clear patterns and trends are to emerge from such technical and diffuse raw data. Too much is often available and relevance must be ruthlessly sought. Much therefore depends upon the quality and organization of the information.

CONSULTATION WITH KEY MANAGEMENT

collects information and views from senior people with power and influence who are in a good position to know what the present and future role and training needs of particular groups of employees are likely to be.

186

these views can be gathered by using techniques such as interviews, group discussions or questionnaires.

Advantages
is simple and inexpensive to conduct.

permits input from a number of individuals each with his or her own perspectives of the needs of the particular group or type of employees.

the views of senior staff can lead to support for or opposition to eventual training proposals. Taking their views into account and involving these managers in the identification of training needs can therefore help to obtain backing for training.

Disadvantages
carries a built-in bias, since it is based on individual, though important, views.

may create an expectation that their views will be implemented though they are an incomplete and biased sample.

OPINION SURVEYS

an opinion poll of all or a sample of employees, seeking their feelings and views on a range of organizational and work related issues.

like other questionnaires it can have open-ended questions with narrative responses or, more typically, closed, structured questions with precoded responses.

Advantages
can be bought 'off-the-peg' and modified.

involve employees and show the company is interested and willing to act on their responses.

useful for indicating general levels of satisfaction as a background to training surveys.

group feedback and discussion of survey results can be a powerful learning device.

Disadvantages
some action is expected as a result. If it is 'shelved' staff feel disappointed and their relationship with the organization deteriorates.

difficult to design.

closed responses are easier to process, but the right questions must have been asked.

ASSESSMENT CENTRES

last one or several days with participants taking part in a range of tasks, tests and discussions (eg in-tray exercises, case studies, decision-making simulations, psychological tests, interviews and group discussions). Trained observers assess each participant's behaviour, and record their views which are then collated into a formal report.

the report is used as an assessment of promotability and as a guide for the participant to help plan his own development.

usually reserved for potential senior management.

Advantages
directors and senior managers can be trained as observers and involved in the process and the follow up.

acts against promotion by patronage.

participation in the process can in itself help to resolve some of the biases and prejudices in the firm and to alter the perceptions held by policy makers and senior managers of their more junior colleagues.

Disadvantages
very time consuming and expensive.

needs expertise, initially from outside the organization.

needs considerable preliminary work (eg repertory grids) to identify what is being looked for.

Performance appraisal

assessment by superiors of the performance of a subordinate employee.

It should be job-linked and can then provide
information on individual training needs.
a composite picture of the training needs of categories of employee.
a basis for succession planning and individual career plans.

discrepancies between present and desired levels of performance, can indicate more training needs.

188

Advantages
systematic and open to analysis.

involves employee and boss and usually a joint commitment to action and improvement.

Disadvantages
because appraisals can be used for a number of purposes, there is a danger that the training needs component will be ignored.

can be unpopular and seen as interfering in the relationship between boss and subordinate.

Advisory committees

can be set up to consider and identify training needs, advise on, and oversee the implementation of, training programmes.

can be functionally based (eg sales, accounting, technical), cover an organization level (eg supervisory, middle management) or cover a craft trade or profession (eg carpenters, civil engineers, buyers).

can be advisory only or decision-taking.

Advantages
generate enthusiasm and involvement.

ensure that committee members release their staff for training programmes.

ensure that broad but knowledgeable views are aired on all aspects of training.

Disadvantages
may become routine or counterproductive.

time-consuming.

can only work in organizations where such committees are encouraged.

depends heavily upon the understanding of the role of training held by committee members and their ability to make relevant and valid contributions.

Work samples

similar to observation, but in written form. Material studied can be collected from records.

can be examples generated in the course of the organization's day to day work, eg tender submissions, new product proposals, market analyses, letters, training designs.

must not be confused with work sampling, a systematic work study-related approach to the observation of people while working.

Advantages
carry most of the advantages of records and reports data.

are the organization's data (its own output).

'cases' of work samples can be used as training material.

Disadvantages
need specialized analysis of content by someone who knows the specialist area covered.

the analyst's assessment of strengths/weaknesses disclosed by samples can be challenged as 'too subjective'.

TESTS

can be profession, function or craft oriented to test a person's proficiency.

proficiency tests can be applied to manual skills, basic job knowledge or high-order cognitive skills like decision-making.

may be used to check learned knowledge and skills, eg trade tests.

clear definition of standards of acceptable performance and the behaviour needed is essential.

Advantages
can be especially helpful in determining whether the cause or a recognized problem is a deficiency in knowledge or skill.

prevent the repetition of training for skills that have been previously acquired.

results are easily quantifiable and comparable.

useful to identify training needs of 'experienced' newcomers to the organization.

Disadvantages
the availability of appropriate tests.

190

expensive to develop and administer.

do not indicate if measured knowledge and skills are actually being used on the job.

SYSTEMS AND PROCEDURE CHANGES

new or modified approaches to work and the planning and control of work create an immediate need for training.

training courses can be built into an action plan for implementing the changes.

Advantages
preparing the training programme encourages a further critical analysis of the new procedures. The need to explain and teach them checks their validity and consistency.

involves the trainer, as of right, in the development and improvement of practices and procedures.

builds training into the management process.

Disadvantages
training should be seen as an important part, but only a part, of the implementation process, or it can be blamed for failure.

CRITERIA FOR SELECTING A METHOD OF TRAINING NEEDS ANALYSIS

The trainer must select an appropriate method or combination of methods for analysing training needs by weighing them on a set of relevant and useful criteria. The most important criteria are listed below. In practice there will often be some additional criteria which are specific to the organization or the trainer. For example the organization may have had bad experience with questionnaires or the trainer may not possess the skill needed to draft them. However the criteria listed below will be relevant in most circumstances.

Employee involvement
Participation makes co-operation more likely. Involvement in deciding needs and designing the training programme gives the trainer access to a crucial body of facts and insights. 'What we think we need to do our job better' will be more acceptable and more likely to succeed than a prescriptive 'we know what is good for you' from management or a trainer.

191

Management involvement

Managers often have strong views about the training needs of people under their control. They often have a strong personal commitment to improving performance, and the process of looking at training needs may itself have resulted from a manager's request for help. They create the climate in which training will succeed or fail. They show enthusiasm and support or signal the opposite; they absorb the costs of needs identification and consequent training. If managers have been involved in the process of data collection and evaluation their commitment and support are more likely. The trainer cannot ignore the realities of organizational politics when deciding who to involve, and may want to 'tie in' some managers in order to reduce the likelihood of opposition, as much as for the contribution they can make to the survey.

Time

The time of all involved, ie managers, employees, trainers and instructors, should be set against the likely results. 'One-off' needs assessment programmes on a project basis require heavy time involvement, sometimes full-time, by the trainer. A deadline for the completed report adds to the pressures. The time dimension generally encourages trainers to select needs assessment methods that are brief and immediate. It also raises the question of the value of 'one-off' surveys as opposed to the continuing identification, interpretation and meeting of training needs as a part of the day to day job of the training specialist.

Cost

There may be a rigid budget limitation which precludes the use of 'better' methods. Low cost methods can include the use of previously produced data, from manpower planning work for example.

Quantifiability of data

Quantifiability aids objectivity, provided that the information has been gathered correctly and analysed in statistically valid and significant ways. Senior executives are increasingly numerate and therefore receptive to conclusions which are based on objective data. Computer advances have made the analysis of data much easier.

The type of trainee

The method of 'training needs analysis' must be geared to the type of trainee. Clearly there are likely to be differences according to whether we are concerned with a senior executive or a 16-year-old newcomer to the organization. Broadly speaking, there are two types of dimension

192

which need to be considered; first whether the potential trainee is already employed or a newcomer to the organization and secondly whether the trainee is experienced or inexperienced in respect of the particular knowledge and skills. These dimensions provide four rather different types of potential trainee:

the experienced current employee, who should be competent but may be displaying performance problems or be ready for further development.

the inexperienced current employee. Sufficient should be known about his existing performance and his potential to provide an assessment of training and development needs in the case of transfer to a different kind of work.

the experienced new employee should be competent but, apart from induction, training needs can be assessed through performance tests.

the inexperienced newcomer will have little to contribute himself and the organization will have to assess potential and examine training needs without much help from this type of trainee.

The recognition of different types of trainee has implications for the role of employee involvement in the analysis of training needs. In some circumstances, the potential trainee can be closely involved; in other circumstances the major contribution will come from supervisors or existing expert or competent performers.

The 13 popular needs assessment methods outlined earlier can now be set against these criteria, as illustrated in figure 2 on page 195. Some version of this framework, in a form which meets the requirements of the trainer and his organization, can provide a basis for deciding which assessment methods to use in a given situation. By combining methods the trainer can reach the right 'blend'. In practice, the range of 'types' of trainee precludes the use of this dimension from figure 2, because it would add considerably to its complexity. However the trainer should try to build it into his own framework.

The best solution will, of course, be the one which gives the trainer a workable approach to obtaining, and analysing data and arriving at a useful and acceptable conclusion. This can then be put smoothly and successfully into practice with the cooperation of all involved parties.

Clearly there is no 'one best method' for the analysis of training needs. For each selection criterion there are some assessment methods that are relatively effective. Figure 2 shows that assessment centres, performance appraisals, questionnaires and skills tests all generate quantifiable data.

Assessment centres, interviews, questionnaires, skill tests and group discussions involve the potential trainees, the employees. The strongest methods overall appear to be questionnaires and performance appraisals, but in practice they may not be feasible in the case of low skill, inexperienced employees or newcomers to the organization. The weaknesses of one method can be balanced by including a second approach with compensating strengths. The first two columns in figure 2 on page 195 are 'organization-specific' and have therefore been left blank for the reader to complete for himself and his organization.

In practice a survey of supervisory training needs on building sites may involve, say, interviews and observation. The nature of the job and the lack of offices and desks preclude the use of written questionnaires. Operator training needs in a factory could involve interviews, observation and direct participation with the trainer learning and performing the job himself.

The methods used provide a potentially objective core of information, but the trainer should be open and eclectic, and supplement his survey with views, opinions and casual observation. He is not conducting a research study and the appropriateness of the training which follows the survey and the contribution it makes to the success of the enterprise are the factors on which he will be judged.

An elegant, methodologically sound and logically convincing survey is useless if it is resisted and rejected by the people involved. Getting a correct 'mix' of needs assessment methods which balance the 'task' requirement of the survey (accuracy, quantifiable data, thorough analysis, sound interpretation) with the 'process' aspects which must be taken into account if it is to be accepted and implemented (managerial involvement, consultations with the unions and with key people, avoidance of previous errors) is vital.

Once the appropriate combination of needs assessment methods has been chosen the collection and analyses of data can begin. For it to be of any value, the data should be analysed in a way which will reveal training needs, so some framework for the systematic objective determination of training needs has to be imposed.

COLLECTING AND ANALYSING TRAINING NEEDS

An integrated tri-partite approach to training need identification was first developed by McGehee and Thayer (1961). It has been developed, and adapted in many contexts but can still form the basis of an ordered

Figure 2
Choosing needs assessment methods using a contingency model

	Trainer skill/ Familiarity	Acceptability/ Previous use	Employee involvement	Management involvement	Time requirement	Cost	Quantifiable data
1 Interviews			High	Low	High	High	Moderate
2 Questionnaires			High	High	Moderate	Moderate	High
3 Observation			Moderate	Low	High	High	Moderate
4 Group discussions			High	Moderate	Moderate	Moderate	Moderate
5 Records, reports			Low	Low	Moderate	Low	High
6 Consultation with key managers	*TRAINER SPECIFIC (Fill in your own)*	*ORGANIZATION SPECIFIC (Fill in your own)*	Low	High	Low	Low	Low
7 Attitude surveys			Moderate	Low	Moderate	Moderate	Low
8 Assessment centres: internal			High	High	High	High	High
external			High	Low	High	High	High
9 Performance appraisal			Moderate	High	Moderate	Low	High
10 Advisory committees			Low	Moderate	Moderate	Low	Low
11 Work samples			High	Low	High	High	High
12 Tests			High	Low	High	High	High
13 System and procedure changes			High	High	High	Moderate	High

195

approach to training needs analysis. The facets of this approach are organization analysis, operation analysis and person analysis.

ORGANIZATION ANALYSIS

This has already been examined as a part of the consideration of ways of recognizing where training needs should be investigated. It looks at the context and helps set the priorities.

OPERATIONS ANALYSIS

Operations analysis seeks to determine what an employee needs to learn if he is to perform the job at the required level. How the tasks are to be performed, the standards of skill and performance expected, knowledge and attitudes needed, are all investigated via the systematic collection of data about a job or a group of jobs. Information of two kinds is usually required. First, quantitative and demographic data to give some measure of the scope and amount of training, (for example, how many centre-lathe turners require training and whether the need is sufficiently wide-spread to justify the training of groups, rather than individuals). Secondly, specific performance requirements for a job so that performance discrepancies are discernible. The techniques which can be used are outlined in table 2 opposite. Many of them are the same as, or variants of, the 13 basic methods that have already been described.

PERSON ANALYSIS

Person analysis seeks to measure how well an employee is performing the tasks which make up the job. There will be major variations in approach according to the level of experience of the employee. A newcomer may not be expected to display any relevant performance skills. However the basic methods or variants of them can be used again. Table 3 on page 198 concentrates on those techniques which are particularly useful in producing data for this part of the training needs analysis.

These three streams of information must now be brought together to identify training needs. The simplest, most general, definition of a training need is expressed in the equation:

Training need = Standard or desired performance − present or actual performance

Training is needed to bridge the 'gap' between the present position and the desired one; between what we have, and what we want to have. So desired levels of performance must be spelled out. Job descriptions, performance standards, etc identify the expectations of the job and so set yardsticks against which the actual performance can be measured. Performance appraisals, performance indices, etc, provide a measure of the efficiency of each employee and a training programme can then be designed to bridge the gap between present and desired performance.

At the simplest level, a kitchen porter may lack the skills needed to wash up properly, so he can be taught them; the 'gap' can be bridged.

Table 2
Operations of job analysis

Techniques/approaches	Useful for
1 Job description specification	Scope and key responsibilities of the job. Lists responsibilities and key tasks and therefore allows a consideration of performance. Specifications extend to the knowledge and skills required of job holders.
2 Perform the job	Most effective way of determining specific tasks but the time required to learn the tasks may preclude it.
3 Observe job—work sampling	Useful as an adjunct to job specifications to look at process.
4 Review written material (a) research in company (b) professional journals (c) government publications	Useful for professional jobs, eg engineers, where role and requirements have been thoroughly examined and discussed.
5 Interviews about the job (a) with the job holder (b) with the boss (c) with higher management (d) with peers (e) with subordinates	Gives different perspectives on the purpose and priorities of the job and may often show varying perceptions.
6 Training committees, conferences or workshops	Inputs from managers or representatives can often reveal differing training needs.
7 Analysis of operating problems (a) idle time reports (b) waste (c) repairs (d) late deliveries (e) quality control	

Table 3
Person analysis
Identifying the training needs of the individual

Techniques/approaches	Useful for
1 Performance or appraisals	Strengths, weaknesses and area for improvement. Easy to analyse and quantify for purposes of determining on-the-job and off-the-job training needs of individuals.
2 Performance data (a) productivity (b) absenteeism or lateness (c) accidents (d) short-terms sickness (e) grievances (f) waste (g) late deliveries (h) product quality (i) repairs (j) equipment utilization (k) customer complaints	Clear quantitative data in many cases, but must sometimes be cautious in assuming a clear link to individual training needs.
3 Observation—work sampling	Subjective but can provide guidance on particular needs of individual.
4 Interviews (a) with the employee (b) with his boss (c) with his peers (d) with his subordinates	Assumes individual or those in touch with him know what he needs to learn. Involvement in identifying his own training needs can motivate an employee.
5 Questionnaires	Same approach as the interview. Easily tailored to specific characteristics of organization. May produce bias through the necessity of prestructured categories.
6 Tests and instruments (a) job knowledge (b) skills (c) achievement (d) potential	Can be tailor-made or standardized. They may measure job related qualities or help the individual to recognize his own strengths and therefore provide a basis for self-development.
7 Opinion surveys	Useful to determine satisfaction of employees with their job and their perceptions of the performance of management and of organization policies and practices, including training practices.

Techniques/approaches	Useful for
8 Checklists or training progress charts	Up to date listing of each employee's skills. Indicates future training requirements for each job.
9 Critical incidents	Observed actions which are critical to the successful or unsuccessful performance of the job and can then be looked out for.
10 Diaries	Individual employee records details of his performance and learns from reality.
11 Devised situations (a) role play (b) case study (c) business games (d) in-tray	Certain knowledge, skills and attitudes are demonstrated in these techniques. Strengths can be fostered and self-knowledge and feedback from peers can be used to form a basis for improvement of job performance. Can be linked to assessment centres.
12 Assessment centres	Combination of several of the above techniques into an assessment programme.
13 Management by objectives	Provides actual performance data on a continuing basis. Performance review and potential review are linked to organization goals and objectives.

But the discrepancy will not always be due to lack of skill or knowledge; the porter may know how to wash up properly, but he may choose not to do so in practice.

Lack of motivation or inappropriate attitudes may be the cause and training may not be the correct solution. Performance discrepancies, the 'gaps', should not automatically be treated as training problems. To find out whether the employee *can do* the job or whether the discrepancy is the result of a lack of knowledge or skill one should ask: 'Does the employee possess the knowledge and skills which would enable him adequately to perform the job?' If the answer is 'yes' this will point towards attitudinal barriers. If the answer is 'no' there is likely to be a need for training in knowledge and/or skills.

Training will solve the skill or knowledge deficiency, it may or may not change attitudes. Where an attitudinal barrier exists, non-training solutions, through alterations in the rewards, communications, supervision or environment must be examined as more likely to improve performance. Features of the design of the jobs, the quality of the equipment and the scheduling of work may also result in performance problems. The 'gap' still needs bridging, but it may need an amalgam of training and organizational changes.

The case study on labour turnover shows how particular training needs can be identified and met by a trainer who is in touch with the aims and problems of the business.

CASE STUDY 3: LABOUR TURNOVER AS A TRAINING PROBLEM

Labour turnover was very high among hourly paid workers in a concrete products factory. Interviewing standards were tightened, pay rates were increased, but to no effect. Management resigned itself to the inevitability of high costs and inefficiency, but asked the training department to survey the training needs on the shopfloor to see if some counterbalancing improvements could be made in that direction.

The training officer:

1 Interviewed shopfloor workers, foremen and recent leavers.
2 Observed all the shopfloor workers and talked to them about their jobs as they worked.
3 Learned to perform several of the shopfloor jobs.

His findings were unexpected, interesting and rewarding. Employees joining the company were told that the jobs were straightforward and could be done by anyone. They involved simple physical tasks with no manual skills. So the jobs were devalued from the start. His observations and experience on the job confirmed that management were right in that the jobs were all physically undemanding but there was an extra dimension: the production information system. To do any shopfloor job you had to be able to read, understand and act on a set of written and diagrammatic instructions from the production control department and no-one taught these. People were being recruited into jobs 'which any fool could do' and then found that these devalued jobs were beyond them. They left to work elsewhere. Interviews with former employees were arranged and confirmed this. A key training need had been identified and simple teaching machines were introduced to teach the documentation at the induction stage.

FORMULATING AND PRESENTING RECOMMENDATIONS FOR ACTION

Having completed the analysis, the trainer should be in a position to present a report outlining the diagnosis, identifying the nature of the problem.

It is useful to consider any report on training needs in terms of the threefold focus identified earlier, namely the concern for organizational diagnosis, operational or job diagnosis and person diagnosis. The organizational diagnosis will focus upon deficiencies within the organization or some subsection, and more particularly within the human or social system. It may, for example, be concerned with the poor performance of a department, a work team, or people in specific roles such as inspectors or supervisors. The implication of this is that the problem lies beyond particular jobs or individuals and therefore the solution may also lie at the organizational level. The recommendation may lie in the broad field of organization development, through improving communication, departmental participation or the speed and quality of decision-making within the management team.

The job diagnosis will typically provide a more or less detailed description of the job. It is usually legitimate for the trainer to comment on the nature and scope of the job, rather than to take this as given; for example many of the problems may result from the fact that the job is too broad or too narrow in scope. The solution may lie both in conventional training and a degree of organizational or job restructuring.

Finally person analysis will result in a report on the qualities, the aptitudes, the existing knowledge, skills, attitudes and deficiencies for an individual or set of individuals. By implication, the deficiencies are based on an analysis of the job as well as the individual. An ideal report will contain elements of all three types of diagnosis although there will be quite legitimate variations in emphasis. The danger, in the past, has been the tendency of trainers to ignore the organizational level of analysis with the resultant risk of recommending inappropriate or ineffective training solutions.

For each element of the diagnostic report, there can be variations in the depth of the analysis. In other words, the trainer will have to use judgement in deciding how wide to cast the analysis and in how much detail. An examination of these issues, in presenting a report of a 'training needs analysis', provides an opportunity to review some of those key decisions.

THE SPECIFICITY OF THE ANALYSIS

Any decision on 'training needs analysis' must consider the boundaries within which subsequent training action will be required. The first issue, which has already been touched upon, is whether to focus more on the individual, the job, the departmental or organizational level. A systems view would suggest that they are all in some respects inter-connected and therefore there are dangers in isolating a specific element without looking at the context. Exceptions to this may arise in certain cases such as the inexperienced newcomer to the organization who is known to have deficiencies in knowledge and skill. In relation to the job analysis, a decision must be reached whether to look at the job as a whole or only at certain critical elements.

In developing training recommendations, it is important to take into account the 'systems repercussions'. One of the most obvious illustrations is the consequence of sending an individual on something like a T-Group. The trainee may return with a dramatically different social style with unpredictable repercussions on unsuspecting colleagues. Similarly any dramatic improvement in performance on the part of a department, a group of workers or an individual will have repercussions elsewhere. For example, if operators handle machinery more carefully, what happens to the maintenance staff? If office staff can solve their problems, how does this affect their supervisors' role? Successful training for one group may lead to opportunities for developmental training or a new set of problems elsewhere. What this means is that the trainer should be thinking of these repercussions when he conducts his training needs analysis and deciding whether the maintenance staff or supervisors should be incorporated in the analysis. It also highlights the dynamics of the situation. There are seldom 'final' training solutions, but a constant cycle whereby new problems, new training needs and new opportunities for development arise.

THE DEPTH OF ANALYSIS

One of the damaging by-products of the levy-grant system of the Industrial Training Boards, particularly in the 1960s, was the tendency in some organizations to devote considerable time and effort to very detailed analysis of jobs. All too often these were sufficient to obtain a grant, but were then filed away and forgotten. The lesson of this is that in carrying out a training needs analysis, the trainer should keep constantly in mind the likely uses of this analysis. It is pointless to conduct a detailed analysis which is then ignored. Whether the main focus is on the organization, the job or the individual, the danger lies in producing a comprehensive descriptive diagnosis which may shed light on the situation but which fails to point to viable or cost-effective solutions. The report will therefore fail to initiate action.

Perhaps the most obvious area in which depth of analysis may not always be worthwhile is the analysis of the job. The conventional

202

approach to training needs analysis is to analyse the job, analyse (or make assumptions about) the individual and train to fill the gap. This chapter has attempted to get away from this potentially narrow and static approach. However in many cases, more particularly for newcomers to jobs, analysis of the jobs is necessary. The question then becomes one of how far to go. Here again, the end product of analysis, the report on training needs and the potential training programme should be kept firmly in mind. This can help to avoid ritualistic, detailed analyses.

The conventional levels at which the job can be analysed, and the report presented, are as follows:

Job description A broad and quite brief statement of the main purpose, scope and responsibilities in a particular job.

Job specification A detailed statement of the duties and responsibilities in the job, the conditions under which the work is carried out, together with an outline of the knowledge, skills and capacities (eg strength, dexterity) necessary to perform the job effectively. This will be the product of job analysis based mainly on interviews, observation and possibly undertaking the work.

Task listing For most jobs a more detailed indication of the content of jobs can be provided through the process of task identification, which involves recognizing, listing and grouping all the tasks that go to make up a job. For some jobs, this can result in a very lengthy list, but it may be the only way of obtaining a detailed picture of the job.

Task analysis This is a systematic analysis of the behaviour required to carry out a task. It emphasizes what has to be done and may therefore result in what looks like a detailed set of procedural steps.

Skills analysis Skills analysis identifies and records the psychophysiological characteristics involved in skilled performance of the job. It emphasizes the cues, the responses and the decision-making functions involved in the job. For conventional manual skills, it emphasizes the use of the senses such as sight, sound and touch. Special training or the possession of a background in occupational psychology is usually necessary for those wishing to carry out a skills analysis.

An example of job analysis is presented in appendix 2 on page 209.

All the stages in the process of arriving at a very detailed job analysis are time consuming and costly. It is helpful, therefore, to develop criteria which can be applied at each level. One fairly well-established approach is to use a combination of the criteria of difficulty, importance and frequency. This means that at the levels of job specification, task listing and task analysis, the questions must be posed; how difficult is the task to learn and perform, how important is it and how frequently is it performed?

The trainer must develop a system of rating each part of the job on these criteria and then ranking them. The process of rating can be carried out in the following ways:

Analysis of more and less difficult elements of the job

Quantitative 'objective' data on accidents, quality control rejects.

Interviews with, and observation of the better and poorer workers and those with different amounts of experience. In particular it is helpful to identify the difficulties faced by those who are new to the job compared with those of considerable experience.

Interviews with supervisors and inspectors.

When the focus is mainly on newcomers to the job, the emphasis should be equally on difficulties in learning and difficulties in performing. When the concern is with improving the performance of experienced workers, it may be more useful to emphasize performance problems. Priority should be given to further analysis of the most difficult elements in the job.

Analysis of more and less important elements of the job
The key question to ask is, what are the costs of making an error? The costs should be considered in terms of safety and human life, the financial cost of damage to equipment and materials and the social cost in terms of damaged relationships and loss of goodwill. This information can again be gleaned from records, from interviews with supervisors and inspectors and, equally important, with 'customers', using this term in the widest sense.

Priority should be given to further analysis of the most important elements of the job.

Analysis of the frequency with which elements of the job are performed
This is straightforward to obtain using methods already outlined. It is less straightforward deciding where the emphasis should be placed for further analysis. Clearly a newcomer must be able to master elements of the job which occur frequently. On the other hand, the trainer cannot ignore infrequent occurrences if they are important and/or difficult. Perhaps the best illustration of this is the emergency; the fact that an airline pilot hopes never to have to perform an emergency landing does not obviate the importance of learning how to do an emergency landing.

An illustration of how this kind of scheme can be applied is presented in appendix 2 on page 209.

The foregoing discussion has pointed to issues which help to determine whether or not any kind of conventional job analysis is required and, if so, how detailed it should be. In practice, what often emerges is that when the main concern is the training of inexperienced newcomers below supervisory level, a conventional and fairly comprehensive analysis may be required. In similar circumstances for jobs at supervisory levels and above, the range and complexity of tasks necessitates selection using the criteria already outlined. This results in what is sometimes termed a 'key tasks analysis'. Finally, when the main concern is the performance of the present job incumbent, it may be more useful to use some form of problem-centred analysis as a basis for training and development or as a way of indicating other appropriate changes.

TRANSLATING TRAINING NEEDS INTO TRAINING GOALS

The final stage in the process of analysing training needs is to set goals for action. Some action may not be what is conventionally recognized as training. However for conventional training programmes there are advantages in being able to establish explicit aims and objectives. A distinction is sometimes drawn between aims and objectives; an aim is a statement of intent while an objective is a specific indication of the expected behaviour at the end of the training. For example an aim might be 'to provide an understanding of the levels at which a job can be analysed' while an objective might be 'to list, correctly, the five main levels at which a job can be analysed'. In practice the distinction between aims and objectives can become hard to sustain.

The main benefits of preparing aims and objectives are:

they provide a bridge between training needs and a training programme.

they should help to indicate the clarity of the analysis of training needs.

they should point to the nature of the material to be learnt and, by implication, the methods and media.

they should provide criteria for the evaluation of training.

The attraction of clearly stated aims and objectives is easy to understand. However they can become beguiling, and, in the same way as job analysis, a time-consuming and rather ritualistic end in themselves. The trainer must know how to develop and specify objectives, but must also learn how to decide when they should be used.

CONCLUSIONS

A trainer must be as involved as possible in the present and future development of the organization or unit that he works in. Because time elapses before the results of his work are seen he must think ahead. He is not a subversive undermining the status quo but a predictor and a catalyst ensuring that the skills, knowledge and attitudes that the company needs now and the different ones they may need in the future are recognized and developed.

Firms change over time, as individuals do. New training needs emerge as soon as the organization's new directions depart from the career abilities, values and aspirations of the employees who make up the organization.

Obsolescence and opportunities loom large in this context and the trainer must collect data about, and show some insight, into the firm's new requirements as they evolve. In this situation conventional training needs analysis techniques applied blindly and in isolation are of little value and the training 'function' which is not alert and involved will find itself in the unenviable position of training for yesterday's needs.

One mark of professionalism among trainers is the ability to use their knowledge and insights about human and organization development to good effect, and to be recognized by their colleagues as competent to do so. Yet many trainers cast aside this strength, ignore the 'soft data' it generates and so limit their contribution to a worthy but restricted use of techniques alone.

Appendix 1: Checklist of useful needs survey information which may already exist in an organization

1 Organization

A Organization charts (formal or informal)
B Statements of work content of departments
C Departmental directives
D Job descriptions
E Future plans affecting organization, nature and size of workforce, management, supervising, patterns of working
F Jobs with specific built-in responsibilities for training

2 Personnel statistics

A Personal records
B Present strength by categories
C Labour turnover and stability indices
D Absenteeism, sickness
E Wage and salary structures
F Age profiles

3 Physical

A Working conditions
B Special physical demands—requirements
C Office set-up, timekeeping and expectations

4 Recruitment and selection

A Sources
B Notification of vacancies and phasing of recruitment
C Selection methods external and internal
D Administration

5 Induction and job training

A Induction training
B Basic training courses
C On the job training
D External courses
E Mandatory technical training
F Apprentice training
G Administration including training reports

6 Management supervisory and professional training

A Recruitment and selection methods
B Formal training schemes and courses
C Relationships with colleges and universities
D Technical training—upon appointment
E Management training—upon appointment
F Knowledge of policies, procedures—approaches
G Performance appraisal and succession planning
H Use of outside courses

7 Education

A Scholarships
B Full time/sandwich courses
C Part-time day and block release
D Evening courses
E Correspondence courses
F Awards
G Use of video for distance learning

8 Communications

A Meetings
B Circulars
C Bulletins/newspapers
D Notice boards
E Video
F Method of internal communication
G Relationship with other departments/regions/companies

9 Trade unions

A   Unions involved and attitudes
B   Formal consultation
C   Informal consultation
D   Disciplinary procedure
E   Promotion/redundancy
F   Demarcation likely to affect training

10 Cost and administration

A   Training budgets and control
B   Authority for expenditure on training
C   Evaluation of results against cost
D   Equipment and premises available
E   Admin services available
F   History of the function

Appendix 2: Presenting the results of job analysis intended to identify training needs

There are many different ways of presenting the results of job analysis and each trainer must develop an approach which they find useful. In most circumstances it will be necessary to go beyond the conventional job description before information can be generated which is useful for training purposes.

The following job description and task listing for a senior sales-person in the camera shop in a large department store was drawn up after interviewing the job incumbent and the manager of the section, as well as a brief period of observation. It illustrates the use of the dimensions of difficulty, importance and frequency.

Job Title: Senior Salesperson: Camera Shop.
Job Description: To serve and advise customers; maintain stock control, ordering and displays; and prepare weekly sales reports. The job involves supervision, including training, of two sales assistants.

Task Listing:

Task	Frequency	Importance	Difficulty	Knowledge and Skill Required to Perform Duties
1 Check stocks on shelves	Daily	Moderate	Low	Knowledge of sales turnover
2 Maintain display	Daily	Moderate	Low	Skill in instruction of sales assistants
*3 Receive goods into store-room and check for damage	Daily	High	Moderate	Knowledge of packing away procedure
4 Orders replacement stock from listings and from outside suppliers	Every two days	High	Low	Knowledge of company procedure; discretionary decision to try new stock based on knowledge of market
5 Takes customer's orders and deposits if not ordinary stock	Occasionally	Moderate	Low	Knowledge of company procedure
6 Makes out receipts for cameras	Daily	Moderate	Low	Knowledge of company procedure and pricing
7 Makes out receipts for printing and enlargements	Daily	Moderate	Low	Knowledge of company procedure and pricing
8 Sells to customers	Daily	High	Moderate	Knowledge of prices and products' characteristics
*9 Advises customers	Daily	most important; customers won't buy without guidance	High	Technical knowledge of camera mechanics and the range stocked—their relative advantages and disadvantages
*10 Loads films and cartridges	Daily		Moderate	Must be able to load full range of cameras etc
*11 Demonstrates cameras, cines & projectors	Daily		High	Must be able to demonstrate use of full range of cameras etc.

210

Task	Frequency	Importance	Difficulty	Knowledge and Skill Required to Perform Duties
*12 Deals with outside sales reps.	Occasionally	Moderate	Moderate	Discretionary decision to try new stock based on knowledge of market
13 Deals with customer complaints—by refund, repair or exchange	A few weekly	High	High	Knowledge of company policy and the goods; skill in handling sometimes difficult customers
*14 Gives training to assistants	Daily until competent	Moderate	Moderate	Skills in instruction; knowledge of all aspects of the job
15 Completes credit card payments	Daily	Moderate	Low	Knowledge of company procedure and the various credit card procedures
*16 Telephone orders for films	Every few days	Moderate	Low	Procedure for use of telephone
17 Prepares sales report	Weekly	Low	Low	Knowledge of company procedure & documentation
18 Prevents shrinkage	Constantly	High	High	Knowledge of prices and stock display levels. Skill in maintaining 'watchful eye' over customers & assistants. Knowledge of procedure if theft suspected
*19 General supervision of assistants	Constantly	Moderate	Moderate	Knowledge of all aspects of the job. General supervisory skills, including delegation and allocation of work

Numbers with asterisk are those tasks for which no training has been given.

References

BOYDELL TH (1976). *A Guide to the Identification of Training Needs*. London, British Association for Commercial and Industrial Education.

McGEHEE W *and* THAYER PW (1961). *Training in Business and Industry*. London, Wiley.

MEADE JP de C *and* GREIG EW (1966). *Supervisory Training—A New Approach for Management*. London, HMSO.

THURLEY KE *and* HAMBLIN A (1963). *The Supervisor and His Job*. London, HMSO.

Additional reading

Job analysis and analysis of training needs

ANNETT J *et al* (1971). *Task Analysis*, Training Information Paper No 6. London, HMSO.

BOYDELL TH (1976). *A Guide to The Identification of Training Needs*. London, BACIE.

MAGER RF *and* PIPE P (1970). *Analysing Performance Problems*. California, Fearon.

SEYMOUR WD (1968). *Skills Analysis Training*. London, Pitman.

SINGLETON WT (ed) (1978). *The Study of Real Skills: Volume 1, The Analysis of Practical Skills*. Lancaster, MTP Press.

THURLEY K *and* WIRDENIUS H (1973). *Supervision: A Re-appraisal*. London, Heinemann.

YOUNGMAN M *et al* (1978). *Analysing Jobs*. Farnborough, Hants., Gower.

Training objectives

BLOOM BS (ed) (1956). *A Taxonomy of Educational Objectives*, Vols I and II. London, Longmans.

KIBLER RJ, BAKER LL *and* MILES DT (1970). *Behavioural Objectives and Instruction.* Boston, Allyn and Bacon.

MAGER RF (1962). *Preparing Instructional Objectives.* California, Fearon.

Chapter eight

Designing and resourcing training

Training, education or learning?

The previous chapter analysed training needs. This chapter outlines the issues and steps involved in designing and resourcing training. It is easy to talk about training as though everyone is quite clear what is meant by the term. Unfortunately this is not a safe assumption within many business organizations. Many identify training with training schemes for particular groups of employees. Thus a large or medium sized business could have, for example, an apprentice training scheme, a scheme for training salesmen, an operator training scheme, a supervisory and a management training scheme. Elsewhere training might be identified with the use of a 'training course', whether of the internal or external variety. In this case a works manager, for example, goes off to learn something about finance on a special 'appreciation' course devised by his company, or a shorthand typist goes to learn how to operate a word processor at a course run by the manufacturer of the equipment. These are, however, inadequate ways of looking at training. Training needs do not always slot neatly into the boundaries of such schemes, if they fit in them at all, and established training courses will frequently be unsuitable means of meeting these needs. In any case, one gathers from these activities an inadequate conception of what training managers do and one should try and define what training staff in industry actually do.

The concept of training

It is usual for trainers to distinguish between education and training, whereby education is a matter for schools and universities and training is industry's task. Here education is seen as being broad, aiming at the whole person and with an emphasis on intellectual formation, while training can be seen as a specific process of training someone for a specific task up to a specific standard. Just as the term 'welfare' became unpopular with personnel managers, and for much the same reasons the term 'education' became an embarrassment to trainers, who ceased to become education officers or education and training officers and appear now much more frequently as simply 'training officers' or 'training managers'. The search has been for relevance, for centrality to the aims of the business. In addition there is the fear that inappropriate, classroom methods of instruction might be imported into industry along with the term 'education'. The achievement of the acceptance of this distinction has not been without cost. Where the process of education can be seen as a sort of 'nourishing', as providing the basis for individual growth, or as helping to draw out the latest capabilities of individuals, training is much more connected with the idea of dragging along a passive passenger. However, the trainer is rarely in a position to drag anyone along. He has little power and very few rewards and punishments at his disposal. His trainees must want to learn and must actively involve themselves in the process or he will not see them reach the desired standard of performance. The focus for the trainer, therefore, is on learning and how it can be helped to take place.

Once we focus on learning it should become clearer why training cannot be equated with apprentice schemes or foreman's courses. In discussing learning here we are discussing the central human property of responsiveness and adaptability to the environment.

Insofar as the training officer is concerned with the organization and its survival he must be concerned with the encouragement of learning. Thus he should have a role to play in the design of the organization and the formulation of personnel policies with a view to increasing their capacity to foster rather than inhibit learning. He may intervene in more specific difficulties and problems. If the response of the organization to technological or market change is seriously jeopardized by poor understanding between production and sales staff then there is an immediate learning problem which will not be rectified by, for example, a sales training course. We have here an operational problem which will often be seen and acted upon in some way without the trainer even having noticed it. But the focus of the trainer on learning processes will make it more likely that he will see such problems and his conference running skills will be helpful in exposing them constructively.

The goal of the trainer must therefore be to facilitate learning, with a view to improving performance. To do this he must create the appropriate environment and provide the necessary resources. This should be a dynamic, proactive role rather than the more conventional, static administrative training activity associated with running courses.

So the trainer's job is to find out what is the essential experience needed for learning, helping people to get this and then helping them to learn from it. For people vary widely in their capacity to learn from experience. Two individuals may meet with the same, or similar experience; one may learn a great deal, the other much less. Helping people to get the most out of their experience is one of the most important and taxing parts of the trainer's function. This emphasizes the value of a competent analysis of training needs, which can point, among other things to those parts of a job that are the hardest for the trainee to learn. We have to discover whether the current structure of the job is the best for the purpose it is meant to achieve. Trainers have to develop the skills of asking the right questions, interpreting what they hear, and understanding the situations in which people have to learn.

CRITERIA INFLUENCING THE DESIGN OF A TRAINING PROGRAMME

In designing a training programme, the trainer has to take into account a number of rather complex factors. The main ones are illustrated in figure 1 below.

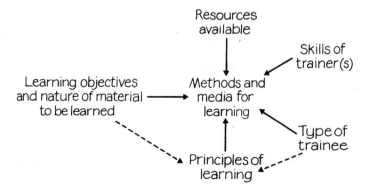

Figure 1
Influences on the design of training

217

In practice, the eventual training programme, and the methods and media employed, will involve a balancing act between these various influences. Achieving the right balance between them can require considerable skill on the part of the trainer.

Each of the major influences can be considered in turn.

LEARNING OBJECTIVES AND THE NATURE OF THE MATERIAL TO BE LEARNED

The training needs, translated into learning objectives should indicate the knowledge, skills and attitudes that the trainee is expected to demonstrate at the end of the learning period. There are obviously going to be different requirements arising in connection with, for example, learning to be an airline pilot, learning to give helpful instructions to subordinates and learning about recent changes in company law. The differences are reflected partly in the behaviour which should follow from successful training and partly in the relative emphasis on knowledge, skills and attitudes. Implicit in any description of the behaviour required at the end of the learning period is an assumption about the complexity of the material. Learning theorists have attempted to classify material in terms of hierarchies of complexity. The distinctions are not entirely satisfactory, but they serve to illustrate the range of levels of learning. Also, as a very general rule, the more complex the material, the more sophisticated the methods required to achieve successful learning.

Knowledge, or what can be termed the cognitive dimension, is usually broken down into five levels.

Knowledge: for example, what is an intelligence test?

Comprehension: how does an intelligence test work? What are the principles involved?

Application: how can an intelligence test be used in the selection of craft trainees?

Synthesis: how far can the principles considered in the application of tests to selection of craft trainees be applied to selection of graduate trainees?

Evaluation: how does one judge the general and specific value of intelligence tests in selection?

It is clear that synthesis and evaluation require more time, more variety of methods of learning and more skills on the part of the trainer. In theory, all levels could be learnt through reading or from a good lecture

218

or series of lectures. But the learning is likely to be facilitated by group discussions, by case studies and even by trying out the tests.

The attitudinal or affective dimensions also contains five levels of complexity.

Receives information passively: listens to the instructor talking about intelligence tests

Responds: answers questions and therefore shows some interest in intelligence tests

Values: seeks opportunities to get involved in discussion, to participate and learn more about intelligence tests

Conceptualizes: forms judgements about the value of tests compared with other methods of selection

Internalizes: natural consideration of use of tests becomes part of the individual's value system.

It is again clear that much more is involved in reaching a stage where an individual values and then internalizes a particular viewpoint than in simply communicating a message where the only concern is that the trainee should listen. There is far less scope for applying a hierarchy of this sort to skilled performance. Instead the types of skill can be put within major categories as follows:

Gross bodily skills: skills involving the whole body such as learning to lift heavy loads properly

Finely coordinated skills: skills involving mainly manual dexterity such as typing or certain types of assembly tasks

Non-verbal communication skills: skills involving delivery and receiving of non-verbal messages using signs such as gesture and facial expression

Speech skills: skills involving verbal communication including speaking a foreign language, giving clear instructions and making a presentation to a large audience.

A central requirement for the development of skilled performance is the opportunity to practice the skills and receive feedback on performance.

In most circumstances, there will be different parts of the job which have to be learnt to varying levels of complexity. Consideration of these levels encourages the trainer to focus on questions such as: do we want shop assistants simply to know what the prices are or do we want them also to know why the prices are fixed at a certain level and communicate this convincingly to shoppers. The first involves straight presentation, possibly through a talk; the second requires at least some discussion.

PRINCIPLES OF LEARNING

The principles of learning are a set of guidelines, drawn up by learning theorists, which reflect good practice in the design of learning (*see,* for example Otto and Glaser, 1970, Stammers and Patrick, 1975). They are described in some detail in a number of books and will only be mentioned briefly here. Many of them seem little more than common sense, but it is unfortunate how often common sense is ignored.

Guidance: the trainer should ensure that the trainee receives guidance on the correct response, to avoid the need for the trainee to adopt potentially costly trial and error learning

Feedback: the trainer should ensure that the trainee obtains feedback on his progress, and in particular feedback on whether his performance is correct or incorrect, appropriate or inappropriate

Reinforcement: the trainer should reinforce or reward correct performance. The reinforcement should be clearly associated with the correct performance and follow as soon as possible after it

Motivation: the trainer should take steps, through appropriate use of intrinsic and extrinsic rewards, through correct spacing and timing of learning and through careful organization of learning sequences, to ensure high motivation to learn

Practice: where appropriate, the trainer should ensure that there are sufficient opportunities for practice under realistic conditions

Transfer: in some respects the most important principle is to ensure that if learning takes place in a context other than that of everyday work, behaviour can be transferred from the learning context to the workplace and applied to the work situation in the work setting

Whole versus part learning: the trainer has to present the material in the appropriate sequence. He can either present all the material at once or bit by bit. If it is gradually presented, he has a choice of progressively adding bits on to an ever increasing 'whole' or treating each bit separately and only combining them at the end. In fact this is less a principle than an issue on which an informed choice has to be made

Continuous versus spaced learning: this is again an issue rather than a clear cut principle, but the trainer has to consider how to present and organize the learning, ie should it be in long sessions or short broken up stages? In deciding this, much will depend upon the type of trainee.

It is important to be aware of these principles, and they can be a helpful checklist to which the trainer should refer in drawing up a programme, but they cannot be used in isolation. They are closely related, as figure 1 suggests, to the material to be learnt and to the characteristics of the trainees.

THE CHARACTERISTICS OF THE TRAINEES

The form of training programme should be influenced by the type of trainee. There are several characteristics that can be considered, although some of them may overlap.

Experience of learning
Some trainees are accustomed to learning and to learning in a particular way. Graduates who have recently completed a university or polytechnic course will feel comfortable in the classroom, may like lectures or talks as a method of instruction and be able to sit quietly and concentrate. In contrast a group of supervisors of manual workers, who may often be in their fifties and might not have been in a classroom for 40 years, will not be used to sitting down indoors for long periods and will find it difficult to listen and concentrate for long periods. Trainees who find themselves in uncomfortable, unfamiliar situations will be less likely to learn effectively.

Level of trainees
Trainees at different levels within the organization will have expectations about the method of learning that is most appropriate. They will also present different types of constraints, such as time availability. Another factor will be the number of trainees. At the shopfloor level there may be large numbers for whom in-company training programmes can be devised; at more senior levels more individually-tailored programmes might be necessary.

Capacity of trainees
The intellectual capacity, the present level of attainment and experience of the specific type of work around which the training is focused can provide a general guide to methods which will be more or less appropriate. Rapid learners will not respond well to slow methods and slow

221

learners with low levels of attainment will find it difficult to cope with methods which involve rapid, standardized group learning.

Age

Much research has been conducted on the impact of age on learning. Belbin and Belbin (1972) in particular have identified the conditions necessary to facilitate the learning of older workers. ('Older' is a flexible term, but it applies in particular to those over 50.) They have encapsulated this in what is known as the 'discovery method'. It provides workers with an opportunity to learn at their own pace, utilizing long learning periods and with an opportunity to learn abstract principles through guided experience. Younger workers seem to prefer shorter, varied spells of learning.

Attitude to learning

The motivation of trainees and their general attitude towards the trainees is something which the trainer should be able to influence both before and during the training. Mager (1968) has examined influences on attitudes to training. Factors such as anxiety, frustration, embarrassment, boredom, wrong pacing, and physical discomfort are all likely to lead to negative attitudes. Positive motivation can be engendered mainly through careful use of the principles of learning, but also through showing positive interest in the trainees, through giving trainees a sensible amount of control over their own learning and adapting to their needs and, if necessary, by eliciting responses in private.

THE TRAINERS

The trainer is best considered as someone who organizes opportunities for learning. It is therefore quite possible that he does not do much face to face instruction himself. However, he does have to identify who is available to do the training and determine who is most appropriate.

The trainee

Although it may seem contradictory, the ideal person to provide training is the trainee. In part, the trainer should encourage the view that learning is a continuous process and it is up to the trainee to seek out opportunities in the environment. The previous section has indicated that this will only be possible for trainees who are highly motivated, with a positive attitude to learning. Many workers take the initiative in self-development, and the distanced learning made available through the Open University and to a lesser extent in the Open Tech facilitate such initiatives. In practice, incidental learning will occur all the time and the trainer must ensure that it leads to the acquisition of good rather than bad habits.

'Nellie'

One of the most popular methods of learning is 'sitting next to Nellie'. This is considered again later in the chapter, and one of the key elements in the success of this approach is the quality of 'Nellie'. She or he must possess two key qualities; one is the knowledge and skills to perform the job to a high standard and the other is the ability to communicate these to the trainees. Often it is the second quality which is lacking and the trainer must therefore be careful in the selection and training of these individuals. Short instructional techniques courses can often lead to dramatic improvements in the capacity of high quality operators, craft workers and supervisors to help and guide trainees.

The trainees' boss

The role of the supervisor as an on the job instructor has already been discussed. Both supervisors and more particularly managers are often held partly accountable for the development of their subordinates and writers such as Hague (1973) have emphasized the value of coaching, controlled exposure to new experiences and other forms of learning which the informed manager can provide for his subordinates.

Instructors

Conventional programmes of in-company training, conducted perhaps in training workshops or training centres will require skilled instructors. They must have the qualities outlined above under 'Nellie', namely detailed job knowledge and skill and instructional ability, but in contrast to Nellie, for them training, or instructing, will be a full-time activity. Not surprisingly, such individuals can often be found amongst the best of the 'Nellies' and can receive more detailed training in instructional technique. In the context of rapid technological change, they themselves may also need constant up-dating if they are to be fully effective.

External resources

The trainer may wish to look outside the organization to find the most suitable people to undertake training. This may mean hiring a consultant who is an expert in social skills training; or, for a small company, it may mean sending one manager on a short locally organized group module. On a larger scale, many organizations make use of the expertise in educational institutions ranging from the local technical college to international business schools. In practice a combination of trainers or instructors is likely to be used. Indeed a combination can often provide a balance between the hard-pressed boss whose help is invaluable, highly relevant but scarce and the external college which has the resources, but may be less directly relevant and may present problems of transfer.

RESOURCES

The final factor to take into account is the availability of resources for training. One of these, the availability of trainers or instructors, has just been discussed. The other key resources can be dealt with quite briefly. First, the trainer has to consider how much he can spend. He will have a training budget within which to operate and this may rule out the use of external resources. The second key factor is the availability of physical and material resources, such as a training centre, office space, machinery and equipment. A third important factor is time. The trainer has to accommodate training within the available time of both the trainers and trainees. In practice this may be highly flexible and considerably influenced by the motivation of the various people involved. Finally the external environment has to be considered. A factory located in a city is likely to have a technical college nearby whereas one situated in a rural setting may find that day release or evening classes are impractical.

Resources, like so many of the other factors influencing the design of training are highly flexible. The trainer should develop a training policy and within this should plan his resource requirements. This requires, among other things, an ability to cost training and prepare a detailed training budget. (For more details of this *see* Cannon, 1979 and Talbot and Ellis, 1969.) It also requires ingenuity and imagination on the part of the trainer in identifying learning opportunities and invoking the aid of others in the organization.

METHODS OF TRAINING

For the trainer who is designing a training programme, once he has established the training goals and taken account of the various factors discussed in the last section, the next step is to consider what methods to use. In many cases, the only question that is seriously considered is whether training should be on the job or off the job. In fact each of these possibilities hides a range of methods and it is quite possible to use several

224

of them. Indeed, the analysis in the previous section, highlighting the varying complexity of the material to be learned, the need to maintain trainee interest and the need to take account of the principles of learning, implies that a combination of methods will often be desirable. Other things being equal, however, it is best for training to take place as close to the job as possible to minimize the problems of transfer and to integrate it into the general activity of the department or organization.

In this section, each of the major methods of training is examined. They are arranged along a crude continuum from on the job to the most distanced form of learning. Each is a structured form of learning, although some may not always appear so to the trainee, and they can therefore be distinguished from casual or incidental learning.

LEARNING ON THE JOB

Learning on the job is almost certainly the most common, both for newcomers to a job and for those well established in a job who have to learn new procedures or adjust to changing circumstances. Textbooks on training tend to denigrate this method of learning, but the justification for this view depends very much on the form it takes. Three major variations can be distinguished:

The 'trainee' is thrown straight into the job with no help. This variant is hard to defend either for newcomers or for experienced workers. The problems may be ameliorated by a carefully presented set of procedural instructions which could enable the trainee to cope. But the consequence is often trial and error learning, with an unnecessary waste of time and possibly materials and with the risk that inappropriate procedures will be adopted.

The trainee learns by sitting next to 'Nellie'. The trainee sits and works alongside a competent worker. For this to succeed, much depends upon the competent worker and the nature of the job. Some of the learning of craft trainees in the workplace invariably falls into this category.

The trainee learns by doing the job under guided instruction. Supervised performance requires an instructor who can give full-time attention to the trainee or trainees. The learning therefore takes place on the job but with considerable instruction. Examples of this include some salesmen training but perhaps the best known example in the UK is learning to drive a car.

The advantages of learning on the job

It is cheap, except when an instructor supervises trainees.

For straightforward jobs, it may be the most cost-effective way of training.

It can be a sensible way of training when resources are very limited.

The disadvantages of learning on the job

It can be slow, wasteful and costly.

It can result in the learning of bad habits.

It is very dependent on the organizational climate and, in the case of sitting next to Nellie, on the quality and enthusiasm of the expert.

It can over-emphasize *what* has to be done when the major learning difficulties might centre around *how* it should be done.

Criteria for successful use of learning on the job (with special reference to 'sitting next to Nellie')

The instructor or Nellie must be competent at the job and competent to instruct.

The type of job must be one where

the job can be seen as a whole

the risks of errors are small and/or the costs of error are small

speed of learning is relatively unimportant.

TRAINING IN THE FIELD

An approach which has been widely used, particularly with graduates is a process of training in the field. It usually consists of sending trainees on a kind of 'Cooks tour' of the organization. There are several possible variations:

A general non-directed look at a department. Often this can entail spending some time sitting around, perhaps talking to some managers, perhaps looking for something to do. This is used as a device to show graduates what 'work' is 'really' like. It has been heavily criticized but organizations persist in using it.

Talking to other employees and managers and learning about operations. This is a more structured approach in which the trainee is expected to interview, or listen to experienced workers engaged in different kinds of jobs. The intention is that trainees should learn through this about the way the organization works and understand the different jobs. It depends heavily upon the willing cooperation of a wide range of employees and managers.

Looking for specific information. The trainees are given exercises involving information gathering. The exercise involves discussion with a wide range of workers and therefore provides a form of active and directed learning for the trainee. The main problems centre around the levels of cooperation and the relevance of the learning that takes place.

Undertaking simple internal consultancy exercises. This is an exercise designed to serve a useful purpose both for the organization and in helping the trainee to learn about aspects of the environment. This requires some skills on the part of the trainee and certain types of trainee may be able to make a contribution whilst also learning for themselves. In practice, however, it may be difficult to find suitable projects which achieve the learning objectives for the trainee.

The advantages of training in the field

It provides an opportunity for trainees such as graduates, sales staff and others to

integrate into the organization

learn procedures

practice techniques.

It requires training resources to set up, but can utilize managerial resources within the organization.

The disadvantages of training in the field

The objectives are often vague.

The trainee can quickly become impatient and disillusioned by being in an organization but not really a part of it and not being allowed to get on with the job.

It can result in interference with day to day activities and create resentment among experienced staff.

227

Criteria for successful use of learning in the field

Requires clear objectives and careful preparation by an experienced teacher.

Experienced workers must be prepared to give sufficient time to trainees.

Trainees must be given access to information.

There must be frequent feedback and reinforcement from the trainer. This might be usefully done with groups of trainees to avoid feelings of isolation.

Many organizations have used this type of training as a form of extended induction. Yet it requires considerable care and attention to be effective and where it is extended unduly, trainees may become impatient and disillusioned. An approach which sets out to develop positive attitudes towards and understanding of the organizations will then end up having the opposite effect.

SIMULATION

When training on the job is for some reason undesirable, the most appropriate alternative may well be some form of simulation. For certain types of situation, simulation may have distinct advantages over other forms of training. There are three central principles or characteristics of simulation:

it represents a real life situation

it provides certain controls over that situation

it deliberately omits certain features of the real situation.

The best known examples of simulation is probably the use of 'simulators' for pilot training, in which the experience of piloting an aeroplane is replicated as closely as possible. However it can be used for a variety of purposes. These can be classified as:

simulation of equipment: examples include simulators of cars, trains, aircraft and the like.

simulation of materials: examples include nuclear waste and first aid dummies.

simulation of situations: examples include flight crash landings, customer contacts and selection interviews.

228

In practice the simulation of situations means that business games and many kinds of role playing exercises can be considered as a form of simulation. This would include, for example, the re-enactment of an industrial tribunal case or a negotiating exercise.

The advantages of simulation

It can dramatically reduce costs. Prior to the introduction of flight simulators, the costs of pilot training in terms of lost aircraft and loss of life among crew was becoming unacceptable. The same is true for activities such as starting up a whole machine when the learning only concerns one part of it.

It can provide feedback and extra information. A diver who makes a serious error may never have the chance to discover what he did wrong. The same is true for others in tasks, such as driving, which might normally be carried out in isolation with no one to provide feedback of performance.

It can remove stress and other inhibitors to learning. It may be easier to learn when there is no danger, when noise, heat or tiredness are removed and when the money used for the business game is not real money.

It can be used when the actual task is inaccessible. It was, for example, impossible to practice lunar landing procedures for the space programme on the moon. Therefore a simulated lunar environment had to be used. Similarly planning the response to a nuclear disaster can, fortunately, only be simulated.

It can 'collapse' or 'extend' time. Infrequent occurrences, such as emergency landings or monthly board meetings can be repeated several times. Rapid events, such as an inflow of information from different sources, can be slowed down.

The disadvantages of simulation

Much depends on the role of the instructor, both in drawing out and reinforcing learning points and in controlling the training process. There can be a danger that because it is a simulation it is treated as a game, the trainee is too relaxed and therefore fails to concentrate and learn. This is a particular danger for those on some form of 'refresher' or up-dating programme.

The use of simulators, solely for the purpose of training, can prove prohibitively expensive.

Criteria for successful use of simulation
The quality of the simulator or simulation process must be sufficiently good to allow for transfer from simulated to real life.

From this analysis, it is clear that good simulation combines many of the best characteristics of on the job and off the job learning. In practice, the main problem lies in devising a realistic simulation. For example, in role playing, the situation may be realistic but the other actors are also trainees. In a business game the conditions can appear too artificial. Simulations where the danger or noise is removed may prove counter-productive if they lead first to over-relaxation and then to shock when confronted with the reality. The emotional interference can then result in the freezing of performance. The introduction to the 'real' job must therefore be handled with care.

CASE STUDIES

A case study is essentially a description of a situation that has arisen within an organization which is presented to trainees for analysis. There is a tendency on many management courses to use specially created cases, and these can certainly be useful to focus upon specific learning points. The problems of transfer are reduced when 'live' or current cases are presented by those actually involved in them, particularly when the organizational context is also relevant. The difficulty with this is that sometimes there can be political problems in discussing contemporary issues and it is also not unknown for trainees to conclude that the main problem in this type of case study is the person presenting it.

Advantages of the case study
It is an active, participative form of learning which can be an excellent vehicle for evaluating and applying knowledge.

The case study is highly flexible, ranging from 10 minute exercises to something akin to a business game.

The active learning in small groups, usually in the absence of an instructor, combined with the need to present and argue for a certain approach should produce high involvement, high learning and high internalization of the learning.

Disadvantages of the case study
If the timing is wrong, poor preparation or insufficient time for discussion can limit the value of a case.

The quality of the case is critical. A poor case may result in no learning, combined with negative attitudes to learning among trainees.

The search for involvement of trainees can backfire if they become over-committed to an inappropriate solution.

Criteria for a successful case study

The nature of the case is crucial. Characteristics that should be taken into account are:

there should be no definite answer

it should avoid extreme value conflicts

it should be easy to understand

it should be sufficiently difficult.

The context must be right.

trainees should possess a suitable knowledge base

the length should be appropriate to the circumstances

there must be time to prepare and discuss, and time to present suggested solutions and discuss these thoroughly.

The trainer's contribution and role needs careful consideration. He can adopt two main approaches, which may overlap. One is to act as a kind of irritant, asking questions and getting discussion underway, but avoiding giving the answers to return questions. The second role is a kind of expert and referee, who guides discussion and may provide expert input. Where someone other than the trainer is presenting the case, it is essential for the trainer to be present to ensure that appropriate learning takes place.

If the various criteria are met, the case study can be an effective means of achieving higher level cognitive learning (ie application, synthesis and evaluation) and attitude change. It is often less suitable for the lower levels of cognitive learning, namely knowledge and comprehension. For this the lecture, the talk or reading may be more suitable and these are discussed below.

THE LECTURE

The lecture, much beloved by academic institutions, has been widely criticized for industrial use and tends to be frowned upon by many industrial trainers. Like all forms of instruction however, the good lecture, used in the appropriate circumstances, can be highly effective. Furthermore the lecture format is extremely flexible, and it is possible to identify the following variations:

The straight, uninterrupted lecture.

A lecture followed by questions.

Short 'lecturettes', possibly combined with other methods of learning.

A lecture combined with discussion. The discussion may follow the lecture. Indeed the conventional form of academic teaching consists of a lecture on a topic followed by a 'class' or seminar to discuss it in more depth. A further variation, when the lecture is delivered to small numbers, is to allow interruptions and discussion at any point.

A lecture combined with a demonstration. This is a widely used approach for the training of scientists, engineers and medical students.

The advantage of the lecture

It can be delivered to large numbers. The use of TV, video and film means it can be 'captured' and repeated many times. The Open University's use of TV, radio and cassettes illustrates the possibilities of this.

Well presented, it can be a good means of communicating low level cognitive information, that is, knowledge and comprehension. For those used to the lecture method, who already possess a knowledge base in a particular subject, it can also cover all cognitive levels effectively.

For the lecturer, and for many trainees or students, the lecture is highly convenient.

Disadvantages of the lecture

It imposes paced learning, which fails to account for individual differences in learning speeds.

It may be difficult to transfer from verbal descriptions to task performances. There are therefore dangers in using the lecture method in isolation.

Trainees' powers of concentration are limited. An uninterrupted lecture is unlikely to attract full attention if it lasts more than 40 minutes

232

and it is wise to introduce a break (by telling a joke or anecdote) after about 20 minutes.

The lecture is a passive form of learning and it is difficult to ensure attention. If note-taking is encouraged this may increase concentration and also ensure that the learning is more active.

There is often little or no feedback either to check that the trainee has understood or to inform the lecturer about the quality of the lecture. A badly presented lecture may result in almost no learning.

Criteria for a successful lecture

The structure and presentation of the lecture must be good. This means making it clear and interesting and structured to take account of spans of concentration.

Given the flexibility of the lecture, it must be structured and geared to the particular audience.

Appropriate visual and other aids should be used. However these must be well prepared and presented. Slides which are too small to read at the back of the room are worse than no slides. Furthermore excessive use of visual aids can become distracting.

In most circumstances, the lecture should be used as part of a learning process. It has an important part to play, but will need to be supplemented by some of the other methods of training already discussed.

OTHER METHODS

In addition to the major methods outlined above, there are several more approaches which partly overlap with some of these methods, but also contain distinctive features. The following are among the more important.

Coaching

This is a variant of on the job learning which has been strongly advocated by Hague (1973), more particularly for the training of managers. It consists of giving the trainee planned experiences, initially under the watchful eye of his manager but with increasing independence. In practice this may mean attending meetings with the boss, probably starting as a silent observer, then making a modest contribution and later standing in as substitute for the boss. This approach deliberately places responsibility for training and development of subordinates in the hands of the manager. Its success therefore depends on his commitment to coaching, the time he can make available and his skill in providing guidance. The principle of management responsibility is a sound one and coaching implies that learning and development is a continuous process. Therefore, often in conjunction with other methods, it has many attractions.

Projects

Revans (1971) has developed a system of management development centred around the use of projects. These entail something close to consultancy activities, usually in unfamiliar environments, and are combined with some academic input and an opportunity to discuss progress. The trainee is therefore learning by doing, deliberately developing specific approaches under guidance and undertaking an activity of value to the host organization. The principle, in amended form, is utilized in a range of learning contexts from schools to polytechnic courses in business studies and NEBSS-type courses for supervisors. Its attraction lies in the opportunity to link theory and knowledge to practice while at the same time doing something useful. There can be difficulties in finding suitable projects, maintaining appropriate supervision and avoiding negative reactions if the host organization fails to accept and implement the recommendations.

A second and rather different form of learning associated with projects focuses on a group rather than on individuals. The start-up of a new factory, a new department, a new maintenance team or sales section provides an opportunity to build up the effectiveness of the team around the primary task (and often on the basis of a very specific task) of the group. The aim of the trainer is to use the situation to ensure an effective process of group working, using the specific task as a kind of case study. As such it may not be recognized as training by the participants; indeed it could come under the label of Organization Development (OD). To succeed, this requires a different set of skills on the part of the trainer, namely the skills of a group facilitator. Clearly it is only appropriate in certain circumstances, but when skilfully utilized, can be extremely effective.

Group discussions

Most structured learning programmes will involve some sort of group discussion. Ideally discussions provide trainees with an opportunity to test out, clarify and extend their knowledge and understanding. Academic institutions therefore use tutor-led but student-dominated discussions as a complement to lectures. In industry a useful variant is the regular departmental meeting. A number of organizations use this to inform staff of new developments and to appraise these developments. For example a sales and marketing department might have monthly day-long meetings, part of which include a presentation by a member of the department or an outsider followed by a discussion of its relevance and of how it might be used. Again, this may not be labelled as training, but it is a deliberate attempt to provide an opportunity for relevant learning.

Self-learning
Much of the learning that takes place in organizations is initiated by the learner himself. Typically this takes the form of reading, occasionally extending to the use of television and tapes. The trainer must consider whether to structure this and build it into the work. It could, for example, be argued that part of any individual's job is to keep up to date in his specialist field. The trainer's role might therefore be to facilitate this by encouraging a supportive organizational climate in which reading a journal like *Personnel Management* is accepted as working rather than resting and by ensuring the provision of appropriate literature.

Discovery learning
In a rather different category, discovery learning is an attempt to facilitate learning by creating an environment in which the trainee is helped to discover principles for himself by following a series of cues. It ensures that the learning is self-paced and relevant. Discovery learning was pioneered by the Belbins (Belbin and Belbin, 1972) for the retraining of older workers. Its strength lies in its careful application of the psychological principles of learning. However it can be time-consuming and expensive to set up and will invariably require outside expertise. The trainer is therefore best advised to consult an expert before investing heavily in it as a special approach rather than a general principle.

MEDIA AND AIDS TO LEARNING

Backing up the various methods of training, the trainer has to consider the type of media and other aids to learning that he wishes to use. Essentially, these must be considered as part of the training resources and the choice will be constrained by the cost and what is available.

235

The major types of aid are visual aids, audial aids, audio-visual aids and mechanical aids and are described below.

Visual aids

These include blackboards, flip-charts, over-head projectors, pictures, maps and diagrams. Particular types of diagram include algorithms which lay out a sequence of events involved in, for example, diagnosis of a machine breakdown. These, and other types of detailed instructional guide can facilitate individual learning.

Audial aids

These include records, tapes and radio. As well as providing a substitute for a lecture, they are particularly useful where audial discrimination is important. Examples of this include engine tuning, language accents and musical pitch.

Audio-visual aids

These cover TV, including closed-circuit television (CCTV) and films. They have the general advantage of tackling more than one 'sense' and therefore of having a potentially greater impact. Both CCTV and films have the flexibility to provide feedback.

Mechanical aids

These are a variation on simulation. Those learning to paint may need a model, car mechanics need an engine, surgeons need bodies and architects need models of buildings. Chemists may need models of molecules to illustrate their make-up. Mechanical aids are therefore used to illustrate, to provide a visual representation and to demonstrate a skill or to practice on.

The aids available to a trainer may range from a blackboard and chalk to a complete and fully equipped training workshop or flight simulator. Whatever the availability, it is essential to ensure that the aids are, in fact, aids rather than hindrances. Two problems must be avoided: one is poor quality aids, which put off the trainees, the other is inappropriate aids. A typical illustration of the latter is the use by the training workshop of last year's machinery, which was generously donated by the production department but which requires outdated skills.

The use of aids is subject to fashion. For many years, attention was focused on programmed learning which never really fulfilled its potential. More recently the training package, developed at a centre and used in

236

large numbers of local units has become a focus of interest. The best known examples are the Open University and the Open Tech. Both the Ministry of Defence and the accounting profession make use of such packages. More recently most attention has been directed towards computer aided instruction. Some of the most intriguing applications are in training in diagnosis, ranging from electronic trouble shooting to medicine and detective training. More obviously, computers can make a major contribution to business games. The trainer should keep an eye on new models and on the use of them by other departments. He should select his aids on a pragmatic basis by asking questions such as: are they helpful, are they available, can I afford them and do I know how to use them?

THE TRAINING PROGRAMME

The final stage, having considered the context, the learning objectives, the resources available, the type of trainee and the strengths and weaknesses of each method, is to put the information together to design and implement a learning programme. In this chapter it has been suggested that the outcome of this exercise will sometimes not be the kind of conventional training, typically associated with off the job courses. Even when a conventional programme is designed, it is often not a question of which method, but more one of which combination of methods. Exceptions may possibly be found in some areas of operator training, but if we consider two examples, those of a craft trainee and a personnel management trainee, then we can see that most of the methods outlined earlier are used. The skill of the trainer lies in understanding what sort of trainees and learning requirements he is dealing with, what choice of methods is available and how to weigh the criteria already discussed to arrive at the best combination and sequence for effective learning to occur.

Designing and resourcing a training programme is not an exact science. It involves judgement and compromise and a certain amount of trial and error. It also requires the possession of considerable local intelligence—about who is a good speaker, about which managers will cooperate and the like—which can only be gradually acquired. For all these reasons the trainer and the training must be flexible and adaptable and therefore responsive to continuous evaluation. The question of evaluation is explored in some detail in the next chapter.

REFERENCES

BELBIN E *and* BELBIN RM (1972). *Problems in Adult Retraining.* London, Heinemann.

CANNON J (1979). *Cost Effective Personnel Decisions.* London, Institute of Personnel Management.

HAGUE H (1973). *Management Training For Real.* London, Institute of Personnel Management.

MAGER RF (1968). *Developing Attitude Towards Learning.* California, Fearon.

OTTO CP *and* GLASER RO (1970). *The Management of Training.* Addison Wesley.

REVANS RW (1971). *Developing Effective Managers.* London, Longman.

STAMMERS R *and* PATRICK J (1975). *The Psychology of Training.* London, Methuen.

TALBOT JR *and* ELLIS CD (1969). *Analysis and Costing of Company Training.* Farnborough, Hants., Gower.

ADDITIONAL READING

BELBIN RM (1969). *The Discovery Method*, Training Information Paper No 5. London, HMSO.

DEAN C *and* WHITLOCK P (1982). *A Handbook of Computer-Based Training.* London, Kogan-Page.

EASTON G (1982). *Learning from Case Studies.* London, Prentice-Hall.

FITTS PM *and* POSNER MI (1976). *Human Performance.* California, Brooks/Cole.

GAGNE RM (1970). *The Conditions of Learning.* New York, Holt, Rhinehart and Winston.

HOLDING DH (1965). *Principles of Training*, London, Pergamon.

Industrial Training Research Unit (1974). CRAMP *A Guide to Training Decisions, a User's Manual.* Cambridge, ITRU.

JONES S (1968). *Design of Instruction*, Training Information Paper No 1. London, HMSO.

KING D (1964). *Training Within the Organization.* London, Tavistock Publications.

238

MORRIS J *and* BURGOYNE J (1973). *Developing Resourceful Managers*. London, IPM.

TAYLOR J *and* WALFORD R (1978). *Learning and the Simulation Game*. Milton Keynes, Open University Press.

WELFORD AT (1976). *Skilled Performance*. London, Scott, Foresman.

Chapter nine

Evaluating training

INTRODUCTION

To evaluate the effectiveness of training is a difficult exercise which has concerned trainers, researchers and managers for many years. As the cost of training programmes has risen so has the need to assess the benefit from this type of investment. This chapter outlines the steps to be considered before undertaking an evaluation exercise, discusses the methodology which has been used and examines some of the other issues relating to the process.

The first problem encountered is one of definition. The word evaluation is subject to many interpretations, so for the purposes of this chapter it is necessary to clarify in which sense it is being used. Various writers have attempted definitions including the Department of Employment (1967) in the *Glossary of Training Terms*, which distinguishes between validation and evaluation. However, in practice this has proved a difficult distinction to make as many writers such as Hesseling (1966), Warr, Bird and Rackham (1970) and Hamblin (1974) have recognized. For the purposes of this chapter the broad view taken by Hamblin, that evaluation of training is 'any attempt to obtain information (feedback) on the effects of a training programme, and to assess the value of the training in the light of that information' is the most useful definition. Training, of course, is another term open to a variety of meanings. As the previous chapter has illustrated, a training programme can range from on the job coaching to a three year course and the training methods used vary considerably. The material in this chapter is not limited to any one type of programme, although some of the techniques are restricted in their application.

Techniques for evaluation are plentiful and seem to be becoming

241

increasingly complex as more research is carried out in this area. Before any decisions can be made on the amount of sophistication required, a number of questions have to be asked in order that the evaluation procedure takes the right direction. However complex the evaluation system devised, if it is not directed at the right questions then the effort is wasted.

WHY EVALUATE?

Where does the impetus to evaluate come from? Training programmes and training departments are expensive to run and therefore the training budget should be justified. However, this is by no means the only objective. Programmes continually develop and the needs of the participants change, therefore both must be investigated to ensure that the relevance of the training is maintained.

It appears that the reasons for evaluating training fall into two categories; either those concerned with justifying the investment in this area (evaluation as an end in itself) or those related to refinement or development of the programme (evaluation as feedback). The two are not mutually exclusive and often an evaluation procedure has to cover both. However, problems can arise if the impetus appears to be in one category, usually the second, but is actually in the first. An evaluation system designed to refine the content of a programme will not necessarily yield the information a training manager needs to demonstrate the value of his department to the organization. Therefore, until it is clearly understood why the training is to be evaluated and the purpose for which the results will be used, it is not sensible to move on to the next stage.

WHAT TO EVALUATE?

Training programmes generally involve a variety of interests. The training organizer, the teaching staff, the participant and the individual responsible for his attendance all have a vested interest in the programme and its results, and one of the perennial problems is frequent confusion or misunderstanding between these interests. Most courses have objectives which are clearly defined but they are often not the same objectives as those of the participant or his manager. In one company a study highlighted that the participants expected to learn about business in general, their managers expected them to be able to do their job better, while the teaching staff were concerned with developing individual self-knowledge. All these objectives were included in those listed for the programme as a whole, but the different emphases given by those involved illustrates the problem of deciding what to evaluate. This is why it is necessary to have a clear understanding of why the evaluation is taking place and the kind of results which are expected.

Having decided which objectives should be investigated, it is also necessary to examine at what level these objectives operate. Some training aims to provide an appreciation only while other programmes have very specific behavioural objectives. In general there is usually a mixture of learning, behavioural and organizational objectives, and it is useful to consider these in what has been called the 'circle of evaluation', adapted from Whitelaw (1972).

Figure 1
The circle of evaluation

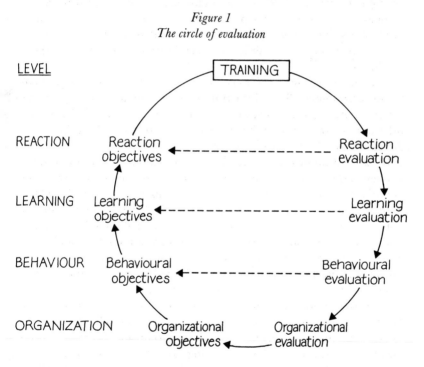

This shows the feedback effect of the process. An evaluation of the learning, for example, will enable changes to be made in the learning objectives if necessary and therefore in the training itself.

The first level in the circle is the reactions of the participants to the training. This can include a variety of aspects such as what they feel they have learnt, how useful the content was, whether the teaching style was appropriate etc. This type of evaluation is most useful for the traditional form of off the job training course.

The second level has been called the immediate outcome level where the learning of the participants is evaluated. This learning can be a combination of knowledge, skills or new attitudes depending on the type of programme. A distinction must be made here between what is actually learnt and what participants feel they have learnt since the latter is included in the reactions level.

The third level of evaluation, sometimes called the intermediate level, is concerned with the impact of training on the trainee's job performance. Here the interest is in the way an individual changes his behaviour at work as a result of a training programme and it is assumed that this is a result of both the reactions and learning that has taken place. It is often only possible to examine this level some time after the completion of the training.

The final level in the circle has been called the ultimate level where the organizational effects of the training are evaluated. This may be in terms of organizational performance or climate and is the level at which the costs of training are related to the benefits gained. However, the difficulties at this level can be considerable.

It has been argued that any evaluation should be carried out at all four levels. This may appear to involve an excessive amount of work, and organizational constraints will occasionally make it impractical. However, the problem of not evaluating at all four levels is that it becomes difficult to explain the reasons for the success or failure of the training. For example if you only evaluate at the organizational level and if the results are negative, it will be almost impossible to explain why the expected changes failed to materialize. It might be because the change in job performance was of no help to the organization; or because there was a failure to transfer the learning from the training situation to the job; or because learning did not take place. Occasionally, only a limited amount of evaluation will be feasible, but it is important for the trainer to be aware of the risks involved in attempting to cut corners for there is a real danger that the wrong explanations for the outcome of training will be accepted within the organization.

WHEN TO EVALUATE?

Having established why an evaluation is necessary and therefore what levels are to be examined, the next question to be considered is when the evaluation should take place. For each level a different time scale may be indicated which adds to the complexity if all levels are to be considered.

At the reactions level it is usual to collect the information either at the end of each session or at the end of the course. There are advantages and disadvantages to both these methods. If the course is fairly short, not longer than four weeks, a review of reactions at the end is likely to give a more considered view of the training as a whole. However, one must bear in mind what is often called end-of-course euphoria. This phenomenon is likely to cause the participants on the last day to look back at their experiences through rose coloured glasses, therefore giving more favourable reactions. By getting the reactions to each session or section of the training as it proceeds this problem does not arise. It also provides an opportunity to take remedial action if a particular session has been notably unsuccessful. However, the reactions collected will not be directly comparable between sessions as the group of trainees are developing and learning as the programme proceeds. Also courses are known to have a fairly consistent pattern of low and high periods of commitment by the participants which are usually reflected in any continuous reaction measurement. In a one week course there is generally a high spot after the first day and a low after the third, followed by a build up towards the last day. The pattern is the same on any programme, only the time scale changes. Therefore, any evaluation of reactions has to take this into account. If possible, reactions to the training can also be measured some time after its completion. This avoids the problems mentioned above and allows a more reflective view to be taken of the experience.

At the second level, evaluating the learning, there is the question of measuring before the start of the training to provide a base from which to assess changes. This can cause practical difficulties but should be attempted if possible. As this level is concerned with changes in knowledge, attitude and skill, as an immediate result of the learning, the evaluation of these should take place at the end of the training before the trainee returns to the work situation. It can be useful to repeat these measures some time after the completion of the training to assess how well the learning is retained.

At the intermediate level, the question of when to measure becomes even more important. Ideally, before and after measures should be made, the latter measure taken after the trainee has returned to his job. If the objective of the training is to learn a mechanical skill, then a measurement at the end of the course will give information on immediate skill development, but a repeated measurement later will demonstrate whether this is incorporated into job behaviour. If the evaluation study is concerned with interpersonal skills or some types of management training, then the measurement of behaviour should be at least three months after completion of the programme so that the participants have had an opportunity to put into practice what they have learnt.

At the level of organizational evaluation the problem of timing becomes more crucial and more dependent on the methodology used. As evaluation at this level has to be on a longer time scale than the previous levels, examining the effects of training on an organization or even a department within a company becomes more complex. The changes in the environment, which are impossible to control are difficult to isolate from any changes which might be due to the training.

Table 1 below summarizes the stages in the training process at which measures are taken.

Table 1

Level	When
Reactions	at the end of each session
	at the end of the training
	around three months after
Learning	before the training
	at the end of the training
Behaviour	before the training
	at least three months after
Organizational	dependent on methodology, but a time scale of at least one year between measurement points is usually necessary.

WHO TO EVALUATE?

This may well be determined by the time available and the methodology used rather than any more theoretical criteria. If the measurement techniques are time consuming to administer then it may not be possible to include all the trainees. However, if possible, it is best to include all those undergoing the training, especially if pre-training measurements are made, as suspicions are often aroused if the trainees discover that some of them have been selected for what appears to be a kind of test.

A control group should also be considered. As the effects of training are often difficult to isolate from organizational or environmental influences, the use of the same techniques on a group who are not receiving training will help to distinguish these. The control group should be matched with the participants as closely as possible and this is where practical difficulties arise. If the methodology is complex and time consuming then there will be considerable resistance within the organization to the use of such a group. However, it is always worth looking at the possibility of a control as it gives credence to the results and enables some sources of bias to be removed. A perfect experimental design is unlikely to be a practical proposition in most industrial situations, but the best possible compromise should be attempted.

How to evaluate?

The selection of an appropriate measurement technique is difficult. A wide range of options is available, varying in sophistication, and at first glance it seems that an evaluator is spoilt for choice. However, the reason for the study, the level and the practical considerations of timing and numbers to be evaluated restrict the choice. There is no methodology which is appropriate for every situation and often trial and error is needed before the technique will emerge which is best in the circumstances. This section attempts to summarize the methods which can be used for each level and to point out some of the advantages and disadvantages.

Reactions level

This information can be obtained from reactions during the training, immediately at the end or some time after. All those who run training programmes have some idea of the trainees' reactions to the experience as a result of informal discussions, watching the process and listening to general conversation. However, this is not usually systematic enough for an evaluation procedure. It is common to introduce a standardized questionnaire for reactions which enables a group view to be assessed. Group discussions, while useful in allowing specific points to be raised, often allow one or two voices to dominate the opinions of the others.

When designing a standardized reactions questionnaire first decide exactly what needs to be measured for each section or session of the programme. The following list is not exhaustive but includes the measures most frequently used on conventional courses:

1 enjoyment of the session
2 relevance to the current job
3 relevance to future career
4 amount of new knowledge gained
5 performance of the speaker/instructor in

    maintaining interest

    use of visual aids

    clarity of subject

    meeting session objectives

    general presentation

    speed of the session

6 Meeting of personal objectives
7 Meeting of programme objectives.

It is usual to give the participants a scale on which to indicate the extent to which each of these were met, eg

> How much new knowledge did you gain from this session? Please tick the relevant position

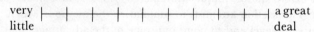

very little   a great deal

The individual responds by placing a mark at the point he feels is relevant to him. An alternative is to use numbers rather than a line, eg

> How much new knowledge did you gain from this session?
>
> Please ring the relevant number

very little   1   2   3   4   5   6   7   a great deal

Both of these allow a group response to be obtained and in the latter case it is possible to calculate an average response for the session. If the reactions are measured at the end of each session, averages or summaries of responses can be fed back to the participants and the trainers regularly, enabling improvements to be made if necessary. There are, however, dangers in this approach if the results are ignored. The programme must be flexible enough to allow changes to be made and the participants must feel that their views are being considered. There is nothing more frustrating for participants than to see, for example, the 'relevance to their job' rating decline continually and no action taken by the course organizers.

If a questionnaire such as this is given at the end of a course and the ratings are obtained for each session, the participants will respond in a comparative manner, rating one session *vis-à-vis* another. This has advantages in overcoming the problem of the mood of the moment or day of the week and is especially useful when there is a logical progression between sessions, the relevance of one not being obvious until later in the course. Also at the end of a training programme general questions can be asked about the programme as a whole and other items such as the domestic arrangements, very important in a residential course, can be included.

It is impossible to give examples of all the many types of reaction questionnaire which have been used, but in general they tend to be tightly structured to enable the summary of a group response. Open ended questions in this context are more difficult to handle, although with a longer programme they can be valuable (for an example of an open ended evaluation of participants' reactions and assessments of a programme *see* Burgoyne (1975)). Examples of structured reactions questionnaires are given in Hesseling (1966); Warr, Bird and Rackham (1970); Whitelaw (1972); Joyce (1980) and Hogarth (1979).

LEARNING LEVEL

Evaluation of this level is familiar to all who have progressed through the educational system and taken school examinations. There is a vast amount of research in this area as criticism is directed at the examination system and techniques such as continuous assessment are introduced. For a comprehensive text on educational assessment, *see* Budd and Blood (1972).

The division of learning into three categories, knowledge, skills and attitudes, can be difficult to make in a practical situation. It is rare to find training which concentrates solely on one area and, therefore, it is usual to have to evaluate learning in all three. However, this distinction is useful when considering what type of methodology is most appropriate.

Evaluating changes in knowledge

In assessing new knowledge there are a variety of techniques available ranging from the traditional essay type of question of school examinations, which are difficult to mark objectively, to programmed learning where multiple choice, sentence completion and other similar types of questions are used. Some examples of these are given below.

1 *Multiple choice*
   eg the most frequently occurring value in a set of data is called
       mean
       average
       mode
       median
   Please tick one

2 *Sentence completion*
   eg correlation coefficient measures ....

3 *Matching items*
   eg here are a list of statistical measures
       correlation coefficient
       standard deviation
       median

   Please put each measure opposite the correct description below
       spread of the distribution ....
       central value of the distribution ....
       association between two distributions ....

The advantage of this type of question is that they can be assessed objectively and they are relatively quick to complete and mark. However, there is the problem of minimizing the number of times the right answer can be guessed or obtained by chance. If tests such as these are used, considerable effort must be put into constructing them and ensuring that these problems are reduced by testing the questions with individuals, some of whom know little about the subject and others who are experts.

These tests are carried out before and after the training, enabling the trainer to assess the level and range of knowledge amongst the group. If the results are fed back to the participants this can increase their motivation to improve in the areas in which they were found to be weakest. However, this can lead to the trainees concentrating only on remembering, or trying to, those parts which were included in the test, rather than trying to understand the whole subject. This could be exacerbated if they feel there is any reporting of results to their superiors. One advantage of the pre-test is that the possibility of a trainee attending who already has the required knowledge can be eliminated. For this reason it is usually best to administer such a test some time before the start of the programme.

Evaluating changes in attitude
The evaluation of attitude change is a more difficult area but nevertheless one which deserves careful attention. Many training programmes have objectives which relate directly to changing the attitudes of trainees. Often these are what could be described as the hidden objectives of the course. For instance, in many internally run courses an objective is to reinforce the participant's commitment to the company whereas one reason for sending an individual on an externally run programme is to enable him to mix with and change his attitudes towards individuals from many other types of organization. Therefore, it is frequently necessary to evaluate attitude change.

There are many techniques which have been used in this area and a detailed description of the methodology is given in Oppenheim (1967). Probably the most useful and simple is the semantic differential. Many of the others take time to construct and are too specific for general use. The semantic differential in comparison is relatively easy to design and to complete. It involves presenting the respondent with a set of opposing words or phrases and getting them to mark the position which most corresponds with their attitude. The example given below is an extract from one used with a group on a training managers' programme to assess changes in their view of their own training department.

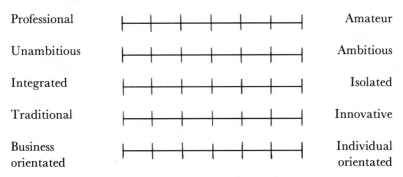

The respondents were asked to place a mark on the scale according to their views. With scales such as these care must be taken not to have all the 'good' words on one side as this might bias the reaction.

The analysis of data gathered in this manner can be made in a number of ways. Average responses for the group can be calculated for both before and after responses and compared. They can also be compared with the attitude of the trainer to see if the course has brought the group to a similar position. This type of data can be displayed in the following manner.

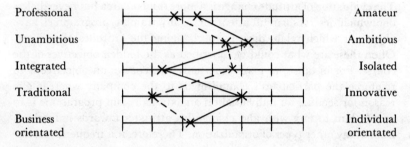

——Pre-course measure
- - -Post course measure

In the above example where the training managers were asked to rate their own training department, the results after the programme show significant changes on the integrated/isolated and traditional/innovative dimensions. It would not be right to assume that because these have moved in an unfavourable direction that the course has failed. In fact it can be argued that the opposite is more likely in that a more realistic appraisal of their departments was now being made. To examine whether this was the case, they were also asked to complete the same scales in response to the question 'where do you think your department *should* lie on the following scales?' When gathering attitudes of this type it is often valuable to ask similar additional questions to enrich the interpretation of the data.

Of course, using group averages will hide the individual variations and therefore changes in an individual's responses can also be examined. This implies that the participant must identify his responses to enable the comparisons to be made. In general there is little reluctance on the part of trainees to put their name on a questionnaire, but sometimes on internally run courses this can be a problem. If this is the case then it should not be pressed because it is more valuable to have the information anonymously than to have no data at all.

The semantic differential may not be the most sophisticated method for measuring attitudes, but it is a useful tool. Hamblin (1974) and Warr, Bird and Rackham (1970) give other examples of the use of this technique.

Another technique which can be used to examine attitude change is the paired comparison. The example given below is an extract from one used with a group of managers to see if their attitudes to the importance of various parts of their job changed. They were asked to consider each pair of activities separately and indicate, by placing the relevant letter in the box, which of the two they felt was most important in their current job. Therefore, the completed form might look as follows:

	B Planning future operations	C Keeping others informed	D Developing subordinates	E Allocating work	F Working with colleagues
A Encouraging new ideas	A	C	A	A	F
B Planning future operations		C	D	B	F
C Keeping others informed			C	C	F
D Developing subordinates				D	F
E Allocating work					F

The scoring is a simple process of counting the number of times each letter occurs. In this case the results are:

	Score
Encouraging new ideas	3
Planning future operations	1
Keeping others informed	4
Developing subordinates	2
Allocating work	0
Working with colleagues	5

A comparison between before and after measures will indicate whether the training has had any effect on the attitudes to the job.

The completed questionnaire from which this extract is taken included 12 activities and takes time to complete. However, it forces the participants to consider carefully each activity and is an improvement on a straight ranking or rating procedure for the activities.

Evaluating changes in skill

The evaluation of changes in skill depends very much on the type of skill and the ease with which it can be specified and measured. The major contrast is between manual skills, usually associated with blue-collar workers, and social process skills, more typically associated with supervisory and managerial roles.

In some respects the evaluation of changes in manual skills might be considered quite straightforward. It is a matter of testing the trainee's ability to perform specific tasks such as changing a car wheel, operating a lathe, assembling a typewriter after repair and the like. In practice, the evaluation of operator and craft training is something which is often rather poorly done in the UK. Ideally, the analysis of training needs should lead to specification of objectives and these point to both evaluation criteria and the method of evaluation. For example, a training objective might be to drive a fork-lift truck, fully loaded with a pallet of goods, through a warehouse, safely unload and return without touching any other goods or parts of the warehouse. This should provide the basis for what is sometimes called a trade test. But there is plenty of scope for variety, including the definition of 'safety' and 'loaded with pallets'. To take a more familiar example, the case of learning to drive a car, the objectives are partly specified (for example the ability to perform a three-point turn and an emergency stop) and evaluated, after training, in the driving test. But the test conditions are seldom standardized either for traffic flow or weather conditions and it is possible to pass the test without ever driving at night or on a motorway. It raises the question, which all those concerned with assessment of training should consider, of what criteria to test, what standards of performance to set and whether to test under ideal, average or challenging conditions. In practice the decisions may be partly a function of administrative and political requirements within the organization. In times of labour shortage, standards may therefore be reduced, dangerous as this may be.

To summarize the implications of this discussion using another well-known illustration, the evaluator, in assessing the performance of an operator skill such as typing, must take into account:

what has to be typed. Should the 'test piece' be easy or difficult to read? Should it be read from shorthand? Should it be a letter or a report?

the conditions under which it should be typed. Should these be noisy office conditions, with telephone interruptions or ideal conditions of peace and quiet?

254

the type of materials to use. What sort of typewriter and paper should be used?

performance standards. What standards of accuracy and time should be set?

Therefore set objectives, which for this type of training should be feasible, can help to clarify each of these issues. For a fuller discussion of trade testing, see Jessup (1983).

Social and process skills are less easy to specify and to assess. However, a number of approaches to the evaluation of such skills, both during and after training have been utilized by trainers.

Role playing exercises are often built into courses concentrating on social skill development as part of the learning experience and they provide an opportunity for the evaluation of skill development. This is often carried out by the other participants on the course as part of their own learning. In this case a structured or semi-structured questionnaire is used to help the observers concentrate on the important aspects of the exercise.

If the role-playing exercise is in the form of an appraisal interview, then the trainer can design forms listing the points to look for such as how is the interview opened, how constructively are any failures discussed etc. These can be used by the observers and space can be left for an overall assessment of the performance of the interviewer.

Another method of recording communication skills has been developed by Rackham, Honey and Colbert (1971). Their system is based on an analysis of the behaviour of individuals in groups and a number of headings are used as follows:

initiating proposing new ideas: building on new ideas.

reacting supporting others: disagreeing with others: defending or attacking.

clarifying testing one's understanding: summarizing: seeking information: giving information.

process bringing others in: shutting others out.

The number of times each individual in the group uses one of the above behaviours is noted and this information can be fed back to the participants. Later the process is repeated to see if changes have occurred. However, this system requires highly trained observers as the counting process must be accurate in order to have any value.

This section has divided learning into knowledge, attitudes and skills and considered appropriate techniques for each. However, there is some argument about whether this distinction is valid or useful and some of the methodology available does not fall neatly under one of the three headings. In management development programmes it is often the objective to broaden a manager's view of his company and the way it operates and also to extend his vocabulary enabling him to communicate more effectively with other functions; such changes in an individual's frame of reference are less easy to measure.

One technique which is used for this purpose is the repertory grid based on the work of Kelly (1955). This is used to build pictures of the frameworks or models which a manager uses to understand the world around him. This can be in terms of his relationships with others, the other functions within the company he deals with or any other models included in the programme objectives. For a more detailed description of models in this context see Davies (1976).

The grid technique involves presenting an individual with three elements; these can be people, functions, situations etc. The most frequently used elements are people, eg boss, subordinate, colleague. In this case the individual would be asked to identify these people and then to indicate which two are alike and why they differ from the third. This process is repeated many times using a variety of people, including the individual himself, and in this way a list of constructs (characteristics which distinguish between the people) can be obtained. After this is completed all the individuals used to generate the constructs are rated on each construct, either on a scale or by a yes or no response. An example of the type of grid obtained is given on below.

2 people	1 person	Boss	Self	Colleague	Subordinate etc
Ambitious	Not ambitious	√	√		
Relaxed	Over anxious		√	√	
Always has time to listen	Never has time to listen		√	√	√
Confident	Diffident	√		√	

In this grid a tick in the column indicates that that person fits the description given under the heading—2 people. If a rating procedure is used a number between say, one and five would be used to indicate the strength of each construct for each individual. The analysis of grids such as this are complex and require computing facilities. However, if used before and after a programme, changes can be assessed in the models the managers use to understand the people around him. A detailed description of the use of the repertory grid for this purpose is given by Smith and Ashton (1975).

One disadvantage of this technique is the amount of data it generates and the complexity of analysis. It is, therefore, difficult to communicate the results in a useful way. It also requires a skilled administrator and is time consuming. However it often gives surprising and unanticipated insights into the results of training.

BEHAVIOUR LEVEL

At this level, the way an individual performs in his job as a result of training is evaluated. It has been argued that this is unnecessary; if there is an improvement in the results achieved by the trainee, then the behaviour used to obtain these results is immaterial and a matter of the individual's own personal choice. However, many training courses have specific behavioural objectives which need to be assessed and sponsors of trainees are often more interested in job behaviour than in any of the other objectives.

Assessing changes in job behaviour can take many forms. Direct observation, indirect observation and self reporting are the three main forms which will be considered.

Direct observation
Direct observation while an individual carries out his work can be either continuous or at discrete periods of time. The former gives a complete picture of the job and the way it is done but suffers from several disadvantages. It is very time consuming, and it is difficult to tell how the very fact of being observed affects an individual's behaviour and that of the people he deals with. It is also likely to cause resentment and therefore should only be used carefully. Observation at discrete periods however is more successful and is based on the principles of activity sampling. At regular intervals an observer records what the individual is doing, in a structured format, which enables him to build up a picture over a period of the job behaviour. A description of the use of this type of technique to examine supervisors' jobs is given in Thurley and Wirdenius (1973). It is also possible to get individuals to complete a diary or activity sampling record for themselves. If this is used then the form on which the activities are recorded should be carefully structured so that it takes the minimum

257

time to complete, enables comparisons to be made between, before and after behaviour and also makes the summary of a group response possible. In an evaluation of a programme for management development advisers, a form was used by the participants to record with whom they were dealing since one of the objectives of the course was to raise their level of operation within the company. They were asked to use one column for each separate activity of the day and to tick the appropriate boxes under the headings.

Who were you with?

How long did it last?

Who initiated the activity?

The final form is given below.

	Activity number					
Who?	1	2	3	4	5	6
Alone Boss A director Other more senior Colleague Other peer Subordinate Other more junior External to the company						
How long? Under 15 minutes 15 minutes–1 hour Over 1 hour						
Please tick this box if you initiated the activity						

The analysis of the data gathered by this process gave the percentage of time spent with various levels within the company and also who had initiated the activity. Comparisons were then made between the before and after situation. Forms such as this, however simple to complete, are subject to error. Participants forget to fill them in and then there is a possibility that they will invent a day's work. However, where there is a specific behavioural objective, as in this case, they can be very useful.

Indirect observation

Indirect observation is the next way of evaluating any changes in behaviour. Here those closely connected with the individual are asked to describe his behaviour in either a structured or unstructured way. Supervisors, colleagues or subordinates are those most frequently involved in this technique. They can be asked for specific incidents which illustrate a change or complete questionnaires on general behaviour such as leadership. Of course, this type of study has to be handled carefully so that it is not seen to pose as a threat to the trainee. Whitelaw (1972) gives examples of studies where this has been used.

The appraisal system of an organization is another potential source of data on the way an individual behaves in his job. If detailed records are made of appraisals then it should be possible to examine these for evidence of behavioural change. As one objective of most appraisal systems is to identify training needs then the following yearly appraisal can be used to examine how these needs were met and whether the necessary changes have taken place. The timing of the appraisals and the ability of the evaluater to assess the evidence from the appraisal are the main drawbacks in using this method.

If all the participants on a programme are in similar jobs then the critical incident technique can be used to develop job behaviour questionnaires. In this situation, managers of the trainees are asked to give examples of incidents which represent the difference between good and poor performance and to describe behaviours associated with each of these incidents. These behaviours, ranging from good to poor performance, enable each trainee to be placed on a point on this scale for all the critical incidents, measuring both, before and after the training. Details of a study using this technique are given in Campbell *et al* (1970). This requires detailed development work to ensure that the categories are understood by all those completing the questionnaire and is limited to those trainees in similar jobs.

Self-reporting

Self-reported changes in behaviour can also be used as an evaluation method. There are many ways in which a trainee can be asked to provide evidence of his own behaviour and a variety of these are discussed here.

The simplest method is to ask the individual an open ended question such as: 'What do you think you are doing differently in your job as a direct result of the course you attended?'. The responses to this do, of course, vary widely and analysis is sometimes difficult. However, it is usually possible to classify them into categories to give an overall picture

259

of the changes. A study carried out on a four-week management development programme yielded six categories of reported changes as follows:

1 better at communicating, eg I listen more carefully to my subordinates, I explain things more carefully now
2 better at planning, eg I don't just rush into new projects now, but plan them in detail
3 increased self-understanding, eg I am more confident in my abilities and therefore more prepared to stand up for my ideas
4 better at dealing with people, eg I am trying to increase the feeling of teamwork amongst my subordinates
5 job specific changes, eg I now review my work regularly and reflect on where my department should be going
6 company specific changes, eg I contribute more to the company effort because of my increased understanding of the organization and its objectives.

Classifications such as these, although not generally applicable, enable the evaluator to see the main areas where changes are occurring and to relate these to the declared objectives of the course. If they can be corroborated by changes reported by colleagues of the individual, their credibility is enhanced.

A variation of the critical incident method can also be used for self-reported behaviour changes. In this case the individual is asked what he feels are the critical incidents in his own job which distinguish between good and poor performance. He is then asked both before and after the training how he behaves in these situations. There are problems in the interpretation of this type of information, but any major changes in the behaviour described can be detected.

Highly structured questionnaires can also be used for self reporting of behaviour change. In the study reported in Hogarth (1979) a detailed list of 50 possible traits which might change was devised and the participants were asked to indicate their agreement or disagreement with statements such as:

I am more inclined to take risks
I am less critical of the company

In this study colleagues of the individual were asked to complete the questionnaire and this was found to add little to what was obtained from the individuals themselves. The most interesting part of these results is that bosses did not perceive differences in the behaviour of the trainees, whereas colleagues and subordinates did. This raises questions such as who should evaluate behaviour changes and who should be believed. If an individual genuinely feels that he has changed his behaviour this may be sufficient for an evaluation exercise. However, the issue remains open and only by returning to the original intention of the evaluation exercise can a decision be made as to whose assessment of behaviour changes is the most useful.

ORGANIZATIONAL LEVEL

This is the most problematical area of evaluation. If the effects of training on an organization as a whole have to be evaluated, these are assumed to result from changes in the way jobs are performed. But job and organizational performance are affected by so many other variables which are impossible to control that any assessment of organizational effects must be tenuous. Therefore, there are no specific techniques for evaluation at this level but measures can be obtained which will indicate changes within an organization.

Some organizational measures are collected regularly within companies and can give some help in this area. Labour turnover, absenteeism and accidents have been used in this context as have various indices of productivity. Changes in these can obviously not be attributed solely to training programmes, but can indicate the contribution training makes to overall results.

Two techniques at this level which have attracted considerable attention are cost-benefit analysis and human-asset accounting. The aim of cost-benefit analysis is to determine whether the financial rewards of training outweigh the costs. In practice this presents all sorts of problems. For the most straightforward example of off the job operator training, Thomas, Moxham and Jones (1969) have shown that it is feasible to identify costs; benefits are more difficult, but can be assessed in terms of time taken to reach experienced worker standard and any changes in labour turnover and absenteeism. However it gets increasingly difficult as the training gets more complex and therefore many trainers have questioned whether the exercise is worthwhile. Certainly it becomes difficult if not impossible to establish cause and effect. Unfortunately many other people will wish to raise the questions about the financial justification of training, and if the trainer does not do so, others in the finance department and the boardroom will. This, then, becomes partly a political issue concerning the viability of the training function in the organization. The need for the trainer to undertake this kind of evaluation will depend partly upon the organizational climate, but the trainer should be prepared at least to present a counter to potentially hostile financial assessments. For a fuller discussion of cost-benefit analysis, *see* Cannon (1981).

Other techniques have been developed to evaluate the organizational climate and whether this has changed. Measures of this type are appropriate if the objectives of the programme are concerned with increasing the commitment of trainees to the organization and its operations or perhaps developing a more participative style of management. Several measures of organizational climate are available of which the best known is Likert's (1967) profile of organizational characteristics. However, these methods still run into the problems of isolating the changes due to training as opposed to those due to other internal and external factors.

Before embarking upon an evaluation at this level it is necessary to examine the original reasons for doing so carefully to ensure that it is an essential aspect of the study. The unpredictability of the environment means that it is never possible to demonstrate that organizational changes are due to the training alone and any lack of credibility at this level can cast doubts on any other results from a study.

OTHER DATA

So far this chapter has concentrated on the various types of methodology which are available for evaluation at the different levels within the cycle. However, it is not sufficient merely to collect data on say, behaviour changes, without looking at the other variables which influence the changes, and help to explain the results. Before looking in more detail at the variables which can be considered, it is helpful to look at the processes which occur when an individual attends a training course, either internally or externally run.

Initially the individual starts the training with attitudes and expectations which are a result of his previous work experience, discussions with his manager and the trainers about the course, the problems he currently faces in his job, his qualifications, the organization climate and, what often gets overlooked, the rumours about the training which are current within the organization, ie the grapevine. Once attending the training other variables become important such as the teaching methods used, the relationships with other trainees and the way he prefers to learn. All this has a major effect on the impact training has on an individual. At the end of the training and on his return to the job the trainee will have reactions to the learning which will affect whether it is transferred into

Figure 2
Training process

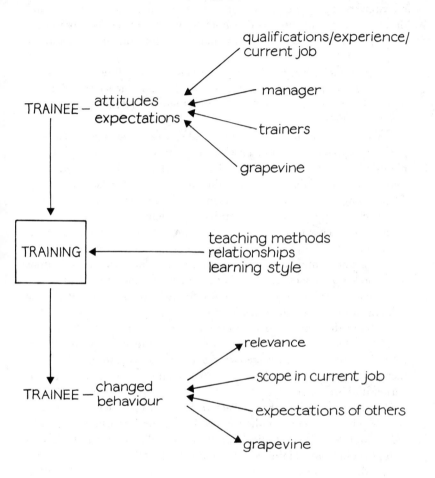

behaviour changes. It is this transfer of learning process which is difficult for many individuals and depends, among other things, on the perceived relevance of the learning, the scope he has within his job to change and the expectations of those with whom he works, especially those of his manager. At this stage the individual will also add to the company grapevine his views of the training.

This process is illustrated in figure 2 opposite. Therefore, at each of the three stages there are different factors which can influence the effectiveness of the training and so information on these is necessary to clarify any evaluation study.

Some of these factors are readily available to the evaluator. Current job title, qualifications and previous experience are usually part of a nomination system for courses and are therefore easily obtained. Attitudes and expectations are more difficult but nevertheless important. There seem to be three broad categories of attitudes to training which can be classified as keen, apprehensive and sceptical. The 'keen' trainee is one who is looking forward to the training and is confident both that it will be helpful and in his own abilities to handle the learning. The sceptic is also confident in his own abilities but for a variety of reasons has a low opinion of the training and its relevance to his job. The apprehensive trainee is less confident in himself, is unsure about why he is being trained and often has worries about neglecting his job. It has been found that this latter type is more likely to change his behaviour than the others and is certainly more receptive to the learning. These attitudes are very closely related to expectations and both can be measured using techniques such as the semantic differential discussed earlier in this chapter.

During the training, the interaction between the teaching style and the learning preferences of the trainees is of major importance. An individual who learns by practical experience is unlikely to gain the maximum benefit from training which is in the form of direct lectures. Therefore, if the learning style of the trainees can be assessed this will assist in the interpretation of learning evaluation data and provide evidence on the suitability or otherwise of the teaching methods. Kolb *et al* (1971) identify a cycle of learning styles and suggest that individuals have a bias towards one or more of these. This cycle comprises experience of a situation leading to reflection, then to the formulation of concepts and generalizations about it, which then lead to experiments and testing of the concepts which will eventually become concrete experiences, starting the cycle again. This can be illustrated in the following way in figure 3 opposite:

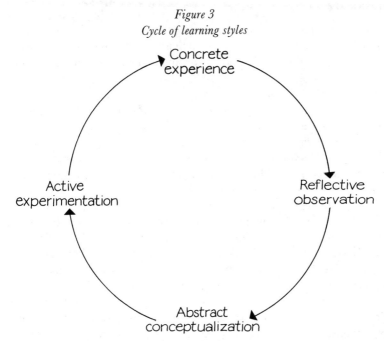

Figure 3
Cycle of learning styles

Concrete experience

Reflective observation

Abstract conceptualization

Active experimentation

This cycle has proved useful in providing an insight into the learning of trainees and, as a result of this, improved the way in which information is presented during courses.

There are obviously many factors which influence the process of learning. Baynes (1975) discusses the interdependence of the trainee himself, his work, his expectations, his learning and the role of the trainer. Pedler (1974) attempts to classify learning methods by levels of learning which are defined as memory, understanding, application and transfer. The most interesting work in this area is being carried out by the Centre for the Study of Management Learning at the University of Lancaster. For an example of their thinking see Burgoyne and Stuart (1977).

The part of the process which has aroused a great deal of interest is the third stage. After the training, how can the learning be transferred into new behaviour in the work situation. The factors which help or hinder this process have been investigated by many evaluators including Hogarth (1979) and Vanderput (1973). Figure 2 on page 263 identified three main factors to investigate, the perceived relevance of the training, the scope in the current job for change and the expectations of those with whom the individual works.

Relevance is of obvious importance. If the trainee does not see that the training has any bearing on his work then he will have no impetus to change his behaviour and is likely to reject the learning as useless or of academic interest only. Sometimes when this happens it is a result of poor preparation for the training by the individual's manager who often does not understand the purpose of the learning himself. The onus is therefore on the trainers to emphasize the relevance of the learning. Even if the trainee sees the learning as being relevant to his job, if he has no scope to make the changes he feels are necessary, then transfer will not take place. In this situation frustration with the organization is likely to arise and can lead to resignation from the job. One manager reported that on his first day back at work after a four-week programme he was told by his boss to 'forget that rubbish and get back to work', not an environment conducive to change. Some jobs are highly constrained by the nature of the work, the technology or the political pressures within the company whereas other jobs allow the individual considerable freedom to exercise choice in his behaviour. Job titles say little about the nature of the job itself and therefore it is dangerous to say, for example, that a salesman has more freedom than a production supervisor. One method for looking at jobs in terms of the constraints, demands and choices they offer the incumbent has been developed by Rosemary Stewart (1976). She has developed a classification of jobs by their pattern of contacts and profiles of demands which can be used to consider the amount of freedom an individual has for change. It might also be possible to develop her demand profile to evaluate behaviour changes, although there is no evidence that this has been done.

The comment reported from the manager to the trainee illustrates the importance of the expectations of others in assisting or hindering the transfer of learning into behaviour changes. A supportive atmosphere created by those around the trainee will enable him to experiment with new behaviours in the initial period after the training. Individuals often feel that they are worse at their job during this initial period because they are testing out the new learning in a real situation, and it is only after some time that they begin to feel confident in their new way of working. The role of their manager is obviously crucial in this process, as is discussed in Weiss, Huczynski and Lewis (1980), but the attitudes of colleagues and subordinates will also have considerable influence.

Conclusion

The cycle of evaluation which has been used in this chapter as the framework for an evaluation study assumes a cause and effect link between the training objectives, the training, the evaluation and back to the objectives at each level within the cycle. This emphasis on the feedback element is important. Evaluation research as an end in itself, while contributing to the general body of knowledge about the subject, is often theoretical and removed from the day to day issues which are important to both trainers and trainees. Therefore, all possible efforts must be made to ensure the relevance of the information obtained during any study of the training process.

This chapter started by stressing the importance of defining the reasons why an evaluation exercise is required. Lack of clarity in this area is often the reason why some evaluation exercises are seen as failures. Time spent at this initial stage in defining clearly and concisely the objectives of such an exercise will never be wasted.

The range and complexity of the methodology available may appear daunting and this chapter has only been able to discuss some of the many techniques available. However, careful definition of the objectives of evaluation will often narrow the choice of appropriate techniques and make the decision on which techniques to use somewhat easier. In practice it is often time and resource constraints which have the most influence on the design and approach taken in a study. Perfection in the experimental design is rarely possible and some would argue that it is never attainable. This is not a justification for not evaluating. Any relevant feedback on the effects of training is valuable. Training has often been called an act of faith but this does not mean that continual refinement and improvement is not essential and evaluation has a major role to play in this process.

References

Baynes M (1975). 'An examination of the major variables in the management training process', *Personnel Review*, Vol 4, No 1.

Budd WC *and* Blood DF (1972). *Educational Measurement and Evaluation*. London, Harper and Row.

Burgoyne JG (1975). 'Towards an evaluation of a business school graduate programme', *Omega*, Vol 3, No 4.

Burgoyne J and Stuart R (1977). 'Implicit learning theories as determinants of the effect of management development programmes', *Personnel Review*, Vol 6, No 1.

Campbell JP, Dunnette MD, Lawler EE and Weick KE (1970). *Managerial Behaviour, Performance and Effectiveness*, London, McGraw-Hill.

Cannon J (1979). *Cost-Effective Personnel Management*. London, IPM.

Davies J (1976). 'An evaluation framework for management development', *Industrial Training International*, October.

Department of Employment (1967). *Glossary of Training Terms*. London, HMSO.

Hamblin AC (1974). *Evaluation and Control of Training*. London, McGraw-Hill.

Hesseling P (1966). *Strategy of Evaluation Research*. Leiden, Holland, Van Gorcum.

Hogarth RM (1979). *Evaluating Management Education*. Chichester, Wiley.

Jessup G (1983). 'Trade testing skills' in Ungerson B (ed) *Recruitment Handbook*, 3rd edition. Farnborough, Hants., Gower.

Joyce L (1980). 'Participants reactions to different types of training courses', *Management Education and Development*, Spring 1980.

Kelly GA (1955). *The Psychology of Personal Constructs*. London, Norton.

Kolb DA, Rubin IM and McIntyre JN (1971). *Organizational Psychology: An Experimental Approach*. London, Prentice-Hall.

Likert R (1967). *The Human Organization: Its Management and Value*. London, McGraw-Hill.

Oppenheim AN (1967). *Questionnaire Design and Attitude Measurement*. London, Heinemann.

Pedlar M (1974). 'Learning in management education', *European Training*, Vol 3, No 3.

Rackham N, Honey P and Colbert M (1971). *Developing Interactive Skills*. London, Wellens.

Smith M and Ashton D (1975). 'Using the repertory grid to evaluate management training', *Personnel Review*, Vol 4, No 3.

Stewart R (1976). *Contrasts in Management*. London, McGraw-Hill.

Thomas B, Moxham J and Jones JAG (1969). 'A cost-benefit analysis of industrial training', *British Journal of Industrial Relations*, Vol 7 No 2.

Thurley KE and Wirdenius H (1973). *Supervision: A Re-appraisal*. London, Heinemann.

268

VANDERPUT M (1973). 'The transfer of training, some organisational variables', *European Training*, Vol 2 No 3.

WARR P, BIRD M *and* RACKHAM N (1970). *Evaluation of Management Training.* Farnborough, Hants., Gower Press.

WEISS E, HUCZYNSKI AA *and* LEWIS JW (1980). 'The superior role in learning transfer'. European Industrial Training, Vol 4 No 4.

WHITELAW M (1972). *The Evaluation of Management Training—A Review.* London, IPM.

Section Five

The final section of the book contains two chapters which deal with financial rewards and with what are usually termed fringe benefits. Payment systems is a vast subject which has been comprehensively covered in a number of books. In chapter 10 Duncan Wood outlines some of the main issues in designing and monitoring such systems. He emphasizes the importance of having a clearly thought out reward policy as the basis for deciding upon an appropriate system. He then outlines the four main types of payment that are offered in industry, examining what each involves and what each can achieve for an organization.

In chapter 11 Clive Moody covers the difficult and often neglected topic of fringe benefits, or what he prefers to call non-cash remuneration. In the opening section he outlines the importance and the extent of usage of this type of benefit. He then outlines the range of fringe benefits, from pensions to subsidized canteens and staff discounts. Because this subject has sometimes received little attention in personnel management texts, it is treated here at some length. This is particularly the case in relation to pensions, which, like many aspects of fringe benefits, is a rapidly evolving topic, subject to changes in government policy and requiring considerable expertise to administer, often beyond the expertise of the personnel department. However, as Clive Moody indicates, the personnel manager, as recruiter and industrial relations specialist, must also be well-informed about pensions and other fringe benefits since they inevitably impinge upon their work.

Chapter ten

Payment systems

INTRODUCTION

This chapter provides an introduction to the very complex subject of payment systems. It is unlikely that many personnel managers in their first or second jobs will have responsibility for pay policy and for developing pay systems. However they may well be involved in certain aspects, such as job evaluation exercises, in the administration of existing systems or in dealing with problems arising from it. It is therefore important to understand the components of pay and the way in which payment systems are developed and maintained. In particular, it is essential to be able to understand and apply some criterion to judge the suitability of particular payment systems and their need for revision or updating.

Payments may be defined as a reward for services rendered, or as the amount paid for the time during which an employee is at the disposal of the employer. Payment systems are concerned with the methods by which the amount and form of payment is decided.

Pay can also be seen as a means to an end. Both the levels of pay and the ways in which the levels, differentials and changes are determined communicate to employees the objectives and values of an organization.

This is not, of course, suggesting that pay is the only way of achieving or communicating company goals. Nor is it always the most effective way of motivating employees. Management should use a wide range of financial, operational, marketing and other techniques for this purpose. However, payment systems are rarely neutral in their impact upon behaviour.

Company objectives will be reflected in the payment policy, the policy in turn should determine the pay structure and systems, and the systems will require payment procedures to ensure that they are maintained.

Thus if the policy is to pay the market rate, then there will need to be a system for evaluating jobs and procedures for handling changes in job content. If the policy is to reward individual contributions or productivity then a payment system will be required which can measure that contribution, together with procedures for handling changes in the workload.

This chapter will therefore begin by considering the factors which determine the payment objectives and policy. It will then outline the systems for matching those objectives through:

basic pay, which reflects job content

contribution pay, whether assessed through individual performance appraisal, piecework or profit sharing

situation pay, which recognizes the demands of such factors as shift or overtime work

deferred pay, such as pensions or sickness or life assurance schemes.

Taken together these components can be termed total remuneration. The final section examines the maintenance and auditing of payment systems and procedures. Throughout the chapter the fact that there is no 'best payment system' will be emphasized. The best system is one which most closely integrates the needs of an organization with those of its employees, and these will change as the environment does in which the systems operate. What is appropriate for a local authority will be less appropriate for a marketing oriented organization, and the needs of both may be different in the 1980s compared with the 1970s. The determination of the best payment systems must be seen as a dynamic art rather than a precise, unchanging, science.

ESTABLISHING A PAYMENT POLICY

The first step in developing and maintaining an effective payment system is to determine and specify a payment policy. Many organizations have not clearly or explicitly considered what their pay policy should be; but an implicit or operational policy is often identifiable by examining their payment practices. Whether implicit or explicit, most organizations tend to adopt one of three general approaches.

One type of policy may be to pay the market rate; the organization is saying, in effect, 'If we want to employ people and to demand their maximum contribution then we have an obligation to provide payments which compare reasonably with similar work in similar organizations within the area from which we recruit (possibly nationally for a specialist or manager, but a 10 mile radius for factory operatives). Questions of productivity can only be determined by management'.

An alternative policy is to say that pay will be determined by the ability to pay. The organization is saying, 'Nobody owes us a living and changes in the cost of living or local pay rates are outside our influence. We can only set pay levels according to our profitability. When profits are high we will pay above the market rates, when they are low we cannot keep up—a different policy would cause redundancy or make us bankrupt'.

A third policy is to say that profits are outside the control of most employees and that pay should be related primarily to contribution. 'As management, we must provide conditions which make it easy for employees to work efficiently and productively. Our payment systems must communicate this requirement to all employees and must reflect their contributions rather than the market rate or profits which they cannot affect.'

In reality many organizations too often vacillate between such policies, following that which seems most expedient at a particular time. As a result their employees regard each of the messages which are communicated by the payment system cynically and believe that they merely reflect bargaining power. In such an environment the systems are bent or bastardized or manipulated according to day to day pressures. Instead of contributing to the needs of an organization they may be undermining them. For example the prospect of extra overtime may be used as a way of overcoming a problem of differentials but at the price of reduced productivity.

The compatibility of pay policies is made more difficult in multi-divisional or multi-site or multi-national organizations, especially when these are managed as semi-autonomous profit centres. In some circumstances such units may be separated only by a wall and in others they may be many hundreds of miles apart or in different countries. Some may be profitable, whilst others are making losses; some short of skilled craftsmen, others working short-time. The local cost of living, the levels of productivity or absenteeism may all vary widely. The need and desirability for common pay policies will depend in part upon whether employees see themselves as part of the same organization with similar jobs, or whether their concerns are closely linked to their own unit. Understandably those in the profitable areas will want to see this reflected in their earnings, whereas others will seek harmonization of benefits across the whole organization. The only certainty is that management will be challenged unless it has developed a coherent policy, whether to justify different or common treatment, and made this credible by the way in which it is applied.

The policy which is appropriate at a particular time can of course combine elements of the three approaches outlined above, but in any case must take account of both specific objectives and of the external and internal environment of the organization. Without a clear payment strategy, rationality and sound principles give way to *ad hoc* adjustments to pay in response to immediate pressures, and ultimately these will destroy the effectiveness of the payment systems.

At any one time there may be specific needs, among others things, to:

recruit and retain particular categories of employees

reduce waste or scrap

encourage greater flexibility of job or time or location

reward personal qualities such as good timekeeping or long service

permit rapid changes in work organization or technology

change or maintain differentials

increase the levels of effort.

The payment policy and systems must be able to cope with changes in these or in similar priorities.

Equally no payment policy can operate in a vacuum. What is appropriate has to reflect first the external environment. This will include levels of unemployment, trends in pay increases elsewhere and in the cost of living, the policies of governments and of employers' organizations and the availability of labour. Secondly the policy will depend in part upon the internal environment, including the order book, relationships between management and the managed, trade union activities, the type of work and levels of skill required and the scope for increased output or productivity or quality.

Finally the ways in which the policy is formulated and communicated (whether it is open or secretive, mechanistic or personal, rewarding high flyers or long service, encouraging cosy or abrasive relationships) will reflect the management style of the organization. It is right that this should be the case. If there is a contradiction between the two then the payment systems will be ineffective. For example a joint job evaluation committee will soon be bypassed if its proposals are overridden by autocratic management, and a participative management style may be hard to operate alongside an incentive system dependent upon bargaining about allowed times. Management and the managed will understandably negotiate about pay levels, but these negotiations will be eased if there is a separation of the HOW from the HOW MUCH. This means finding ways in which employees or their representatives can:

> participate in agreeing the objectives and in listing the obstacles to the achievement of those objectives

> be involved in finding ways of overcoming those obstacles

so that they are committed to, and feel a sense of ownership for, the resultant systems. In the environment of the 1980s it is difficult for the systems (whether for job evaluation or incentive payments or other elements) to be effective unless that commitment is present.

BASIC PAY

In most organizations basic pay will be the most significant part of remuneration. In some cases, (for example where there is no shift or overtime or incentive or merit pay) it may represent total remuneration. In a few, such as where pay is based solely upon commission or piecework, it may be absent but such circumstances are rare. In all organizations basic pay will depend in part upon an evaluation of the content of a job, ie how much skill is required, how long does it take to learn and the level of physical effort. Where there are only a few employees the owner may make these judgements unilaterally and may include an assessment of the individual's contribution. 'I pay Joe £X per week because he is doing an unskilled job, has only been with me for six weeks, and doesn't produce very much. I pay Charlie £X + 20 per cent because he has an easy job but has been with me for twenty years and is thoroughly reliable. I pay Fred £X + 50 per cent because he has the most skilled job and that's the market rate.'

When an organization and the range of work grows the judgements of one man, even if he is the owner, will be challenged by employees and perhaps by department managers who have a better knowledge of differences in job content. It becomes necessary to have consistency between and within departments, and a system is needed to evaluate new or changed jobs. At this point the process has to be formalized and a structured system of job evaluation may become necessary. It has to be emphasized however that there will still be many medium size or large organizations which do not use such a system but where both management and employees prefer to retain a more flexible structure based upon *ad hoc* (but acceptable) judgements which reflect local understandings and/or management values.

JOB EVALUATION

Job evaluation is concerned with assessing the differences in the content or demands between different jobs. Only the job is evaluated, not the person doing it or their level of ability. For payment purposes jobs will normally be grouped with others which have been assessed as having similar levels of content; this is the process of job grading. The principal stages in introducing or updating a job evaluated structure are summarized in the following paragraphs. For a fuller discussion see Thomason (1980).

The jobs to be covered
Is the system to apply to all jobs or restricted to all factory jobs or all clerical jobs; is it to include the supervisors or managers or salesmen? In determining the parameters of the system it is useful at an early stage to complete a job census which will list the jobs to be included and the numbers of employees in each. This will not only clarify the scope and define the border areas between employee categories but it will be useful when it comes to deciding which method to employ. The census will also make necessary some basic decisions about what is a job; for example do all or some secretaries share the same job description, do the assembly operators interchange and thus have a common job or do we have to evaluate separately each job on the assembly line?

Is it a management system or a joint one?
In most, but not all, unionized situations the trade unions will want to share in the management of the job evaluated structures, in the decisions about which methods to use, and in the evaluation process. For non-unionized groups it may be equally important to have the involvement of their representatives in order to get the support of the whole workforce, especially when the implementation and maintenance of the final structure raises problems, as it inevitably will. It is of course possible to have partially joint systems such as where trade union or other employee representatives share in deciding the method to be used but leave the evaluation to a management panel. There are also a few examples where the whole process is determined solely by trade unions without any management involvement. But in the environment of the 1980s it is probable that job evaluation will be most successful when it is devised and implemented on a joint basis.

278

Which method is to be used?

There are many different methods of job evaluation but the most widely used can conveniently be divided into three groups:

1   Whole job methods: these rely upon comparing the whole of one job with the whole of another job. The best known use some form of paired comparisons, or broad classification (such as skilled, semi-skilled and unskilled). They work best when the job category or family is narrowly defined, for example the foremen on their own or laboratory assistants on their own, or clerks on their own; when the number of jobs is limited probably to less than 100; and when changes in job content are infrequent.

2   Analytical methods: these require each aspect of a job to be assessed separately. These might include the requirements for previous experience, the responsibilities, the mental and physical demands. Analytical methods begin by agreeing the factors to be used and at some stage have to decide the relative values of these factors, ie the weighting process. Jobs accumulate points for each factor which is relevant (some, for example responsibility for the supervision of others, may not apply to all jobs) and the total points determine the rank order.

3   Two part methods: these are an extension of the analytical approach and the best known are profiling and factored direct consensus. In the first, jobs are assessed for each of the agreed factors at one of four levels (for example basic, medium, high, exceptional). They are then ranked by direct consensus and a mathematical formula is used to decide the weighting which is required for each factor to balance the two sets of judgements. In factored direct consensus, jobs are first ranked separately for each of the agreed factors. As with profiling there is then an overall ranking, and a mathematical process used to decide weightings for each factor which will match the two sets of judgements. These and similar two part methods have been increasingly used over the last decade to resolve the problem of factor weightings—the most difficult aspects of traditional analytical systems. This aspect becomes particularly important when it is necessary to embrace a wide range of jobs in the same job evaluated structure, which becomes increasingly likely with moves towards single status employment.

There are no golden rules for determining which method to use in which situation; in many cases adequate results could be achieved through several different methods. But factors to be taken into account when choosing between the alternatives include:

acceptability to management and to employees. This is the most obvious but critically important factor and may be determined by previous experience, by the apparent competence of the consultant or by other subjective reasons

simplicity. This might be related to acceptability but it is not always possible to achieve. For example it will be extremely difficult to ensure a simple system in multi-site organizations with a wide variety of jobs. Nevertheless it is still important to go for the simplest method of achieving the results required

job method stability. If there are frequent changes, then it is more likely that analytical methods will be needed

range of jobs. If there is a wide variety of jobs to be evaluated by the same method then an analytical method will be required

employee participation. If this is particularly important then direct consensus or profiling (which incorporates direct consensus) may be more attractive, since it allows more scope for the involvement of large numbers of managers and representatives

interface with other requirements. If the job analysis aspect of job evaluation is to contribute to, or be integrated with the job analysis used for other purposes such as selection, training or O & M studies, then an analytical system will be more useful. If it is important to have reliable comparisons with salaries paid for similar jobs in other organizations or to make comparisons between different subsidiaries within a larger group then the Hay MSL package will be more attractive than a tailor made system designed to fit one organization alone.

Evaluating the jobs

Whichever method is used, the job evaluation panel will need, as a minimum, job descriptions which relate to the selected method and factors, and which have been agreed with the job holder/s and the supervisor or manager. Additionally they may want to visit the job and/or to interview the job holder and manager or supervisor. The extent to which this is necessary depends upon the range of jobs and therefore the level of understanding which can be expected among the panel members.

How many grades?

The evaluation will produce a ranked list of jobs, and it then becomes necessary to group together those of similar value, that is, to decide the grades. Analytical systems may produce natural break points in the ranked list. For example there may be a cluster of jobs between 95 and

105 points, then another group between 120 and 130, and a third with 150 to 165 points. But in most cases judgements will be required about both the break points and the number of grades that will be most appropriate. If there are only a few grades each will embrace a wide range of jobs (thus making flexibility easier) and the pay differentials between each grade may be larger, making argument about upgradings more critical: those at the top of the wide grade will justifiably argue that their jobs are closer to those in the next grade than they are to those at the bottom of their own. If the results are being used to replace an existing pay structure then the new grades will often include employees who previously had different pay levels and some will question why those previously getting less pay are being brought up to their level. If there are many grades then some of these problems will be removed or diluted, but every time there is a small change in job content there may be an appeal for an upgrading—hence a detrimental effect on flexibility. The problem of getting acceptance of the resultant grades is probably the biggest reason for wanting to involve the representatives of employees in the process of job evaluation.

An appeals procedure

Job evaluation is not an exact science—at best it is a systematic, consistent, disciplined series of judgements. But there will invariably be some cases both initially and when changes arise or new jobs are introduced, when the job holder (possibly with the support of his manager) disagrees with the judgements that have been made. There is normally therefore a requirement for an appeals procedure. This may have one or two stages and may be an appeal to the original panel or to a separate group. Whatever the arrangements, it is important that the job holder should be encouraged to continue co-operation in his job whilst awaiting the results, that the appellant is given a proper opportunity to state the reasons for his appeal and that successful appeals do not cause other job holders to become dissatisfied creating the danger of the leap frogging.

Maintenance of the structure

All job evaluated systems will deteriorate unless there are two forms of maintenance procedure. The first has to cope with new jobs and with changes in the responsibilities of existing jobs. This will require arrangements for job descriptions to be prepared (possibly on an interim basis if the job is totally new) and for the job evaluation panel to meet at regular intervals. Additionally an auditing system is required since changes will take place which will gradually make the job description obsolete. The audit may require all descriptions to be checked once every two years eg 10 per cent every two months or 25 per cent every six months; they are circulated to the job holder and manager who have to check that the description is still valid. Where changes are identified by the audit they are then processed by the job evaluation panel.

The preceding paragraphs can only summarize the main constituents of a job evaluation programme. However they show that although there is no major mystery about the technique it requires considerable skill and commitment from top management if the results are going to provide an acceptable basic payment system and strengthen employee relations.

OTHER ASPECTS OF BASIC PAY

Job evaluation can assess differences in job content or worth within an organization, but in most cases it will also be necessary to assess the comparative market value of jobs. If pay levels follow closely those determined by national, industry-wide negotiations then this element may be largely determined at that level. Trade unions and employers alike will seek to defend their claims by reference to what they see as comparable jobs in comparable industries in (perhaps) comparable locations.

Whatever the national negotiations most employers will additionally want to be aware of comparable pay levels and where pay is determined by the company, with or without trade union involvement, then access to and/or participation in pay surveys will be critically important. Such surveys can take several different forms. They may arise through a 'club' of employers or personnel managers (possibly through the local branch of the Institute of Personnel Management) who exchange information about an agreed cross section of jobs. This may be on a local basis or may be at a national level covering a particular industry; the latter arrangement will obviously be necessary where information is required about the pay of those, such as managers or senior specialists who are recruited nationally.

A second source of information is the published surveys. The preparation and publication of salary surveys has been a growth industry in the last decade. The sponsors include professional bodies concentrating on the earnings of their members, recruitment agencies specializing in secretarial or clerical positions, management consultants principally concentrating upon management level positions and specialist publishing groups.

Whatever their sources, the value of such surveys will depend first upon the balance of the contributors; ie is it a representative sample comparable to the situation of the enquirer? Secondly the value depends upon the exactness with which the jobs have been defined; is it possible to match them realistically with the particular jobs being studied? Finally there will be questions about the pay statistics themselves; do they refer to basic pay or average earnings or total remuneration or what; and should there be reference to the value of other benefits such as a company car, contributory or non-contributory pension scheme and profit sharing?

Another point of comparison is with the shape of the pay curve. It is not a question of saying that one curve will be more appropriate than another, but it may be useful for an organization to question their own differentials if their curve is markedly different from that of other comparable organizations.

As with other aspects of payment systems, it is important to know the facts about the existing situation and whether there are logical or acceptable reasons for the shape of the resultant curve.

Basic pay depends therefore upon both internal and external comparisons. Other related matters concern the way it is calculated and the structure if any for growth in pay levels. The traditional distinctions in calculation between hourly, weekly and monthly paid arrangements with the allied differences in status are now being eroded. Many companies, either as part of a deliberate move towards single status organizations or for reasons of administrative convenience, now encourage employees to be paid monthly by credit transfer into their banks. Some make this more attractive by providing the payment in the middle rather than at the end of the month.

STAFF SALARY STRUCTURES AND INCREMENTAL SYSTEMS

Having established basic pay, growth within a pay level, that is, incremental systems, is largely confined to traditional staff or white collar positions. With less responsible jobs the growth may be limited to two or three modest annual increments, for example 2 per cent of basic salary per occasion. If incremental scales are going to apply to more senior positions then it is logical that there should be more steps, for example over five to seven years. In the private sector such scales do not apply widely to manual jobs but it has been argued that moves towards single staff status should mean the extension of incremental structures to such groups.

In most respects staff salary structures are based upon the principles described in this chapter. The main difference will be in the use of salary bands (rather than a single 'rate for the job') and in the private sector progress through the band will probably depend, at least in part, upon a judgement about individual merit or performance. In the past it was less likely that staff would be paid for overtime at premium rates or receive other plus payments but the growth of white-collar trade union-ism has meant that in some organizations such differences have largely disappeared. The principal distinction will be for management positions where overtime, call-out or similar payments are unlikely to apply (with consequent problems about the dividing line and the issue of how much compensation is built into the salary when promotion leads to a loss of overtime earnings).

Formal job evaluation systems are more widely used for staff salary structures whereas incentive payments are rare. Profit sharing plans or other company wide bonus payments (as described in the next section) tended to be fostered by the various statutory incomes policies of the 1970s and the continuing interest in financial participation as an aspect of more wide-ranging employee involvement, means that such payments now apply to many staff in private sector organizations.

CONTRIBUTION PAY

In one sense all pay is a reward for the contribution of an employee but this section is concerned with a separate reward related to a contribution which goes beyond an agreed base line. There are of course some who would argue that any such reward is to be deplored since it implies that basic pay is given for mere attendance at work; they believe that to reward the contribution made to the results of an organization suggests a wrong sense of values and too easily encourages a them/us, bargaining climate of relationships.

In practice however this is a minority view. Most companies and most employees believe that distinctions can and should be made to reflect differences arising from:

> personal experience or merit

and/or individual effort or results

and/or group effort or results

and/or factory or divisional or company-wide results.

More debatable and less clear in most payment systems is whether contribution pay is meant to act as a direct incentive which will affect behaviour or as a communicator which may affect attitudes. Obvious illustrations of the first are individual piece-work schemes or commission only earnings which directly reflect the behaviour, effort or results of the employee. At the other extreme would be the profit sharing scheme of ICI where the individual contribution cannot be separated from those of thousands of other employees, but where the scheme may still be of value in influencing attitudes towards the company and towards the introduction of change or new technology or more efficient working arrangements.

As with other aspects of the payment system the starting point has to be a consideration of the objectives of contribution pay. Only then is it possible to assess the potential usefulness of alternative ways of measuring or rewarding that contribution. This analysis will need to consider three groups of questions:

how/where/when to measure the contribution

how to link the measure with the payment

how to maintain and develop the consequent arrangements.

THE MEASUREMENT OF CONTRIBUTION

In most organizations it is possible to measure contribution in one or more of four ways. Physical measures such as tons or numbers of units produced or pages printed, are the easiest to understand but produce problems if there is a wide range of products. Time standards when properly applied can be the most objective, for example minutes per unit of work, but are less easy to apply to creative work, may be expensive to maintain and can encourage restrictive, protective attitudes. Financial ratios will always be present but in a large organization special efforts may be needed to make ratios such as Added Value per £ payroll costs, meaningful to those whose contribution is to be rewarded. Finally, subjective measures, including the quality of service, levels of housekeeping or merit, in some cases may be the only measures which are possible. But if their subjectivity is going to be acceptable as part of a payment system then considerable efforts will be needed to ensure consistency and a sense of fairness about the results.

The measure may be pitched at the individual, group, departmental, plant or company-wide level. The choice should be influenced by the type which is thought to best fit the previously defined objectives. If it is profit then the location probably needs to be company-wide, if it is merit then it will be individual, if it is a physical measure then this may be applicable at a group or departmental level.

Two general points need to be made about measurement. The first is to emphasize the need for, and value of, 'telling us how we are doing'. This is an essential element of motivation at all levels, as important to the director as to the machine operator, and it is vital that the link with payment systems does not dilute the effectiveness of the motivating aspect. This means also that the measurement must not be seen or used as a policing tool, a way of imposing sanctions and penalties. Secondly it is useful to follow the pyramid concept, illustrated below, which begins by looking for the broadest measurement to satisfy the objectives, and only examines more local or individual measures if the former is shown to be unsuitable:

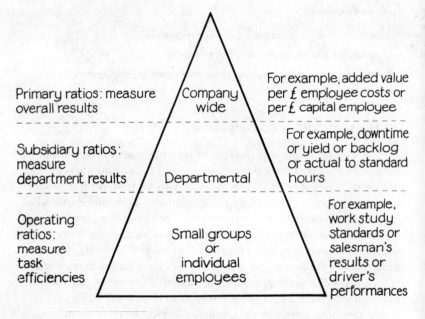

Primary ratios: measure overall results — Company wide — For example, added value per £ employee costs or per £ capital employee

Subsidiary ratios: measure department results — Departmental — For example, downtime or yield or backlog or actual to standard hours

Operating ratios: measure task efficiencies — Small groups or individual employees — For example, work study standards or salesman's results or driver's performances

Too often the examination begins with the individual shopfloor results and only, as a 'second best' accepts the broader alternatives.

LINKING THE MEASURE TO A REWARD

In simplistic terms broad measures encourage co-operative attitudes whilst individual measures encourage effort, but as with most generalizations this statement has to be qualified by the environment of the work

286

place. Thus in a factory assembling consumer electrical products the development of more automated assembly lines, which dictated the pace of work, made incentive schemes obsolete and they were replaced by high day rates. But when subsequently a job enlargement programme gave operators the opportunity to assemble a whole product they asked for the introduction of individual incentives to recognize their different levels of skill and effort and as an aid to their pacing of the job.

A full examination of all the forms of contribution pay has to be beyond the ambitions of this chapter but the following schedule compares some of the more widely used alternatives.

System	Comments
Merit or performance appraisal payments linked to the systematic assessment of the behaviour of the individual.	Principally used in staff (rather than manual) areas; often criticized as being too subjective ('blue eyes' systems) and/or because they direct attention away from the key purpose of performance appraisal, that is to improve performance by identifying and removing the obstacles to such an improvement. (See chapter five).

Earnings vary by output and operators control output

Piecework

Rewards are based upon a constant and specified price per unit or piece produced regardless of time taken.	A strong incentive to make quantity, possibly at the expense of quality. Usually only suitable where there is an unlimited supply of work and output is not restricted by production requirements.

Payment-by-results

A financial incentive in which the employee's earnings are related to the work done or other factors within the control or influence of the individual or group to which he belongs. The standard time based upon work measurement or estimates.	As with piecework, adequate work should be provided and output must not be restricted. A good incentive to effort, but a disincentive to method changes. May be a source of friction between employees and management over measurement, or payment for lost time.

Multi-factor schemes

A payment-by-results scheme where rewards are based upon more than one factor, eg quality, machine utilization, process yield, output.	Suitable if the factors which are important can be defined. Often suffers from problems in measurement and usually includes some weighting which causes imprecision.

287

Earnings vary by quantity but operators only partially control output

Contract plans

An operator undertakes to perform at an agreed pace, for which he receives a fixed weekly addition to his basic rate: the operator can re-negotiate the level at which he will work.

A system that attempts to combine the advantages of a measured daywork system and a payment-by-results scheme. It may be administratively difficult.

Profit sharing

Company-wide schemes where payment depends upon profitability of the company or some other overall measure of results eg Added Value per £ employee costs. Differentials can be built in for differences in responsibility or length of service and to allow for the prior payment of a fixed return on capital.

Equitable in principle and identifies employees with overall company goals. But remote from individuals and so an indirect incentive. Requires trust, good communications, and situations where chosen measure (profits, added value etc) is not excessively influenced by external considerations or by financial or investment or sales promotion policies. Will have tax advantages if payments available as shares.

Productivity plans

An extra payment based upon the success of employees in reducing costs, expanding production or increasing sales, usually measured by an overall index eg Scanlon or Added Value.

Similar effects as profit sharing, but the index can be chosen to insulate employees from major factors outside employee control. Measurements and/or payments can be linked to particular groups within an organization.

Earnings vary by quantity but management controls output

Measured daywork

A fixed payment for achieving a performance level or output rate, mutually agreed; payment is only withdrawn if failure to meet target can be demonstrated to be the fault of operators. Can include steps for different levels and may be tied to either individuals or to groups.

A good incentive to maintain customary effort levels and flexible in operation. But good supervision is essential and it must be possible to hold waiting time at low levels. Attractive to operators since it provides stable earnings, and convenient to management since they control output.

Whichever the system that seems to be most appropriate there will be many associated questions. How big should be the potential reward as a percentage of basic salary, how frequently should results be measured and rewarded (it does not have to be the same for both), who will be eligible to participate, what happens to the contribution and to the rewarding of new employees, what happens (if anything) when adverse factors outside the control of employees affect their results?

Overall the effective use of contribution pay depends upon twelve key factors which can serve as a checklist for those trying to determine the viability of this approach:

1 Output or results or effort can be measured or assessed to an acceptable standard; in most jobs people can sense the levels which are being achieved from experience but if payment is to be tied closely to these levels then the measurement has to be based upon agreed criteria.

2 The results are directly or mostly attributable to the individual or group to whom payment is being made; thus profit sharing may be highly relevant for executives, for other groups however it may be justified not as an incentive but for other social or morale-building or attitude changing reasons.

3 The pace or output or quality or effort or whatever else is being measured, is to a significant degree under the control of the employee/s concerned.

4 Management is able to maintain a steady work flow so that employees are not penalized by stoppages and the system is not distorted by a complexity of 'lieu' payments.

5 The effects of changes in methods, materials and equipment are minimized.

6 The mechanics and philosophy of the system ensure that when results deteriorate, discussion is concentrated upon what can we do to overcome the problems, rather than upon sanctions/blame/arguments.

7 Earnings are reasonably stable; this is expected so that employees can meet family/social obligations and if not provided employees will try to distort the system in order to achieve stability.

8 The proportion of average earnings (excluding overtime) which takes the form of a variable bonus does not exceed one quarter; this reflects the BSI relationships between a day work rate and an incentive rate of working; a minimum level may also be necessary but the size will depend upon a variety of circumstances, eg directness, frequency of payment.

9 The 'earning curve' or 'improvement effect' is either taken into account when establishing or revising standards, or overcome by setting a maximum or cut off point on the earnings curve.

10 Employees understand the measurement and payment systems and their representatives have had training in the techniques being used.

11 The incentive encourages the trial and implementation of new methods.
12 The incentive will motivate the company and management (eg through providing a fair return on capital and/or good quality) as well as employees.

Given these requirements it is understandable that the design of suitable financial incentives is the most difficult aspect of payment structures. For most companies however payments related to results will be necessary at some stage in their development and these may be as necessary for managers as they are for direct production operatives. The tax concessions on profit sharing and the adoption of Added Value based payment plans are not only indicative of the recent interest, but will themselves encourage wider use. The need to relate earnings to a company's 'ability to pay' must also promote the use of financial incentives.

MAINTENANCE AND DEVELOPMENT

A bonus or merit related increase will not by itself do anything to increase the contribution of employees. This will only happen if next week, month, year they are working differently from the practices of last week, month, year and this requires a change in attitudes and/or behaviour. The skilful introduction of a new contribution-related payment can give impetus to the required changes but this will only endure if the system is both maintained and developed.

Maintenance requires procedures for updating the standards periodically and checking that they are being applied correctly. Thus an added value ratio or a work measured standard may need to be reviewed if there are significant changes in product mix or capital employed, or in raw materials or manufacturing methods. Unless there is a regular and structured audit most systems of contribution pay will degenerate and will end up with working practices which are contrary to the needs of the organization.

Development requires a recognition that today's objectives may be different from those in two years time. Today the pressure may be on increasing output, tomorrow it is possible that quality will be more critical, or that we need to encourage managers to develop a readier acceptance of new technology or methods. It is rare that a system of contribution pay will endure for more than five years; by the end of such a period the demands on the organization will require a change in the ways in which contribution is assessed and rewarded.

Perhaps the biggest danger comes from assuming that a bonus payment can provide more than is within its power, of assuming that it can offset the effects of poor supervision or the problems of inefficient production systems, or that a profit sharing plan will act in the same way as a direct incentive. The analysis suggested in the previous pages can produce a well constructed bonus system but it cannot be wholly effective unless that system is in tune with the total working environment.

SITUATION PAY

The permanent characteristics of a job will normally be recognized and rewarded within basic pay. But there will be other features such as overtime, shift working or other unsocial hours, a requirement for call-outs or for temporary unpleasant work, which will be rewarded separately.

The first distinction is whether the payments related to such features are made when the event occurs (normal for overtime or shifts) or on a regular basis to allow for such occurrences. In the latter group can come call-out payments which may be a regular amount to allow for the possibility of a specialist being required to respond to a call or emergency at any time and at short notice. With some supervisory groups where it is wrong for them to have an incentive to work overtime, a fixed payment may be made to recognize the periodic but unmeasured requirement to work extra hours.

The second distinction is whether situation pay is calculated as a percentage of the basic rate or as a fixed sum. There is a tendency for overtime to be expressed on a percentage basis, for example time and a quarter for the first two hours, time and a half for further hours, double time for all Sunday hours. Some shift premium systems use a similar structure but in other cases employers and trade unions prefer a fixed sum, for example £1000 per annum for continuous seven day shifts or £15 per week for night shifts, £10 per week for afternoon shifts. One of the arguments in favour of such arrangements is that the inconvenience of unsocial hours is the same for somebody on a low wage as it is for a higher paid, more skilled employee.

The inevitable growth of more capital intensive industry must encourage its use over more hours in the week so that the case for more shift work is strengthened. This development is also now found widely in administrative areas with an increasing use of computer installations on a shift work basis. It is likely therefore that shift premiums will tend to increase as the demand for such working expands.

Where working conditions are constant it is usual to recognize any differences within a job evaluation structure. But in manufacturing there are often occasional but extremely unpleasant jobs either resulting from a breakdown, for example in the sewage system, or from the needs of a periodic overhaul. Although theoretically the likelihood of such occasions can be forecast and rewarded through a regular small addition to basic pay, it is often more realistic to provide a larger and more attractive sum at the time that the extra effort is needed.

Finally many organizations will include under the heading of situation pay, extra rewards which are dependent upon the geographical location of the job. These may be intended to offset the extra costs of an area and London Weighting in the Civil Service and in many other national but dispersed organizations is used for this purpose. Alternatively they may be required to offset the remoteness or unpleasantness of a location such as a North Sea oil platform.

DEFERRED PAY

In many companies up to 40 per cent of total remuneration is in the form of a payment which comes when the employee is not at work. This includes contributions by the employer to pensions, life assurance, sickness, long-term disability and similar schemes. These are often broadly grouped with other forms of employee benefits such as canteens or company cars. Both are the subject of the next chapter.

Two aspects, however, concern payment systems. The first is that all such payments need to be seen as part of total remuneration. In most companies it is unrealistic to consider only that part of payroll costs which are provided in cash. If pay is a means to an end—the recruitment and retention of able and motivated employees—then there will be cases when the deferred pay can be a significant contributor to that end. Hence the need for example when using salary survey information, to take account of total remuneration. It is even more important that managers are aware of such figures when deciding whether to recruit, and an increasing number of employers also provide an annual personal statement to each employee so that everybody is aware of the total cost of their employment. Too often, however, money is spent in this area because it is vaguely assumed to be desirable or necessary, without any serious attempt to calculate the benefits which are assumed to come to the employer.

The second aspect concerns the use of systems which enable an employee to decide how much of his total remuneration should be in cash and how much in deferred pay. Known sometimes as 'cafeteria systems' these normally apply to executive positions. They entitle the employee to tailor his remuneration package to his personal needs and situation. Thus the younger executive with a young family may opt for a larger but mass produced car, low pension entitlements, high life assurance and low private medical insurance. As his family grows up the mix of his preferences will change.

Where such systems apply there are three key requirements; the first is that all recipients are required to accept certain minimum levels of benefits such as a minimum level of life assurance to ensure that a widow and children have some protection. Secondly that changes to the package can only be made at stated intervals, possibly every two or three years, so that the administrative burden is eased. Finally that recipients are given some independent counselling by a tax and accountancy expert on the implications of their various options.

We have now examined the characteristics of the four main types of payment system and identified some of the main criteria which help to determine which one, or, in most cases what combination of systems, will be most suitable. There is unlikely to be a system which is clearly 'better' for a given organization and the final choice will depend heavily on the judgement and skill of the personnel managers. As a form of summary, the four main types of pay structure are expressed diagrammatically in figure 1.

THE AUDIT

The chapter began by defining payment systems as 'means to an end', and emphasizing that both the 'means' and the 'ends' have to reflect the external and internal environment of an organization. Since these environments and the consequent management goals are constantly changing, the payment systems must themselves be constantly decaying as with time they become further removed from the conditions which existed at their inception. Hence the need for regular audits which monitor the components of pay and tune the systems to meet current needs. Unless this is done the decay reaches a stage when the cost and effort needed for a revival becomes so large that both management and employees are

Figure 1
Pay structure summary

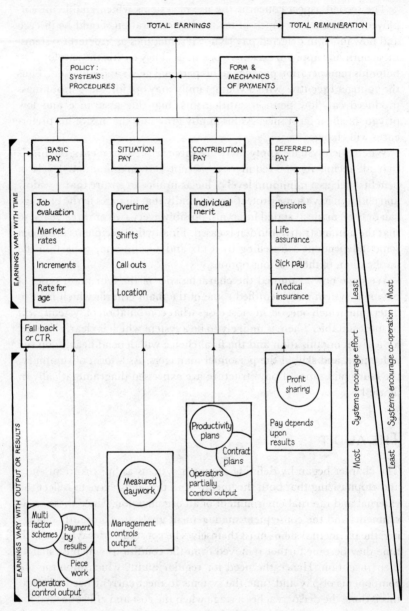

inhibited from taking the necessary initiatives. Job evaluation schemes become distorted, incentives lose their impact, shift or overtime premiums become ends in themselves—but nobody is prepared to propose a reconstruction for fear of what it will do to the uneasy truces or agreements which will have been fashioned to maintain a superficial stability.

The role of the Personnel Manager must therefore include the responsibility for a systematic review of the key indicators, probably on an annual basis. This might be timed as part of the preparation for annual pay negotiations or as component in the annual update of the organization's corporate plan. In the latter case it would be normal to look ahead over a three to five year span and thus seek to ensure that any changes to the payment systems will be targeted to match the anticipated long-term needs.

Given the primary purposes of pay and the need for employee acceptance of both the objectives and the systems there will be obvious advantages if employees and their representatives are involved in the audit. This will support the separation of the HOW from the HOW MUCH referred to previously so that however contentious the pay negotiations become they are less likely to threaten the payment systems. If employees are involved in the audit, identification of the problem areas and in the development of changes so that they feel a sense of ownership for the results then they are more likely to resist moves that will weaken the systems.

The stages in the audit will vary according to the complexity of the existing arrangements but they will probably include:

1 A review or re-statement of pay objectives: what are they now, will marketing or technological or external changes suggest a change in the medium term or longer term future?
2 A re-matching of objectives with components: which objective is achieved or helped by that long standing Christmas bonus payment, are the weightings of the job evaluation system still relevant, does the incentive scheme for salesmen contribute to the priorities that we now demand from our salesmen?
3 Checking the effectiveness with which the components are applied: this must begin with a statistical analysis covering such aspects as:

   job evaluation drift, that is, changes in the number of jobs and employees in each grade—are they beginning to cluster too heavily in the senior grades?

   overtime earnings: how do they vary between departments or

crafts, how regular have they become, are they affecting differentials?

incentive payments: is there any drift in bonus earnings or in the percentage of lieu time or make-up payments?

the shape of the pay and earnings curves: are these changing and if so do the changes cause any problems, do they indicate why problems are being found in other areas such as recruitment or promotion?

the cost of employee benefits as a percentage of total payroll costs: are changes in line with a long-term policy or arising in an *ad hoc* unmanaged way?

comparisons with the local labour market: are we still at the level which reflects our recruitment needs and the calibre of employees being sought?

4 Modifying the payment systems or individual components to bring them into line with the pay policy and with the anticipated requirements of the organization over the next year or two.

The purpose of the audit is not merely to check that we are getting 'value for money' but to identify those areas where a small change or correction now will avoid the possibility of a major difficulty at a future date. The audit and the subsequent consideration of the results by line management reminds managers of the role of payment systems as an essential aid to the achievement of results.

CONCLUSIONS

As stated at the beginning of this chapter there is no such thing as 'the best payment system'. The system can only be evaluated in terms of its effectiveness in helping management to achieve certain objectives, and there will be many factors which help determine which components of a payment structure are most appropriate for a given set of objectives. The potential complexity is illustrated in the scheme developed by Lupton and Gowler. This presents a twenty-three factor framework which takes into account the technological, labour market and structural dimensions of an employment situation together with its susceptibility to labour disputes. Alternative models have been produced by management consultants and academics but they all share the need to tailor the system to a particular environment.

The only certainty is that payment systems tend to decay as requirements change. Unless they can be adjusted and tuned periodically, the decay will reach a stage when the system is actively working against the needs of an organization. The role of the personnel specialist is not merely to know the mechanics of payment systems but also to have a sensitivity for the indicators which suggest that changes are required and the judgement to determine the direction in which the changes should go.

FURTHER INFORMATION

There are several professional or other organizations which can provide detailed information or literature; these include:

> Institute of Personnel Management
> Advisory Conciliation and Arbitration Service
> Industrial Society
> Management Consultants Association
> Institute of Management Services

Additionally many of the larger employers' associations (and some trade unions) have specialist offices advising on payment systems eg Engineering Employers Federation, Chemical Industries Association, EETPU.

FURTHER READING

ARMSTRONG M and MURLIS H (1980). *A Handbook of Salary Administration*. London, Kogan Page.

BOWEY A (1981). *Handbook of Salary and Wage Systems*. Farnborough, Hants., Gower.

GENDERS P (1981). *Wages and Salaries*. London, Institute of Personnel Management.

LUPTON T (ed) (1972). *Payment Systems*. Harmondsworth, Middx., Penguin.

Office of Manpower Economics, *Measured Daywork*. London, HMSO.

THOMASON G (1980). *Job Evaluation: Objectives and Methods*. London, IPM.

WOOD EG (1978). *Added Value*. London, Business Books.

Chapter eleven

Pensions and other forms of non-cash remuneration

INTRODUCTION

A company seeks to attract and retain well-motivated employees through a variety of cash rewards, of which wages, salaries and bonuses are the most obvious and well understood. In recent years more attention has been paid to non-material rewards, either to satisfactions intrinsic to the nature of a job or to its social and environmental aspects. This chapter is concerned with a less frequently discussed but nevertheless highly important area, that of benefits bought by the employer on behalf of the employee, often referred to as 'fringe benefits'. The actual size of current pension, car and other benefits in financial terms has made this term a misnomer. In replacing it with 'non-cash remuneration' it has to be remembered that these benefits could be purchased at some level directly by the employee himself. He might have more cash to do so if the company were not to do it for him.

The reasons for a company's decision to offer fringe benefits will be better understood after some discussion of their nature and extent, as will the criteria for the company's selection of one particular kind or level of benefit rather than another. Pension issues will be examined in some detail, but only a more cursory look can be given here at other forms of benefit. It is hoped that personnel staff involved in policy formulation or administration of these benefits will gain some practical help from these pages and that some links between benefit strategies and personnel strategy generally will become clear.

Pensions and life assurance schemes

Personnel policies and pensions

Pension and life assurance schemes are probably the oldest form of non-cash remuneration in most organizations and usually the most important to the employee. However, the visible glamour surrounding the company car and its immediate value often pushes pensions into second place for the younger employee.

Most of this chapter is devoted to pension schemes because it is the area where personnel managers often need most help. The simplest technicalities of pensions can baffle them. Most personnel managers reach at once for help from the company pensions manager, from external consultants, insurers or whoever is available. This is not always wrong: personnel staff should scarcely try to answer the more detailed or complex questions themselves. But if personnel managers can cope with the complexities of bonus incentive schemes, job evaluation systems and financial information, there is no reason why they should not also develop a reasonable understanding of pensions.

Pension matters crop up for one reason or another almost every day in the life of a personnel manager. It is not simply a matter of pensions on normal retirement. Policies and practices in recruitment, employee motivation, collective bargaining, participation, terminations and redundancy all interact with pension questions. Traditionally, pensions have been the responsibility of the financial or secretarial function within an organization but there has been a tendency in recent years to allocate responsibility for pensions to the personnel function and it is interesting to note that the Inbucon Salary Survey now places the job of pensions executive firmly in the personnel area.

The state pension scheme

The basic pension (old-age pension) is a flat rate amount payable from age 65 for men or age 60 for women and has been more or less index-linked. The full pension is payable to people who have paid the requisite National Insurance contributions but married couples receive a higher total pension even if only one person has 'earned' a right to full pension. The basic pension is set at just about subsistence level.

The Earnings Related State Pension (the additional component) is the second

300

tier of the State Scheme and is an interesting blend of the 'average' and 'final salary' concepts discussed below. Benefits at the rate of 1/80th of Upper Band Earnings (earnings in the band between a lower level £32.50 pw in April '83) and an upper level or cut-off point—around seven times the lower level (£235 pw in April '83) are credited to the member in respect of each year of membership. The best 20 years in the employee's post-1978 career will count. In addition, the credit for each year is revalued in line with the general level of earnings. In a sense, it is an average salary scheme with inflation proofing, both pre- and post-retirement. The maximum benefit is therefore 20/80ths or 25 per cent of Upper Band Earnings and no one will achieve this before April 1998. There is no lump-sum death benefit under the State Scheme but there are provisions for both widows' and widowers' pensions.

All employees must contribute to the State Scheme at the full rate up to the Lower Earnings limit but employees who are members of a contracted-out scheme enjoy a reduction in the level of contributions related to Upper Band earnings. There is no tax relief on contributions to the State Scheme, which form part of the overall National Insurance contributions. Employers with contracted-out schemes also enjoy a reduction in National Insurance contributions.

TYPES OF PRIVATE OCCUPATIONAL PENSION SCHEME

Flat-rate schemes merely provide a fixed amount of pension payable from retirement date, for example £5 per annum in respect of each year of service. These are mainly works or shopfloor schemes and were often purely designed to contract out of the now-defunct State Graduated Scheme. Some may still be found where companies 'live on top' of the State earnings related scheme but they are clearly unsatisfactory in themselves and quite inadequate for contracting-out purposes.

Average salary schemes were the most popular type of staff scheme in the 1950s and early 60s. The pension entitlement was built up on a brick by brick basis at the rate of, for example, two per cent of salary each year. Given that two per cent is 1/50th this would be quite satisfactory if there were little or no inflation on salaries. The obvious drawback is that the pension earned in respect of a member's early career bears no relation to the salary earned at the time of retirement. Such a scheme is rather like the State Earnings Related Scheme but without the revaluation (pre-retirement inflation proofing).

301

Money purchase schemes were often popular amongst employers because the company's level of contributions was fixed rather than involving a 'blank cheque'. Under such schemes a fixed amount of contribution (usually a percentage of the employee's salary) was used to purchase pension in the year in question. Although it was normal for earnings to rise with age, the main drawback was that since pensions cost more as people get older, the contributions paid into the scheme near to retirement produced very small amounts of pension. The size of the pension was not really related to final or career-average salary but was more a matter of pot-luck depending on the pattern of salary increases in relation to age.

Final salary schemes are the most common form of private occupational scheme and it is hard to imagine that they will be superseded, whatever changes there may be in the exact level of benefit offered. Such a scheme relates the pension to a member's pensionable salary at or near to retirement age. The most common fractions used are 1/60th and 1/80th, the former producing a pension of 2/3rds final salary for 40 years membership and the latter a pension of half final salary. This is the only satisfactory scheme for the purpose of contracting-out of the Earnings Related Scheme, and even then, the rules must contain certain safeguards for people leaving service and widows' pensions.

Supplementary or top-hat schemes are merely schemes which either top up the main company schemes or offer an alternative to them for a select group of senior executives. Such schemes often build up pension at an accelerated rate so that a full Inland Revenue maximum pension of two thirds final salary, the maximum permitted under an approved scheme, may be earned for only 20 and sometimes as little as 10 years' membership. Additional death benefits may also be provided. It is normal for these schemes to be non-contributory as far as members are concerned, particularly if they contribute to the main company scheme.

WHAT DO PENSIONS COST?

It is important for personnel managers to understand the basics of pensions funding. Without this, it is impossible to make a useful contribution to questions of policy in such areas as recruitment, early retirement and redundancy. A pension is merely an income payable from a given age. Whether it is an *ex gratia* amount payable out of the till or an insured annuity, the two most important factors in determining cost are *interest* and *mortality*. For example, the actuary of an insurance company offering immediate annuity policies uses mortality tables to determine how long the pensioner is likely to live and makes certain assumptions about the likely amount of interest to be earned on the lump sum premium paid by the purchaser.

Other factors are also taken into account such as whether or not the pension is guaranteed for a minimum of, say, five years, whether pension is payable monthly, quarterly or annually, whether there is any widow's pension built in, whether there is any form of inflation-proofing and, of course, what additions are necessary to cover administration expenses and to provide some profit. Nevertheless, interest and mortality remain the two most important factors.

Traditionally, insurance companies offered deferred annuity policies for the provision of pensions under occupational schemes and there were two main types of costing: level annual premium and single premium. The annual premium method is very similar to that used for a private endowment assurance policy and results in a fixed annual premium per £1 per annum of pension at retirement age. The premium is payable from the age when the pension liability arises, that is, on joining the scheme or from an annual renewal date following a pay increase, until the pension matures at retirement age. This method would work well if there were no inflation or no salary progression. The problem is that these factors have become much more prominent in the past two decades. Given that employees' contributions are fixed at anything between 0 per cent and eight per cent of salary, the employer's cost rises dramatically under the annual premium costing method due to the cumulative effect of increasing the pension entitlement year by year and building up more and more additional premiums which become in any case higher per £1 of pension as the employee gets nearer to retirement.

The single premium costing method was more prevalent in the 1950s and '60s. Under this system the employee's pension entitlement is purchased outright by one 'single' premium payable in the year that the liability arises. For example, let a non-contributory scheme give a pension entitlement of £20 *per annum* pension for someone aged 40 in respect of that particular year's membership of the scheme. A single premium is payable by the employer to purchase the deferred annuity of £20 from retirement age, the cost of which is governed by the annual rate of interest or investment yield (both up to retirement age and the eventual death of the pensioner), the age from which the pension is payable, the likely period of time that the pension will be payable plus the normal administration and profit expenses.

303

This method of paying for pensions has also proved to be unsatisfactory. Both the annual premium and single premium methods relied on the natural process of replacing people leaving service with younger people earning lower salaries to maintain a stable employer cost. Inflation, improvements in the level of benefits provided under pension schemes and the inability of employers to replace leavers at lower salaries have made this impossible in practice. Insurers and self-administered pension fund managers alike have sought to try and find stable funding methods which enable employers to budget their pension costs accurately several years ahead. They wish to avoid an annual surprise, or even shock, once the renewal costs of the pension scheme have been determined in the light of salary and membership changes. Employers want to know what pensions will cost *before* pay increases are awarded.

The modern concept is to get away from the precision of exact deferred annuity premium rates and to delay the purchase of the promised pension until the need arises at the point of retirement. In fact, many large schemes do not use insurance companies at all but merely pay pensions directly out of the private pension fund. Nowadays, employers rely very heavily on the actuaries and investment managers associated with their pension schemes. Very simply, having determined the shape of the pension scheme in terms of benefit levels and retirement ages, the actuary recommends a funding level as a percentage of payroll and the employer hopes that this will hold good until the next actuarial review of the scheme (usually every three years, unless there are any major changes in benefits or retirement ages). In making his recommendation the actuary will have asked the employer to give him some guidance as to the likely level of pay increases which may be assumed and he will also have consulted the investment managers about the likely yield on investments. He is then able to take a broad view of the scheme and to predict what rate of funding is required to meet the liabilities.

The whole process is of course interactive because the employer cannot determine what level of benefits can be afforded until he knows how much they are likely to cost and the actuary cannot make his recommendations until he has some guidance on the salary increase and investment yield assumptions. It will be seen that the bulk of the contributions to a scheme in any one year, both employer and employee, are directed towards the provision of benefits for the older members who are about to retire. Unlike State schemes, it is not normal for private occupational schemes to rely on current contributions to provide the pensions of existing pensioners on a 'hand to mouth' basis. The actuary aims to keep the scheme funded so that it is, at least, capable of providing all the

304

benefits promised in the event of discontinuance. This means pensions already being paid and pensions to members who have not yet reached retirement age. However, some schemes may be funded below discontinuance level for a few years if, for example, they have a heavy liability for previously unfunded past service pensions which will gradually reduce and which would otherwise result in an intolerably high immediate funding rate.

The final point in this section underlines the fallacy of linking company contributions directly to individuals. Over the years we have moved away from the attempt to measure and to meet the costs for the provision of each individual's pensions entitlement year by year. We now commonly use a more stable employer's overall funding rate, expressed as a percentage of payroll, which builds a fund to provide pensions as and when they are required. (A portion of the contributions is also used to provide the lump sum death benefits associated with a pension scheme and which are normally insured.) This means that although an employer's contribution may conveniently be expressed as, for example, 10 per cent of each employee's salary, it is quite wrong for anyone to think that such contribution is allocated solely for the benefit of the individual concerned. In fact, under the typical contributory final salary scheme it is quite normal for the employee's contribution alone to be sufficient to buy the whole scale entitlement up to the age of 40 or more, without benefit of the employer's contribution. The difficulty is that most people think in terms of private insurance contracts and find it hard to grasp the modern cross-subsidy aspects of pension schemes. The problem may be exacerbated where there is a need to tell scheme members or their union representatives how much the employer is contributing to the scheme, for example, 10 per cent of payroll. Insofar as this 10 per cent is viewed by the union as deferred pay for each individual member there is scope for arguments about the benefits available for leavers, particularly if they are made redundant. Some individuals will have less benefits than they might have obtained had they been paid out 10 per cent of their pay and invested it themselves.

THE KEY FEATURES OF A TYPICAL MODERN PENSION SCHEME

Constitution and approval

Most modern schemes are set up under a trust deed and rules, and administered by a body of trustees appointed by the employer. Alternatively there may be a separate Trustee company of which the trustees are directors. Many companies include members' representatives as trustees (this will be expanded on later). Schemes are approved by the Inland Revenue under the Finance Act 1970 and this results in a tax-free build-up on investments, together with full tax relief on both employer and employee contributions. If members of the scheme are contracted out of the State Earnings Related Scheme, then the scheme must satisfy the requirements of, and be approved by, the Occupational Pension Board. Lump sum death benefits are normally insured under a bulk policy which is renewable annually and which requires minimal administration.

Pension benefits in smaller companies with up to 500 members in the scheme are normally insured and, in that event, the employer relies on the insurance company's actuaries, investment managers and administration. However, most employers use pensions consultants for the purposes of independent advice, broking (selecting insurers for provision of death benefits and immediate annuities), coping with changes in legislation and general advice on benefit levels and scheme design.

Most medium and large companies operate self-administered pension schemes and appoint their own consulting actuaries, investment managers (either external such as a merchant bank or their own employees in larger companies), and usually use pension consultants. They may also retain yet another organization for the purposes of performance measurement (a check on their investment managers). It is now normal to find a pensions department which is responsible for all aspects of scheme administration. This has often proved to be cheaper and more satisfactory than relying, as in the past, on the administration provided by an insurance company. The obvious link between a company's payroll and pensions administration now leads to the use of sophisticated computer software packages which eliminate the drudgery of annual transference of data, while greatly improving speed and accuracy of operation.

Scheme design and benefits

Most occupational pension schemes now provide pension related to final salary and the most common formula for staff schemes is 1/60th of final pensionable salary for each year of pensionable service. Quite often, works schemes also provide pensions on the 1/60th basis and one scheme may be used for all employees. However 1/80th is probably more typical of works' schemes. Most pensions are payable from age 65 (men) and 60 (women).

By the end of 1978 some 22,000 pension schemes covering over 10 million employees had contracted out of the State Earnings Related

Scheme. The 1981 Survey by the National Association of Pension Funds revealed that 76 per cent of the schemes representing 93 per cent of the total membership of all schemes in the Survey had elected to contract out. The main reasons for doing so seem to be:

- companies and employees prefer to have benefits provided under a funded private scheme

- to avoid any need to devise complex methods of integration between State and private schemes

- to enjoy full tax relief on contributions to private schemes (unlike those to the State Scheme)

- it is not easy to cut back on private scheme benefits and few companies (or employees) can afford full contributions to a private scheme and to *both* State Schemes.

Although there is no legal or tax reason why schemes cannot provide full final salary benefits on top of the full State Scheme benefits, it is normal for non-contracted out schemes to be adjusted to take account of State benefits so that all schemes taken together provide the target pensions. Contracted-out schemes often contain some form of integration with the basic flat-rate State Scheme (eg a portion of earnings may be ignored in determining pensionable pay) but since 1978 many schemes have abandoned such an approach. Perhaps the added complication of coping with the contracting-out administration is felt to be enough without the complexities of integrating with the basic State Scheme.

Most pension schemes are contributory and the most common rate of contribution from employees is 5 per cent of pensionable earnings for staff schemes, equivalent to 3.5 per cent net of tax relief at 30 per cent and 3.5 per cent for works schemes (2.45 per cent net). Many provide for members to pay additional voluntary contributions to obtain better benefits. Contracted-out schemes must also provide widows' or spouses' pensions and this is now a common feature. Almost all schemes provide the option to take part of the retirement pension in tax-free cash form up to the Inland Revenue limits. This is very attractive to members and almost universally elected in practice.

Many schemes have only reached an adequate level of generosity in recent years and it is dangerous to think that the target of 2/3rds or half final salary for someone with 40 years' service will be reached before the scheme has been in force for many years. For this reason most schemes have an additional entitlement for past service but this is expensive and the whole cost has to be met by the employer.

Finally, almost all schemes provide lump sum death benefits in addition to widows' pensions. These are usually a multiple of pensionable or actual earnings at the time of death, two or three years' pay being the most common. Such benefits are usually payable tax-free at the discretion of the trustees and are a valuable, if morbid, advertisement for the scheme.

PENSIONS AND RECRUITMENT

Personnel staff involved in recruitment should know something about their company pension scheme and, in particular, the eligibility rules. For instance, is membership of the scheme compulsory? Is there a waiting period and how does this tie in with any period of probation in the job? When are the scheme entry dates and when does life cover begin? The ability to provide immediate life cover is a valuable attraction when recruiting new employees, particularly when trying to entice someone to join you who already enjoys good life cover in their present job. The question of transferability is often raised by the potential recruit, though this is one of the factors least important to him. Unfortunately, the media have given it such prominence that many job applicants prefer to talk about transferability rather than the level of benefits or contributions. Clearly it is tidier for all pension to be ultimately payable from one scheme but this tidiness can be dearly bought if, as is not uncommon, a transfer results in a lower pension than would have resulted if pension earned to that date were left until retirement in the previous employer's scheme. In theory, transfers are possible provided that both pension schemes are compatible as far as their transferability rules are concerned. In practice, it has become harder rather than easier in recent years to achieve transfers, largely due to the complications in providing the guaranteed minimum pensions (GMP) required under the contracting-out provisions of the State Earnings Related Scheme. Few pension schemes are prepared to take on board the escalation liability associated with a GMP from an employee's previous employer's scheme on anything other than conservative assumptions about the cost involved. This means that the transfer value offered by the previous scheme is often thought to be insufficient to match the pension entitlement under that scheme.

Those people who read the pension columns in weekend newspapers will already know that there is a serious loss of pension benefit involved in changing job from one employer to another. This has a relevance to

recruitment since such loss can be a stumbling block in clinching acceptance from a highly desirable recruit. It is necessary to explain why the
loss occurs. Suppose a person is working for company A and has a
potential 40 years' membership of the pension scheme which provides
1/60th of final salary for each year of membership. He is, therefore,
looking forward to a pension of two-thirds of final salary. He changes
jobs after 20 years and is then earning £6,000 pa. He joins company B
which has an identical pension scheme and eventually retires after 20
years in that scheme at a salary of £12,000 pa. His total pension from
both schemes is:

Company A	$20/60 \times £6,000 = £2,000$ pa
Company B	$20/60 \times £12,000 = £4,000$ pa
	Total pension $= £6000$ pa

Had he remained with company A and retired on the same final salary
(which is, of course, questionable) he would have received a pension of
$40/60 \times £12,000 = £8,000$ pa.

Clearly, people do not usually change jobs unless they expect to earn
more money and they may think that an extra 15 per cent on the change
makes the move worthwhile. They probably seriously underestimate the
pension loss. In the above example there is only one change of job but a
25 per cent loss of pension. Nowadays many people have four or five
different jobs during their career and there are often gaps in pension
membership due to the incidence of scheme entry dates or waiting periods
so the overall pension loss can be devastating. It is, therefore, not unusual
when filling very senior vacancies, to have to offer some form of additional
pension entitlement under a supplementary (top hat) scheme in order to
make the move attractive enough.

Finally, no one can reasonably be asked to accept an offer of employment without first having been given adequate literature describing the
pension scheme. This can be in a form of a leaflet provided that it contains
the most important features of the scheme. It is interesting to note that
the National Association of Pension Funds (NAPF) has drawn up a voluntary code of practice in an attempt to ward off future legislation and
amongst the recommendations is that of giving much fuller information
at the job interview.

PENSIONS AND LEAVING SERVICE

A decade ago this was a fairly straightforward question of a choice
between a preserved pension (which could possibly be transferred to a

new scheme) or a refund of the member's contributions only. There may have been an element of interest payable on the refunded contributions and there was certainly a 10 per cent tax deduction to offset the fact that full tax relief was allowed when the contributions were originally paid into the scheme. In many schemes the employee leaving service received no benefit from any employer's contributions but could get a preserved pension based on his or her own contributions only. More generous employers would ensure that employees with, say, five years' membership of the pension scheme were entitled to 'vested' rights, in other words, the full scale benefits calculated as at the date of leaving service. It has not, in the past, been possible under the rules of any Inland Revenue approved scheme to refund the employer's contributions to the employee as well as his or her own. But employees sometimes receive an *ex gratia* sum equivalent to the employer's contributions.

The advent of the State Graduated Scheme and now the preservation requirements of the 1978 State Scheme, together with changes in Inland Revenue practice have complicated the leaving service rules and options. Prior to the new State Scheme there seemed to be strong indications that the choice of taking a refund of contributions would eventually disappear and that members would become entitled to better pensions on leaving service. The position now is that refunds of contributions are limited to those under age 26 or with less than five years' qualifying service. (No scheme wants to hold small pensions for many years.) Others have to be given a deferred pension or a transfer value. There are variations depending on whether the scheme is contracted-out of the State Earnings Related Scheme and whether the employee concerned has paid contributions prior to 5 April 1975. There is not room in these pages to elaborate on all these variations but readers are urged to understand their own scheme and to keep up to date on the leaving service provisions through contact with their pensions managers or consultants.

The problems of transferring pensions have been discussed in relation to recruitment and they arise again when trying to transfer pensions out of a scheme. In short, transfers are difficult and will remain so until legislation forces employers to make them happen. In the meantime, few companies are going to offer transfer values which are high enough to enable the receiving company to match the preserved pension in the previous company's scheme.

What determines the amount of the deferred pension entitlement, which is the all-important factor to the employee concerned? The member must be given a scale pension based on the benefits provided under the scheme as at the date of leaving service (but not necessarily including

310

any future improvements to the scheme) or, if greater, a pension equivalent to the value of his or her own contributions. An earlier paragraph on pension costs touched on the modern method of funding pensions whereby an employer's payments year by year are not allocated for the benefit of individual members. This means that members' own contributions alone are often more than sufficient to buy the scale benefits until age 40 or more depending on the details of the scheme. What then constitutes value for money in relation to the pension secured by the employee's own contributions? Many schemes have offered very poor value for money by using employee contributions to provide the scale benefits and, if contracted out of the State Earnings Related Scheme, the full guaranteed minimum pension required (including future cost of living increases). Only if there were anything left after that did the employee get any extra deferred pension. The employer had, therefore, contributed nothing towards the preserved pension, nor had the employee received any benefit for interest earned to date within the scheme on his or her contributions. Other schemes have ensured that the employer at least pays his share of the cost of the guaranteed minimum pension, and government regulations will soon make this obligatory.

An alternative approach may be for the scheme to provide an element of pre-retirement escalation, for example 3 per cent *per annum*, on the deferred pension. Personnel managers increasingly need to be aware of what happens under their scheme and, if the basis of it is alleged to be unfair, either to seek to change or be prepared to defend it. If employees are leaving service involuntarily, there may be a good case for providing continuing lump-sum death benefit to bridge the gap between jobs. This can be done quite easily by making arrangements under an existing company Group Life Assurance Scheme. There are also insurers prepared to set up a special scheme purely for this purpose, which may also cover at their own cost people leaving voluntarily.

PENSIONS AND RETIREMENT POLICY

Normal retirement

It is usual to link the normal retirement date to the State Scheme and for members of private schemes to retire at age 65 (men) and 60 (women). This is sensible especially if the scheme benefits are integrated with those under the State Scheme. It is important that employees' contracts of employment deal with the question of compulsory retirement at the normal retiring age rather than relying on the fact that the pension scheme rules require this.

Early (ill health) retirement

Most schemes provide for early retirement over the age of 50, or earlier in the case of ill-health, subject to the consent of the employer. The amount of pension available is normally the scale benefit to date less a reduction due to the application of an early-retirement factor as recommended by the scheme actuary. The rate of reduction is, therefore, quite vicious because:

- the scale pension ignores the lost years of membership between early and normal retirement dates
- there is normally no account taken of lost salary progression between those dates
- the pension is potentially payable for a longer period of years
- there is a loss of interest on the money which would otherwise, in theory, have remained within the scheme until normal retirement date.

The rate of reduction in scale benefits will vary according to the early retirement factor currently in force but, as a rough guide, a pension payable five years early may reduce by about 30 per cent and this is *before* taking into account the loss of future pension accrual and salary progression.

Most schemes offer a larger pension to people in ill-health by ignoring the actuarial reduction on the scale benefits. This can be very useful when trying to encourage someone to retire early without imposing excessive hardship. However, the amount of early retirement pension available in absolute terms is rarely sufficient in itself and it may be necessary to consider some form of *ex gratia* addition.

The normal rules concerning taking pension in cash form also apply in the case of early retirement with most people taking as much cash as they can, particularly as the conversion factors recommended by the actuary are often very favourable. However, if the employee is in serious ill-health the Inland Revenue will permit a member to take the whole pension in cash form, subject to meeting any widow's pension requirements under the State Scheme. This can be useful but is, in practice, a very delicate matter. It is not easy to discuss this with a seriously ill employee. Are you able to talk to his doctor or relatives? If death is imminent, would the scheme death benefit be greater than the encashed early retirement pension? These are all factors which must be considered before rushing to conclusions and appearing to be conveniently getting the employee out of the way as soon as possible, so that his job may be filled or eliminated.

312

Earlier normal retirement ages

It is fashionable to talk about bringing down the retirement age to help to reduce the number of unemployed, and to remove the anomaly of women retiring five years earlier than men, to make way for younger people by removing 'burnt-out' executives or simply to reward employees by giving them a longer and more active retirement. However valid these reasons may be, it is an enormously costly thing to do in practice. Because most schemes have only been improved fairly recently to provide good pension benefits, most people still retire with inadequate pensions even at the normal retiring age and it will be many years before employers can afford to bring down the retiring ages and also offer decent pensions. Any lead here may well need to come from the State.

Another problem is that people 'wear out' at different rates and not everyone wants to retire early. How do you reduce the retirement age for those already in service? This represents a major change to contracts of employment and employee agreement would be necessary. They may well ask for escalation and other guarantees which would make the change impossibly expensive. Given the cost problems, most employers are likely to confine early retirement to those cases where there is a clear company interest in allowing it, perhaps to senior executives and to all those whose effectiveness is thought to decline more rapidly with age. In practice, it may be better to recognize the fact that not everyone wants, or needs, to retire early and to deal with the problem on an *ad hoc* individual basis introducing any wider changes only gradually as the pension scheme matures. Current high levels of redundancies and growing fears of endemic, high level unemployment may make this judgement appear too sanguine, but it is from the point of view of the decision makers in an individual company rather than from a national perspective.

PENSIONS AND COLLECTIVE BARGAINING

Traditionally, unions were interested in cash now and not pensions. The picture has changed somewhat due to the impact of the 1975 Social Security Act with its compulsory consultation provisions and to the need to look at fringe benefits in times of government pay controls. Many employers still feel that the pension scheme should be quite outside the normal range of matters covered by substantive and procedural agreements, perhaps a little strangely when it is recalled that most pension schemes are contributory for the employee.

The compulsory consultation over the contracting-out decision re-

313

quired by the 1975 Act did much to focus the attention of employers and unions alike on the subject of pensions and many union negotiators grasped the opportunity to cross the thin dividing line between consultation and negotiation. In practice, much depends on the union structure within a company and on the negotiating procedures in force. If there is only one union involved or if several unions bargain jointly with the employer, then pensions may well be a suitable benefit for negotiation. If, however, the company is part of a group or conglomerate with one overall scheme, if the company is involved in national negotiations in respect of one or more sectors of its labour force, or if the labour force is only partly unionized, there may be practical difficulties in bargaining over pensions. In such situations it may well be preferable for the employer to try and keep pensions out of the bargaining arena but, when the need or opportunity arises, to take the positive step of inviting consultation over changes or improvements to the scheme.

PENSIONS AND TRAINING, COMMUNICATION AND PARTICIPATION

These are areas where personnel involvement is unavoidable and where there are real opportunities to make progress on a wider front. The compulsory consultation requirements of the 1975 Act meant that there was an urgent need for people who understood the issues involved to communicate them to others. This meant that personnel and other staff had to be trained to understand the company's scheme and the new State Scheme. In any case, personnel staff usually need training in pension matters. Trustees, whether they be management nominees or members' representatives, need training, and if pensions are to be negotiated, so do the parties involved. The National Association of Pension Funds (NAPF), to which most schemes belong, is a good starting point for ideas about training but the company pensions manager and the scheme consultants are also useful sources of help and information.

The complexity of pensions means that visual aids are essential and there are professional organizations which can help companies to produce tape-slide or video tape presentations (the major pensions consultancy firms offer this service). Much can, of course, be achieved by using traditional flip charts and overhead projectors. The scheme booklet is very important and personnel need to be involved in its production to ensure that it is as easy to understand as is possible and that it achieves a positive public relations impact. Needless to say, personnel staff have to know their way around the booklet. Many companies have moved towards some degree of participation as far as trustees from the worker

314

representative side are concerned. The 1975 Social Security Act gave some impetus to this trend and it seems that experience so far has been generally favourable. As unions push for better pensions, it can be useful for them to be involved in the administration of the schemes so that they develop a better understanding of and a sense of responsibility towards them. One conglomerate wanted to introduce nominated trustees but had the problem of over 40 member companies with some seven unions representing employees. They overcame this by inviting the four major unions to nominate full-time officers to represent the members' interests.

This author's own company had the problem of a large number of non-union staff to be represented as well as those covered by three main unions. The compromise was reached of letting the unions nominate candidates on a geographical basis to fill the four member trustee vacancies. All members (union and non-union alike) have a vote and there must be more than one candidate for each constituency. In practice, this has worked extremely well and external observers find it hard to distinguish members' trustees from those nominated by the employer. Whichever way participation is achieved, it is, of course, only prudent to ensure that the rules protect the employer from being outvoted on major issues.

Trustees' annual reports to members are becoming understandably more and more prevalent, given the members' stake in the pension scheme and the growing publicity concerning pension fund investments. Information about the state of the pension scheme and statistics covering the past year are of interest to the members and less contentious than financial information about the company. An employer contemplating a start or an increase in the provision of financial information to employees would find it beneficial to introduce trustee reports around the same time, or even pave the way with them. Similarly it is good practice to issue annual benefit statements to members of the pension scheme.

Finally, it is necessary to commend the use of pre-retirement training courses for people coming up to normal retiring date. These can be run on a cheap in-company basis. Even a one-day course to which members and their respective spouses are invited can be invaluable to the people concerned. The Pre-Retirement Association can provide the necessary speakers and a typical one-day course would cover health and medical care, social security benefits, how to use leisure time and personal finance.

PENSIONS: A SUMMARY CHECKLIST

The question of the objectives of a company pension scheme awaits discussion in the final section of this chapter but it is clear that the personnel manager must play his part in clarifying, and if necessary, reconciling them. Whatever the precise set of objectives, it will help ensure that key issues are covered if the following questions are asked:

Are pensions related to final salary?

If so, is the fraction used both adequate and competitive?

Do portions of a year count for benefit?

Is entry to the scheme monthly, quarterly or must people wait until the scheme anniversary?

Does the scheme provide immediate cover for lump sum death benefits on joining service (if otherwise eligible)?

Is the lump sum death benefit payable under discretionary trust thereby avoiding delay or capital transfer tax?

Can part-time staff join the scheme? If so, is membership compulsory and how are benefits calculated when members change from full to part-time status or *vice versa*?

Can life cover continue for a period after leaving service for people made redundant?

Does the scheme provide for the maximum cash permitted *in lieu* of pension on retirement?

Does the scheme give fair value for money to people leaving service before retirement?

Do the rules contain the requisite transfer-in and out provisions?

Are the definitive deed and rules available or, as is often the case, are they still in draft form?

Is there a simplified and readable explanatory booklet describing the scheme?

Are members given any form of annual report from the trustees and regular statements of their benefits?

Are members in any way involved in the running of the pension scheme?

Is the personnel department closely involved in pensions policy and the running of the scheme?

Is the scheme used positively as an aid to recruitment and are leavers fully aware of what they may be losing?

Is there a pre-retirement training scheme?

Is there any form of post-retirement escalation on pensions in course

316

of payment or pre-retirement escalation for people who have left service?

Does the scheme contain the flexibility to cope with early retirement problems?

Are there provisions for pensions to be augmented at the discretion of the trustees?

Do the rules permit members to make additional voluntary contributions (which attract full tax relief) to augment their benefits in whatever way they choose?

The above list is by no means exhaustive but it should serve as a basis for looking at a scheme and querying whether and how far the scheme can achieve positive benefits for the company.

Cars, medical and other benefits

Company cars

The overwhelming majority of senior managers and nearly half of middle managers in private industry are now provided with company cars, which today account for over half of the UK new car market. Despite closer attention by the Inland Revenue to these very large benefits the employee with a company car continues to gain great tax advantages. The motivational aspects of company car provision are so dominant that the personnel department tends to take a leading role in car policy, despite the very large financial and operational aspects of the question.

If company cars were allotted on the basis of operational need there would be few problems, but the size and splendour of the executive's car usually bears as little relation to his own travelling needs as does the size of his desk to the amount of his paperwork. In determining a policy which includes the provision of cars as an element of remuneration the personnel manager should consider the following questions:

Who should get a company car as a result of status within the organization?

What is the practice in competitor companies?

Can the status definition be linked to a grading system?

317

Who should get cars on the basis of need and how should need be defined?

What level of car should be provided for various levels of management?

What degree of choice should be given to employees?

Should employees be allowed to get a better car by adding their own money towards the cost?

What is the policy regarding extras?

What should be the replacement frequency?

Are cars to be purchased or leased?

Who is allowed to drive company cars?

Should they be taken abroad on private use?

Should employees be allowed to buy cars handed in for replacement?

MEDICAL BENEFITS

Private medical insurance schemes (BUPA, PPP, etc.) paid for by the employer now cover well over half of British executives and have recently been extended to some government and even trade union employees. Although at first there was often a clear 'company need' criterion for its provision it has become more and more a standard benefit as National Health Service levels of care decline. As the facility to join such a scheme is extended further down into the hierarchy, so it becomes common for these employees to join voluntarily, paying their own contributions but at the favourably low rates which the company has obtained by setting up a group scheme.

A further type of benefit is the so-called 'permanent health' insurance scheme. A typical scheme would offer the sick employee an income of half current pay until normal retirement date, or death if earlier. Unlike employer contributions to the private medical insurance scheme they do not result in a tax burden on the employee, while in both cases the employer enjoys tax relief. The company can be saved the difficult decision as to what to do in the case of an employee struck by illness who needs to give up work.

In many companies there is also some form of policy covering employees against accidental death or injury. These are often schemes pre-dating the company's life insurance benefits and may well duplicate already satisfactory benefits. However, while wastefulness must obviously be avoided, accident insurance is not expensive, is tax-effective and is usually much appreciated.

Finally, there is a growing practice of annual medical check-ups paid for by the company. This can be highly beneficial to the individual but at this stage is confined largely to those whose continued good health is of vital interest to the company.

OTHER BENEFITS

There are a vast number of other potential benefits. Some benefits are, where given at all, usually granted widely, as for example free or heavily subsidized meals or staff discounts on company products. These benefits are not related closely either to the individual or the demands of his job. Another group of benefits, including, for example, the provision of assistance with children's education or the provision of financial advice, are usually closely connected with the individual and his status though not with the precise needs of his job. A third group of benefits is related closely both to individuals and their status and also to the needs of their jobs. These benefits include the quite widespread assistance with telephone bills and the purchase of newspapers and periodicals as well as the more outlandish provision of suits and television sets. In these cases the benefits can be considerable but it can be difficult to measure precisely how much benefit is being received, granted that it may not be practicable to ascertain the exact amount of reimbursement needed to cover the original real, work-related expense. Some benefits may be seen as belonging in more than one of these groups. For example, a housing loan may be generally available for bank employees, but in a manufacturing company it would be closely tied to operational needs and often to status.

Granted the vast array of possible benefits it is impossible to discuss them individually here. It is now time, however, to examine more closely how the provision of such benefits may relate to other aspects of personnel strategy.

PENSIONS AND OTHER BENEFITS AND PERSONNEL STRATEGY

It has been tacitly assumed so far that every employer has a pension scheme and discussion has centred round the different choices in the construction of such schemes. Yet while most employers certainly have such schemes it is still a reasonable question to ask whether an employer might sensibly choose not to have one. Why should the employee want one and why should the employer offer one?

From the employee's point of view a scheme could be attractive in that endemic inflation and a long run rise in general living standards have ensured that some form of pension is vital to retain a standard of living in retirement not too far from that enjoyed by others in working life at that time. The company scheme aids him here because he enjoys full tax relief on his contributions to it and the scheme itself can utilize very important tax advantages. A scheme can gain important advantages of scale. Further, being designed for a continuing legal entity, it can employ a benefit shape which minimizes the effect of inflation on the pension expectations of its employees working through to retirement. The employee is also saved the not inconsiderable burden of shopping around to make his own pension arrangements, possibly enriching insurance brokers and agents on the way. From the company's point of view it may have been originally the aim of having a scheme to retain staff and that at a later date it became necessary, in order to remain competitive, to offer new recruits a pension scheme. Now as well as the objectives of attracting and retaining staff it may well be that a further objective is to be able to dismiss at least older and redundant employees more easily with the help of suitable pension provisions. These objectives, while not mutually exclusive, nevertheless impinge on one another and the company needs to be aware of this.

The company has until recently been able to convince itself that it could meet these objectives while providing a pension more cheaply than the individual could do himself. It also had the comfort of knowing, if employees were in the company scheme, that they were indeed genuinely provided for. If an employee has had adequate funds but has failed to provide the necessary pension or life cover for himself it is frequently the case that the company finds itself driven to providing, more expensively, *ex gratia* what could have been much more cheaply provided and with less effect on cash flow. The case for the company pension scheme seemed impregnable.

Now the unthinkable has become thinkable. The recession has dramatically increased the number of early leavers who believe that they have had a poor deal from the company pension scheme and smart young executives begin to look around for 'portable pensions'. At the same time groups close to the present Conservative Government begin to press for a system whereby an employee can opt either to join the company scheme or to have the employer pay an equivalent contribution into an agreed savings contract, which would eventually be converted to an annuity contract to pay his pension. The increased cost to the employer could be dramatic if he ends up with all the older employees in his own scheme and the younger employees with their own individual arrangements. The end of the company scheme could then be in sight. While the ferment of discussion continues it is too early to predict the eventual outcome, but big questions about the possible unreality of pension expectations, the distribution of benefits, the rates of contribution, and the voluntariness or otherwise of membership are now upon the pensions agenda.

The biggest single reason for the existence of fringe benefits is high taxation in a society where tax avoidance is treated sympathetically by law and public opinion. Thus the employer can purchase a given benefit for the employee, rather than the employee paying for it out of his own taxed income. As long as the Inland Revenue does not assess the whole benefit to the individual as ranking as income due for his full personal tax rate then there is a clear benefit to the individual. The company gains also as it achieves a given motivational effect for less money. There are also economies of scale which can benefit both employer and employee. For example, the cost per individual to a company in respect of many insured benefits is always likely to be lower than the cost to an individual of those same benefits. Thus part of the reason for the provision of the benefit is the direct long run minimization of cost to the company. There is also in many cases a more indirect cost saving in view.

Managers tend to work under great pressures and to work relatively long hours. Thus it not only makes sense for a company to get a sick and off work executive treated speedily and returned to work quickly through private medicine, but also to have treated speedily those not so sick and not off work executives who nevertheless experience the waiting for treatment as an additional source of stress. Further, it is found useful to reduce the amount of time which the executive has otherwise to spend on organizing his own affairs and to lessen the stress which might otherwise be occasioned him. The company pension and life assurance scheme ensures not only that he is covered, but that he knows he is well covered, that he does not have to wrestle with problems of trade off between current income and future pension or spend time shopping around for the best pension or life cover deal. The company car gives him freedom from worry not only about the cost of accident or repair bills and the even bigger worry about the eventual replacement of the car but also relieves him of the need to concern himself with searching for a suitable insurance and remembering to get his vehicle licence. The sum total of executive time saved from all the company benefit arrangements is thus not inconsiderable.

An anomaly of the situation is that while employees place great value on these benefits, they rarely grasp their full value or, having once grasped this, soon forget. As a result personnel staff try to bring home to employees at least the direct monetary value of the benefits and their cost to the employer, often by means of a statement of individual annual benefits. In these days of computerized payrolls and personnel administration systems this is not too difficult to arrange, and in addition there are specialist organizations, like Benefacts, for example, which can provide this service. The benefits can also provide incentives where a straight cash payment is not appropriate. Since the benefits tend not to be as visible as a cash payment a company can pay a good 'market rate' wage or salary, remain competitive there, while bidding up against its competitors on more or less hidden benefits. Some benefits are also likely to avoid a national wage freeze or incomes policy since, for example, the increasing maintenance costs of a company car will still be paid throughout the period of restraint.

Finally the provision of an array of benefits can be seen as an indication of how the company sees itself and wants others to see it. The large and would be 'good' employers will rarely be found sailing as close to the fiscal wind as many smaller and more buccaneering companies, but when the phrase 'usual big company benefits' appears in job advertisements it is nevertheless the generosity of these benefits which is implied. A wide array of substantial benefits is not seen by employers or employees as a paternalistic device to use employees' cash for them better than they can use it themselves, nor is it seen as a 'slippery' tax dodge. It is seen as the mark of a sound, stable company setting out to look after its own future by concerning itself with a search for the most effective ways of attracting, motivating and retaining employees, and being drawn ineluctably to the kind of provisions discussed in this chapter. If the personnel manager of a medium sized or large company is not offering candidates the kind of benefits discussed he has an extra hurdle in establishing the desirability of his company even to the young, entrepreneurial and ambitious characters who might have been expected to be relatively uninterested in company provisions of this sort.

It is clear enough why companies involve themselves with fringe benefits, but what determines the choice of particular benefits, the groups to which they are offered or the level of them? It is tempting to seek to avoid these questions by invoking the so-called 'cafeteria approach'. Under the cafeteria system people can choose from a selection of benefits on display those which appeal to their personal taste and needs, provided that they fall within the total amount of money available to them personally. Thus one person opts for a luxury car, whereas another opts for extra pension, and another for a higher salary. In practice, people are not restricted to one benefit but merely vary the mix. Such an approach is designed to maximize satisfaction, motivation and job performance. Clearly there are administrative problems and therefore such flexibility has to be restricted to a small number of senior staff, at least for the foreseeable future.

There are a number of more fundamental problems which have to be faced. The most immediately serious is the effect on pension benefits if any salary is given up for benefits. The temptation is to opt for benefits rather than pay high marginal rates of tax on salary increases. This, of course, results in a lower pensionable salary than would otherwise apply and, therefore, a lower pension. There are ways round the problem in that few schemes provide the absolute maximum pension permitted by the Inland Revenue. For example, any tax payable on company cars or free medical insurance can be included in the definition of pensionable salary. In addition, there may be room for extra widow's pension or escalation or a replacement of benefits by salary in the year before retirement. This means, of course, that such fortunate staff may need to be covered by a separate pension scheme which permits considerable flexibility. Other problems are inherent in the concept itself. Increased satisfaction for the favoured employees is not directly linked to any company preferred type or level of motivation or better job performance. The further the cafeteria approach goes in allowing employee choice the less the company can use remuneration policies to shape desired behaviour.

Why and when might the cafeteria approach be used? Cash theoretically offers the widest opportunity for the individual to select the benefits which suit him best. It is therefore principally the existence of various constraints, which are mostly in the form of taxes, which negate this and make the cafeteria approach attractive. Fringe benefits are likely to be adopted more successfully in organizations which have the flexibility and capacity to handle the inevitable administrative issues it raises.

There are more problems here than can be solved by the cafeteria approach. In some cases companies tend to provide those benefits which they are uniquely well fitted to provide, like loans from banks and insurance companies or staff discounts from food stores. In others the nature of the work and the type of workforce have an influence on choice, so that, for example, a company with a large labour force of young women with relatively high turnover would not be wise to devote much of its efforts to providing bigger and better pensions. In most cases a mix of benefits, covering the normally accepted range, is offered which tries to balance the benefit to the employee against the cost to the employer and which also will be defensible to employees, shareholders, unions and the general public if brought to the light of day. Efforts have to be made to adjust this balance continually, since taxation and other changes make any static system impossible. Few personnel managers have so far managed to measure costs and benefits very precisely, but a crude calculation can be made. The cost overall can be held to norms for the industry or type of company, while the most effective operation of particular benefits is sought. Meanwhile, the relationship of the benefit structure to the total remuneration system has to be held continuously in review if the larger system is to meet its objectives.

There are, however, a range of other factors not yet fully considered in connection with the selection of fringe benefits. The discussion in this chapter has not so far been carried on in terms of employee status or industrial relations. In some ways it would not be useful to do this since many of the tax benefit and other considerations which apply to the provision of, for example, pensions for 'management' or 'staff' personnel apply for the most part to pensions for 'works' personnel. However, this should not blind us to the fact that there are nevertheless some important differences in the level and manner of provision of benefits which deserve consideration.

In the field of pensions this is very clear. It is only comparatively recently that a significant number of 'works' personnel have been covered by modern contributory contracted out private schemes, and even now there is often a sizeable difference in the level of provision under 'works' and 'staff' schemes. The 'works' schemes tend to lead to smaller pensions, not only because the average 'works' earnings tend to be lower than 'staff' earnings, but because the benefit formula used tends to be less generous. As this difference becomes increasingly hard to defend some companies have responded by retaining the 'works' scheme as a lower provision, lower employee contribution scheme open to all, with the better provision, higher employee contribution scheme also open to all. The normal experience is that the 'works' normally resist the temptation of the lower contribution and opt for the 'better' scheme.

In large companies there may also be an even more expensive executive scheme above the 'staff' scheme and possibly a top directors' scheme beyond that, so that a simple dichotomy between 'works' and management does not correspond to the facts.

At this point we need to consider the concept of 'single status'. Has social change with its apparent elimination or modification of class barriers, and technical change, with the comparative decay of heavy industry and its sharp distinction of 'shopfloor' and 'office' staff, made the move to one status for all employees inevitable? Will we all soon eat in the same canteen, take the same holidays, work the same hours, be members of the same company pension scheme?

However inevitable such a trend, it raises problems not least in the benefit field. One reason for retaining a 'works' pension scheme is that it provides the opportunity for trade union participation and involvement without their possibly embarrassing participation in the 'staff' scheme. If the staff are fully or partly organized in trade unions then a more senior scheme will often be set up through which senior executives can be provided with benefits at a level which could rarely be afforded to a much wider group. Thus the important distinction is not that between a 'works' and a 'staff' scheme but between a scheme which is potentially the subject of collective bargaining and one that is not.

Trade unions have been inhibited in the development of a deep interest in company pensions by a variety of structural, legal, political and practical issues. In the typical medium or large company there will be more than one union and frequently many subsidiary companies and plants, yet one common pension scheme is generally sought to cover all these. The formation of a group of worker representatives with negotiating power at the level of the holding company would often be seen as a challenge to union structures and to the authority of senior trade union officials. As a result the potential power and weight of the unions are rarely mobilized fully in pension matters, and the unions are often satisfied with the appointment of some of their officials as trustees of a scheme, even though the particular legal status of the trustee ensures that he is henceforth in this capacity very limited in pursuing special union interests. In recent years, partly as a result of a slow growth in cash income due to earlier pay restraint policies, and today as a result of recession, a much greater interest in pensions is now being evinced by the unions. Despite many problems this could be very useful for the development of good industrial relations within the firm. A matter of legitimate joint concern, cutting across union structures, involving longer term rather than 'cash now' issues, pension matters could provide useful practice for 'both sides of industry' in working together, as other countries have found. Most companies, however, will entertain reservations about this wherever they feel that greater trade union involvement in pensions will result in unnecessary conflict in the collective bargaining arena. Greater rigidity in the operation of schemes and the insertion of extraneous political criteria into the investment decisions of the pension fund.

Other 'fringe benefits' may not lend themselves so well to trade union involvement. A pension scheme must be well established and guarantee benefits nearly half a century into the future. Other benefits, towards which union members are not directly contributing, need to be much more flexibly administered, started or stopped. Even so there is a clear trend to more union involvement in this whole area, and we have seen that free access to private medical arrangements is now negotiated by some unions. It is clear that there is a trend, albeit very slow, to eliminating some of the more obvious disparities between benefits for 'works' and 'staff' personnel. The example above does not show that it is leading to common, across the board, benefit levels. The private medical schemes offer a variety of benefits and the firm which concedes some benefit to lower level employees will reserve higher levels of benefit for more senior employees. It appears likely that at some stage the same *type* of benefits will be offered to all, with benefit *levels* remaining for the most part very different, if only because the high cost of some benefit levels preclude the possibility of their ever becoming general. In some cases, as with holiday provision, there may come a time when senior levels of provision for holidays becomes so great, eg six weeks in some countries, that this remains a static limit to which other groups of employees catch up.

There remains a basic difference between companies and trade unions in their approach to fringe benefits. The most substantial benefits, pensions and cars, are usually largely non-contractual. That is to say, that although it may be a condition of employment to enter the pension scheme, the company is rarely bound to continue to offer the same or any scheme into perpetuity. Likewise very often the company provides a car, but tries to avoid the contractual need to provide one, or at least of any particular model. There is thus an important area of flexibility for the company, or, as possibly seen by the trade union (which looks on pension not as a 'fringe benefit' but as 'deferred pay') of arbitrariness. In its aim to reduce the company's flexibility in this area the trade union will diminish the attractiveness to the company of fringe benefits and non cash remuneration but as long as the taxation system continues to favour them they will remain an indispensable part of the total reward system of the company.

REFERENCES

CUNNINGHAM Michael (1981). *Non-Wage Benefits*. London, Pluto.

ARMSTRONG, Michael *and* MURLIS, Helen (1980). *A Handbook of Salary Administration*. London, Kogan Page.

GILLING SMITH GD (1974). *The Managers Guide to Pensions*. London, Institute of Personnel Management.

PILCH, M *and* WOOD, V (1979). *Pension Schemes: A Guide to Principles and Practice*. Farnborough, Hants., Gower.

VERNON-HANCOURT, AW (1980). *Rewarding Top Management*. Farnborough, Hants., Gower.

Kluwer-Harrap (looseleaf, up-dated regularly). *Handbook on Pensions and Employee Benefits*. London, Kluwer-Harrap.

Index

central tendency, in rating 116
Centre for the Study of Management Learning 265
Child, J 15, 16
circle (or cycle) of evaluation 243, 244, 267
closed appraisal 129
closed circuit television (CCTV) 236
closed questions 96
coaching 233–34
cohort analysis 158
committee method 113–14
communication skills 255
company cars 317–18, 321
company policy and training needs (case study) 178–79
comparability, in appraisal 129–30
comparative scales 115
computerized personnel information system (CPIS) 56, 59, 60
computers and models 166–68
contract plans 288
contrasting questions 97
contribution pay 274, 284–91
contributory pension schemes 307
control group 247
Cook, J D 15, 16
cost-benefit analysis 165, 261
CPIS *see* Computerized personnel information system
criterion, problem of, in assessing potential 125–26
critical incident technique 114, 122–23, 259, 260
critical questions 97
'crown prince' syndrome 127
Cuming, M 36

curriculum vitae 84, 85–86 *see also* application form
cycle of learning process 264, 265

data processing (DP) staff 57
decision making 6–9, 21, 22
deferred pay 274, 292–93, 325
deferred pension entitlement 310
demand forecasting 155
demand profile 266
Department of Employment Gazette 148
development potential (from a referee) 101
diagnosis of company problems, methods and skills 6
differential transit 157
direct observation 257–59
discovery learning 235
DP staff *see* data processing staff

early (ill health) retirement 312
earning curve 289
Earnings Related State Scheme 300–301
education 215, 216
education *see also* eight point person specification
eight point person specification 73, 74–76
eight point plan 77 *see also* eight point person specification
elements of a job 204–205
employee involvement 191
employee participation 280
employee requisition form 52
employment agencies 78, 79
employment legislation 61–62
Employment of Women, Young Persons and Children Act 1920 49

333